D1691367

Treason and Triumph

A Novel of the American Revolution

Martin R. Ganzglass

A PEACE CORPS WRITERS BOOK

ALSO BY MARTIN R. GANZGLASS

Fiction

The Orange Tree

Somalia: Short Fiction

In the American Revolutionary War Series

Cannons for the Cause

Tories and Patriots

Blood Upon The Snow

Spies and Deserters

Non-Fiction

The Penal Code of the Somali Democratic Republic (Cases, Commentary and Examples)

The Restoration of the Somali Justice System, Learning From Somalia, The Lessons of Armed Humanitarian Intervention, Clarke & Herbst, Editors

The Forty-Eight Hour Rule, One Hand Does Not Catch a Buffalo, A. Barlow, Editor

Cover Image: Surrender of Lord Cornwallis by John Trumbull

In Memory of the Life Long Friends I Have Recently Lost
(They were the best)

Treason and Triumph
A Peace Corps Writers Book.
An Imprint of Peace Corps Worldwide

Copyright © 2018 by Martin R. Ganzglass
All rights reserved.

Printed in the United States of America
by Peace Corps Writers of Oakland, California.

No part of this book may be used or reproduced in any manner whatsoever without written permission except in the case of brief quotations contained in critical articles or reviews.

For more information, contact www.peacecorpsworldwide.com
Peace Corps Writers and the Peace Corps Writers colophon are trademarks of PeaceCorpsWorldwide.org

This novel is a work of fiction. The historical figures and actual events described are used fictitiously. All other names, characters, places and incidents are products of the author's imagination. Any resemblance to living persons is purely coincidental.

ISBN 978-1-935925-93-4
Library of Congress Control Number
2018943533

First Peace Corps Writers Edition, June 2018.

"*Treason of the blackest dye was yesterday discovered! General Arnold who commanded at Westpoint, lost to every sentiment of honor, of public and private obligation, was about to deliver up that important Post into the hands of the enemy. Such an event must have given the American cause a deadly wound if not a fatal stab. Happily the treason has been timely discovered to prevent the fatal misfortune. The providential train of circumstances which led to it affords the most convincing proof that the Liberties of America are the object of divine Protection.*"

Major General Nathanael Greene, General Orders to the Troops, September 26, 1780, Tappan, N.Y.

Part One
Treason of the Blackest Dye

Chapter 1 - The Raid on the Ford House

They left the west side of the city in the predawn darkness and crossed the frozen ice of the lower Hudson and New York Bay. The horses were skittish on the unfamiliar surface and the troopers struggled to keep their mounts under control. A strong wind blew from behind, billowing their newly issued red wool capes around their shoulders. Ahead, Paulus Hook and the Jersey shore were barely discernible. The only sounds were the wind, the occasional nervous whinny of a frightened animal and the clop of the horses' hooves. Two thin shadowy ribbons of cavalry, almost three hundred in number, spread out in long lines, parallel to the shore, a precaution although the ice had been tested and was thick enough to bear the weight of a twenty-four pounder. The troopers converged as they neared Paulus Hook. Their horses nimbly picked their way through the jumbled slabs of ice, randomly scattered by wind and tide into a frozen white breakwater, constructed by the harsh forces of nature. Many of the local Loyalists claimed it was the coldest winter in memory. [1]

The troopers of the 17th Light Dragoons regrouped on the snow covered common, hunched against the fierce winds still blowing behind them. Ahead, Lieutenant John Stoner could make out the Hussars of the Queen's Rangers in their distinctive high fur hats. Those would keep my pate warm, John thought, pulling his tricorn down more tightly. It would also make me a more distinctive target. He would have preferred to wear the leather helmet of the Dragoons, with a death's head on the facing and a stylish crest of dyed red horsehair. But he was not one of them as Lieutenant Chatsworth frequently reminded him, and not entitled to wear their distinctive headdress.

John was normally averse to the dangers of the battlefield. However, with each exaggerated retelling by Judge Thomas to British officers of rank at the numerous New York City dinner parties the good Judge attended, John was starting to believe his own bravery in repelling the Rebel raiders and preventing the Judge's wife from being slaughtered. The Judge referred to John's coolness and courage in confronting the three menacing and heavily armed whaleboatmen.

John was part of this mission because he had been responsible for the maps, made by those Loyalists who knew the back roads of Essex County, from Elizabethtown and Hackensack to Morristown and more importantly to General Washington's winter headquarters at the Ford Mansion. They were common mechanics, millers, farmers and ferryboat men, people driven from their homes in New Jersey by roving bands of Rebel militias. Barely eking out a living in exile in New York City, they were grateful for the Crown's protection and harbored strong animosities toward their former neighbors. It was John who had brought them to the attention of Major Pritchard, milked them for information without ever revealing the ultimate purpose and produced the maps that were in the saddlebags of Lt. Colonel Samuel Birch, the commander of their combined cavalry units.

As the cavalry headed northwest toward Hackensack, instead of south toward Elisabethtown, John knew which plan of attack had been chosen. There was a road from Hackensack over the Acquakanunk Bridge that skirted the Cedar Swamp and led to General Washington's isolated headquarters, five miles east of Morristown and the main Rebel encampment. The troopers would overwhelm the General's Life Guards, abduct their Commander and bring him to the Newark Mountain meeting house. [2]

There, they would be met by a regiment of light infantry to provide additional security in case of Rebel pursuit.

It was as if Nature itself had conspired against the Rebels, freezing the waters separating the British from New Jersey, and then sending one snowstorm after another to obstruct the roads and curtail Rebel patrols. The heavy snows three days before had postponed their mission.[3] It had also covered the roads with three feet of soft and powdery snow, and their passage was unmarked by any other man or horse, sled or wagon. With the snows higher than the fence posts and stonewalls that demarked the fields, only one with a strong familiarity of the terrain could discern the edge of the road from the white, bland adjacent flat countryside. Their local guides conferred frequently and led the cavalry on until, under the ominous grey skies, they saw the spires of churches in the distance.

At the outskirts of Hackensack, they passed stoic British sentries manning the checkpoints and enduring the frigid winter air, with nary a fire to warm them. The town was secured by two regiments of light infantry. No wagon, horse, carriage or foot traveler was permitted to leave under any circumstances.

John handed the reins of his horse to Chatsworth's batman, ignoring the fellow's scowl at being tasked with watering and feeding another mount. He floundered through the knee-high snow and followed Chatsworth to the Sign of the Drum, one of the taverns adjacent to the drift-covered village green. Once inside, he removed his heavy damp cloak and joined the other officers around a roaring fire, warming his frozen fingers and turning his rear and shoulders toward the flames. Gradually, he felt the stiffness in his neck and back easing. From the amount of mulled cider, ale, rum and wine being imbibed, he anticipated they planned to spend the night. Tomorrow, the cavalry would leave for Morristown, roughly twenty miles away.

The sound of hail and sleet on the tavern's roof woke John in the early morning hours. In the upper loft, three to a bed, he was the first to react. Chatsworth and the other officer stirred. John pulled his boots on over his stocking feet, drew his cloak that had served as his blanket around his shoulders, and peered out the window.

A lantern glowed from the barn and cast light on fast falling pellets of ice, ricocheting off the snow. Perhaps, the mission would be postponed another day. He could tolerate being holed up in this comfortable tavern instead of riding out in this miserable weather.

Two orderlies stomped along the well-beaten path to the barn. A bad sign, John thought. They would be readying the officers' mounts. Sounds of men being roused throughout the tavern confirmed the raid would be today. Soon they were all assembled in the main room, spooning hot porridge from pewter bowls and drinking tea laced with rum. Colonel Birch ordered the officers to have the men mounted and moving out by the hour of four.

"I intend to be half way to the Ford Mansion by daybreak and cover the other ten or so miles before midday. This hailstorm is a God-send," Birch said rubbing his hands together. "It will keep the Rebel scum inside with their heads down."

The barn was crowded with troopers silently readying their mounts, cinching the saddles tightly and checking the bridles. The men buckled the straps holding their sheaths across their chests and drew and reset their sabers, the sound of the steel against metal, echoing off the low oak beamed ceiling. They had no muskets or fuzees this time. Only pistols. John made sure his was loaded and carefully placed it in his saddleback under a canvas flap to protect it from getting wet.

The troopers lined up in twos, John paired with Chatsworth, only a few rows behind the Colonel. He thought his chances were better up front. The element of surprise would be in his favor. If any of the Rebel guards were aroused, they would be shooting at those behind him, assuming their powder was dry.

The crust of ice that had formed on the snowy surface crunched under their horses' hooves as they proceeded down the road from Hackensack to the Acquackadonk. In less than a mile, they crossed the bridge over the narrow frozen river and entered a vast white countryside. Their progress was initially slowed by wind blown snowdrifts, some as high as their horses' chests.

Although it was still sleeting, as the road turned westerly toward the mountains, the going became easier. The sloping foothills had shielded this part of the land from the brunt of the early snowstorms. It was almost dawn of a day that was bitterly cold with the hail and sleet continuing to fall, peppering them with icy pellets. John sensed a quickening of excitement from the officers ahead. They had reached the half-way point. He would reap the glory from this mission. Oh yes, he definitely would. Perhaps even parlay it into a field promotion and a permanent staff job in the warm confines of New York City. Another ten miles, then overwhelm the unsuspecting guards, a quick skirmish and they would carry off General Washington, the greatest prize possible and end this rebellion once and for all.

The snow-covered shelters of the Black Brigade, made of tent canvas lashed to bent saplings, looked like random boulders in the shank of the sloping hills. Adam and Colonel Tye lay flat on the cold ice and peered through the sheets of sleet at the red ribbon of the British cavalry, visible even at that distance against the limitless whiteness. The wind blew toward them and Adam distinctly heard the sound of a horse neighing in pain. He shielded his eyes against the stinging sleet and tried to make sense of what he could see.

The troopers' progress along what he assumed was the road to Morristown had come to a halt. A few of the leaders dismounted and were bent low against their horses.

"Damn them for their reckless stupidity," Tye said as he eased himself up on his elbows and brushed the crushed snow from his chest. "Now what the devil are they up to?"

Several men plodded forward through the drifts leading their horses to the front of the line, while others behind them dismounted. Adam watched a cluster of redcoats as they went from horse to horse working their way down toward the rear. Occasionally, a trooper floundered through a deep drift, the visible upper part of his body like a red buoy bobbing on a frothy sea.

"Are they lost?" Adam asked, squatting on his heels. The snow that had melted under the weight of his body began to freeze again on his waistcoat.

"No," Tye said shaking his head. "T'is somethin' more than that."

They stayed motionless in the biting wind for what seemed to Adam a frozen eternity as he struggled to keep his teeth from chattering. Finally, those in the lead turned their horses around, creating a disorganized, confused clump of men on foot, struggling toward the rear. Only a few of the troopers rode, the rest led their mounts back along the road. Even from this distance, Adam could see the pronounced limping gait of many of the horses.

He looked quizzically at Tye for an explanation.

"They must have come up lame. Maybe from the snow and ice," he said with a triumphant grin.[4] "Now it is our turn but we must be quick about it. With so many cavalry this close to Morristown, the Rebels may have been warned." Tye motioned for Adam to follow him to their nearest shelter. "I do not give a damn if it snows or sleets or the worst storm rages against us," he shouted over his shoulder into the wind. "We will leave after midnight and by tomorrow this time, we will be back here with the Gen'rl and one of our own chasin' after those cavalry with the good news - Colonel Tye's Black Brigade has captured Washington." He clapped Adam on the back. "And you will have your Sarah."

Adam grinned back. "Yes Colonel. That is true. We will be together again."

The storm had not abated when they left their makeshift shelters. With no moon to guide them, Adam was anxious he would be separated from his comrades and lost in the icy whiteness. Fear of becoming lost motivated all of them as they struggled to keep up with Colonel Tye and the two Indians in the lead. They were armed with an assortment of pikes, swords and pistols, the latter being tucked away in haversacks to keep dry. Adam had his under the extra white linen shirt he had decided to carry, although it would hamper his quickly pulling the pistol out. He wore every piece of warm clothing he had- a neck stocking one of the Brigade had ripped from the throat of a dead militia officer and then thrown in the communal pile of looted goods, a rough woolen scarf taken after the first raid on Shrewsbury, a waistcoat too big for him but it fitted well over his own, and a large brown coat he wore on top of his worn Mariner short jacket.

On orders from the Colonel they followed in the steps of those in front, heads bent, eyes intently looking for the imprints in the snow, bodies hunched against the strong wind. Adam found his snowshoes better than walking in boots but not as efficient as during their practice marches. The snow was irregularly coated with a crust of hail and ice. In some places the snowshoes held his weight while in others, he sank in up to his ankles. He already had snow and ice inside his boots, his toes were frozen and he could feel a rawness on the instep of his right foot. He clasped his pike, using it as a walking stick to steady himself. The hail stung his face and bare hands.

Their pace was erratic. Sometimes they made fast progress across fields. Other times, they plodded through deep, windblown drifts, sinking into the snow up to the mid thigh. Adam could not tell whether the Colonel and the two Indians deliberately left what they thought was the Morristown road or wandered off track by accident. A barely discernible change in the light signaled it was dawn. The sleet and hail changed to snow, heavy wind blown flakes falling thick and fast, coating them in cloaks of white. Well, Adam thought, the Colonel would have his wish - to attack in a blinding snowstorm, if first they did not freeze or fall from exhaustion before they reached Washington's headquarters.

They had regrouped in a relatively flat area, marked by scattered stumps of grey dead tree trunks. Adam looked around, counting heads. There were only twenty-six left of the thirty-five of the Black Brigade who had set out. Those who made it so far were done in. Adam could see that. They leaned against the remnants of the dead swamp trees, resting their backs, seeking some shelter from the wind and snow. He thought he recognized Nero's squat stolid shape and the tall lean figure of Blue Jacket, although it was difficult to discern, given how they were bundled up, with scarves covering their throats and faces and hats pulled down low and tight. He scrutinized the figures and concluded that Samson and Sam the Traitor were not among them. Were they lost, or had they fallen exhausted in the snow and succumbed to a frozen lonely death? His calf muscles were cramped from cold and fatigue, and his lungs, which felt with each gasp as if he were inhaling icy needles, longed for a breath of warm air. If they remained here too long, Adam feared his legs would not respond with the strength he needed for the final sprint.

Colonel Tye moved among the men, talking briefly to each. Adam marveled that Tye had the energy to do so. He approached Adam and squatted down next to him. "Some of the men want to turn back. They say to continue on is madness." Tye squinted at Adam whose back was to the driving snow. "What say you?"

Adam recognized the gesture of respect in Tye's question. He brushed the snow from his arms and shoulders and thrust his wet, cracked hands deep into his pockets. "Colonel. Even with fewer men, the snowstorm is to our advantage. No one will expect an attack in this weather." He sucked mucus from his nose to his throat and spat out a thick wad of phlegm. "It will be hard going on the return, pulling the General on one of those frames."

Tye smiled and patted Adam on the shoulder. "I've been thinkin' bout that," he said. He put one hand in front of his mouth, trying to warm the breaths he was taking. "Maybe four men to do the pullin'. You and Nero behind the two Indians. Time enough to decide once we have Washington. With Sarah free, I expect you will pull with the strength of a bull to get her to safety."

"Once she is free," Adam responded, repeating the Colonel's words wistfully.

"I told the others we are a mile away. It is more like two but if they believe we are nearer, it will buck up their spirits."

"The men will follow you, Colonel. They have come this far." Adam flexed his fingers in his pockets, trying to regain any sense of feeling, his pike stuck in the snow next to him. He bent closer to Tye. "With this storm, there are certain to be Life Guards in the house. Probably in the front rooms. There must be a door to the kitchen in the back. I propose to break in through there."

"If most of Life Guards are trapped in their huts by the drifts, you can go through the kitchen. I will lead the main attack from the front." Tye grabbed Adam's arm and pulled his hand firmly forward, turning it palm up and tracing the knife scar with his finger, made by the Colonel's blade when Adam had become one of the Brigade. "Remember Adam," he warned. "We are here to capture Gen'rl Washington. Then free your Sarah." He held on to Adam's hand until Adam met his gaze. "Not the other way around."

"From the kitchen it should be easy to get to the General's living quarters upstairs," Adam replied, tucking his hands back under his armpits. "Or his office. Depend on me."

They continued through what Adam guessed was a swamp, the snow deep over the tufts and mire and in some places blown in shoulder high drifts halfway up the dead tree trunks. The wind was now at their backs, driving them forward as it blew thick wet flakes against their shoulders and froze the muscles of their calves. For Adam, every step was agony, intermittently shuffling forward on the snowshoes and then lifting each foot higher over accumulated mounds of snow. There was no rhythm to it and it made their progress more laborious. There was a tightness in his chest. Try as he might he could not control his breathing. It came in quick gasps and gulps of cold air. At one point he imagined his breath had frozen in a puff in front of his face and he made a motion with one hand to knock it away. He felt himself drifting away, his mind becoming as numb as his body. This must have been what happened to the others who had fallen behind. He bit his lip hard, tasted the blood in his mouth and was grateful for the pain restoring some degree of alertness.

As they emerged from the swamp, the Colonel and the two Indians were moving painstakingly up a slope through wet, heavy snow drifts. At the top, with the snow swirling around them, one of the Indians pointed with an open palm to his left. He moved his arm up and down bending it at the elbow, indicating the invisible line he saw as the road to Morristown. The Colonel nodded and the three of them led, followed by the rest of the band, struggling in the deep snow, sinking, snowshoes and all in some places up to their thighs. Adam paused to shorten his haversack straps and raise it and the pistol above the drifts. He hoped his powder was still dry. When he looked up, he could no longer see the Colonel and the two

Indians. Blue Jacket was struggling slightly ahead of him, using his pike to push himself out of the deep snow. Another figure appeared on his left, plowing forward, the back of his hat capped with white from the crown to his neck.

Adam felt the fatigue overcoming him again. The rate of falling snow lessened and then changed to hail. His frozen legs were heavy, as if he were anchored to the ground. Each step was an effort. Ghostly white figures plodded by, disappearing in the mist ahead. He found it easier to walk in depressions made by those who had preceded him. Sometimes, one foot would sink down up to his thigh while the other remained on the surface. Each effort to extract himself caused him to groan out loud.

He was surprised to see Tye coming toward him, struggling into the teeth of the wind. When he reached Adam he grabbed him by the elbow and held him in place.

"Just ahead are the huts of the Life Guards. They are snowbound with drifts piled up almost to the roof. You can see wisps of smoke from their chimneys. And beyond, through the drifts lies the Mansion." Tye's eyes darted beyond Adam. "I will tell the others. Push on, Adam. Take one or two men with you and break through the kitchen." Tye rose, a bit unsteady on his feet, leaning on Adam's shoulder. "Move on. Move on."

Despite the Colonel's sense of urgency, the snow banks and drifts continued to impede their progress. Adam could now better guess where the road was by the line of snow shrouded shapes each with plumes of smoke coming from their chimneys, which were swiftly blown away by the storm. He struggled slowly past the huts with the unsuspecting Life Guards trapped inside. No light shown from the Guards' quarters. Either the huts were without windows or the high snow was so thick, no firelight could penetrate through.

For a moment, he thought he had lost his way. Perhaps there were others ahead of him but he could not see them. A mist hung below tree level. Everywhere he looked, it seemed the same. Adam turned. The huts were no longer visible although he knew he could not have walked more than thirty yards. He turned around and then around again, feeling lost as if at sea.

The Raid on the Ford House

Suddenly, the Mansion loomed ahead, set higher to his right, a few candle lights twinkling, beckoning him on through the storm. He saw the massive central chimney and the lower roof to the rear. That must be where the kitchen is. He heard Tye shout something to him but the wind carried his words away. Adam ploughed ahead through drifts that seemed even deeper than before. He sank in up to his thighs, struggling to lift his tear-drop shaped snowshoes high enough to take the next step. He was twenty yards away, oblivious to everything, the storm, the driving wind blowing snow off the nearby trees, his frozen body and his cracked fingers holding on to the pike.

He reached the corner of the building which shielded him somewhat from the storm. The snow was not as deep here and the snowshoes enabled him to stay on the surface. He turned to see Nero, grimly following him, his pike now held menacingly forward instead of as a staff for balance. The two of them crept along the windowless outer wall until they reached a low wooden door. The snow had blown up against it to the height of more than three feet. Adam noticed the door opened in so there was no need to clear the snow.

Nero made ready to run at the door with his shoulder, but Adam held up his hand and pointed to their feet.

"Snowshoes. We must take them off. Otherwise, we will not be able to move once inside."

Nero bent down to undo the rawhide lacings. Adam hoisted his pike high and with two hands on the shaft, thrust it down through Nero's back, the point coming out his chest and passing through the deep snow until it struck ice.

"That is for the poor militiamen at Shrewsbury," Adam muttered as he struggled out of his snowshoes. He threw himself against the kitchen door that shuddered and then gave way. Adam tumbled inside, momentarily blinded by the bright light of the fire and the candles in sconces about the room.

"Sound the alarm," he shouted hoarsely. "There are British raiders outside."

To his dismay no one moved. Adam saw Isaac, the General's cook standing behind a butcher-block table, a cleaver in his hand.

"Isaac," he yelled. "It is me, Adam Cooper. Sound the alarm man, and be quick about it."

Isaac hesitated for a moment, turned and ran up the few steps toward the interior. Looking about, Adam saw there was no way to bar the door. He pushed a stout oak table against it as he heard the sound of muskets being discharged from above. He leaned against the table, feeling the intense pain in his toes and fingers as they thawed too quickly in the warmth of the kitchen. Three of the women servants stood on the far side of the room, huddled for protection against whom? Then realized it was he they were afraid of.

"Where is Sarah?" he asked hoarsely. They did not answer.

"Tell me where Sarah is?" he shouted.

The ice and snow from his hat, jacket and boots had melted in the warmth of the kitchen. A puddle formed at his feet, as he stood hunched and panting heavily, staring angrily at the women. There were two more volleys of musket fire. A sense of relief flooded over him. The raid had failed. His job was done. He lowered himself on a stool, as his calf and thigh muscles contracted causing him to groan in pain. He stretched both legs out and rubbed them vigorously to no avail. The muscles felt as tight as a frozen fishing line.

Isaac returned and stood blocking the doorway from the kitchen to the rest of the house.

"Captain Gibbs sez you are to stay here." He held the meat cleaver loosely at his side, should Adam attempt to move. Adam was shivering uncontrollably, his teeth chattering, while his toes felt they were being jabbed by hot needles. He hoped he did not have frostbite.

"Adam. Is that you?" Sarah said. She held a tray of empty dishes in both hands and brushed past Isaac. From her look, he thought he must seem very strange. Quickly, she put the tray on a table and ran toward him.

"Careful," Isaac warned. "He may be armed."

"I am," Adam said, glowering at the cook. "Sarah. My haversack. A pistol inside." He handed her the strap and his hand brushed against hers. The touch of her skin was hotter than the agonizing tingle in his frost-bitten fingers.

"Get blankets and a mug of mulled cider," she ordered. "Can you not see he is half frozen to death."

She knelt in front of him, her fingers struggling with the ice encrusted buttons. "We must get you into some dry clothes. You will shake yourself to death with all your shivering."

"Sarah. I came back for you. As I promised."

"I know, Adam. I know." She slid his heavy wet outer coat off, then undid his waistcoat, and the one underneath that, both as soaked as his outer garments. Adam groaned in pain as he bent over to remove his boots. He was not going to allow her to pull them off for him. The stocking on his right foot was pale crimson from his dried blood. No longer frozen, the ugly raw flesh oozed blood. He was more concerned for his toes. They were blue grey in color, numb in feeling, except for the pain caused by the rapid warming.

"Get me some cool water for him to place his feet in," she called out. "Not too warm now or he may lose the toes. And lard. Bring some lard and linens."

Gently, she reached up and touched his nose and ears and then his chin. "'Tis well your scarf protected your lips and chin. Your ears are red and that is a good sign."

"And my nose. Will you still marry me if I lose my nose?" he asked smiling.

"Perhaps. Perhaps not. If they cut off only a small piece, I may still look favorably on you." She mischievously held the tip of his nose in her warm hand. He inhaled the smells of cooking on her fingers mixed with smoke and even a tinge of wine. She handed him the mulled cider and commanded him to drink it slowly. He held the mug to his lips and sipped slowly, his eyes staring over the rim into hers.

Captain Gibbs elbowed Isaac aside and stood in front of Adam, who was now wrapped in a dry blanket covering his naked torso, his stout canvas breeches wet and stained, with his feet in a pan of water. Two of the Life Guards replaced Isaac at the kitchen entrance.

Adam looked up at the commander of the Guards. "Private Adam Cooper of General Knox's Regiment, formerly of the Marblehead Mariners. I would stand and salute sir, but my present circumstances prevent it."

"Him's a deserter," Isaac said. "Run away 'bout a year ago. Demanded His Excellincy free Sarah, there." He pointed to her, sitting on the floor next to Adam.

"I recall that incident." Gibbs said. "If you are indeed he, then all the more reason to keep you under guard until it is determined how you came here in the company of British raiders."

Adam motioned toward the kitchen door. "One of the raiders lies outside, killed by my own hand. It is my pike through his back," he said in a flat tone. "You must speak to General Knox to verify what I will tell you in the strictest confidence, and that I willingly will do once we are alone."

Gibbs hesitated, taken aback by Adam's reply. "It is impossible to consult with General Knox immediately. His headquarters are to the west of Morristown and all the roads are impassable. My own men, seventy-five yards away have not been able to get to the mansion for three days."

"Yet not so impassable Captain for British raiders on snow shoes to get close enough. We passed your men snowbound in their huts," Adam said with more pride in the feat than he intended. "But for my warning, the British would have been inside this house," He paused to allow Gibbs to digest the fairness of his comment and his invoking Knox's name. "You may place a guard over me. However, I am entitled to decent food and a warm place to stay until you have conferred with General Knox."

Gibbs motioned to one of the soldiers who pushed the table away and opened the kitchen door.

"There is a dead man with a pike in his back," the soldier confirmed, shutting the door against the icy wind.

"You may give me your account in private," Gibbs replied.

"Once he is warmed and clothed escort him to the Guard's barracks room," he said to one of the soldiers.

"Thank you Captain for that consideration. I will make every effort to be there soon. I have much to report." He almost saluted Gibbs before the Captain swiftly turned on heel and left the kitchen.

"Oh, Adam," Sarah said. "I fear you will be punished for your desertion and our troubles will have no end."

He patted her hand, resting lightly on his knee. "Find me a decent shirt and dry my Mariner's jacket as best as you can. Everything will be well once the good Captain has conferred with General Knox. Then I intend to ask you to marry me." He smiled at the astonished look upon her face, and saw in her green eyes a quick glimmer of admiration and then tenderness.

The morning dawned frigidly cold with a clear blue sky, promising relief from the incessant snow, sleet and hail of the past week. It was the third day after the last blizzard had ended. Except from struggling through the drifts to the low barn to feed and water Big Red, and the other horses, Will had not been out of the farmhouse where General Knox made his headquarters. Nor had anyone been able to reach them. Neither messenger, nor courier, nor officer on Washington's staff.

Will was beside himself with anxiety. Elisabeth was at the Ford Mansion in the care of Mercy Ford Hadley, an accomplished nurse and now the wife of his friend Captain Hadley. Five days ago, when Will left Elisabeth, Mercy had opined the birth of their child was imminent. Surely, she has given birth by now, he thought. Or, he shuddered with horror and leaned against Big Red's neck to steady himself, she has died in childbirth and our babe with her. He could not bear this uncertainty any longer. Jockey Hollow was less than five miles from the Ford Mansion. If it took him all day, he would ride there and be with Elisabeth by dark.

Will's resolve weakened, as he strode along the well-trodden snow on the short distance from the barn to the house, If he became snowbound with Big Red, he could freeze to death before anyone found him and then it would be Elisabeth and the babe who would be alone.

With these melancholy thoughts and torn between anxiety and prudence, Will stomped the snow off of his boots and hungry, went into the low roofed kitchen. Captain Hadley was seated at the long table, his back to the fireplace, one hand around a wooden bowl of porridge, the other holding a spoon.

"Come warm yourself by the fire and fill your bowl with hot porridge. It will do you good for today, I think we may attempt a ride to Morristown."

Will spooned the hot cereal from the cast iron pot hanging from a hook over the fireplace, feeling the flames from the fire singeing his bare hands.

"The General is more than restless. He is positively agitated. Nay, he is like a bear that has been baited and is eager for the fight." He chuckled at the image and Will grinned.

"He has finished all his dispatches and correspondence and has no where to dispatch them to. His ink has frozen in the well. He is beside himself to spend time in the company of General Washington and the senior staff."

They heard the heavy steps of Knox first ascending the stairs from upstairs and then shaking the floorboards in the hallway to the kitchen.

"Ah, Will. There you are. Good lad to attend to the horses. Today, we will need them. Captain Hadley. Select three men, plus Lieutenant Stoner here. We cannot deny him the opportunity to visit his courageous Elisabeth and perhaps to see his wee babe, if it has arrived already." He clapped Will on the shoulder with his big meaty hand. "We five shall blaze a trail through this snow with the smoke from the chimneys of Morristown to guide us. We rode through worse in the blizzard of '75 through the Berkshires. Is my recollection not correct Will?"

"Yes sir," Will said pushing back the bench from the table. The General's enthusiasm was infectious.

"We crossed the Delaware in the teeth of a storm and then beat the Hessians at Trenton, capturing almost one thousand of them,"

Knox continued in his booming voice. "On a clear day as today, our ride will be a jaunt in the snow in comparison."

The first mile or so was the hardest. The snowdrifts were exceptionally deep and the road from Jockey Hollow to Morristown difficult to determine. Once, with Big Red in the lead, they halted in front of a drift that came midway up the horse's chest. Despite Will's urging, the horse refused to budge. Will dismounted and floundered forward to bang into a snow covered stone wall bordering a field. They had lost their way and were off the road heading into pastures. They turned their mounts around and backtracked until Hadley found what they agreed was the road, covered in drifts but marked by snow-laden trees as a border.

It took them the better part of four hours to cover the distance that, when the road was clear, could be accomplished at a trot in less than one. As the General had predicted, the smoke from the chimneys of the town was clearly visible, and gave them a point of reference in determining where the road lay. For the last mile, the General on his large dappled mare was in the lead, plowing a trail for the rest to follow. As they approached the town, the drifts became smaller and the snow was more compacted by men, horses and sleds that had been out since the storm had abated.

The General rode up to the Ford Mansion, stopped where he recalled the dismounting block was, swung his ponderous girth over the saddle, found nothing but soft snow for his foot to rest on and fell on his back into a snow bank. Three of the Life Guards on duty rushed forward to haul Knox up as the General laughed heartily.

"You see my lads," he said to Hadley, Will and the others as they hurriedly dismounted to come to his aid, "I may have lost my footing but gained in reputation as the only one of His Excellency's General Staff to enter his headquarters so humbly." He brushed the snow from his blue coat and epaulets and lumbered up the entrance stairs, still chuckling to himself over his mishap.

For once, Will readily left Big Red and the other horses to the care of the Life Guard's stable hands and bounded through the door. Recalling the room where he had last left Elisabeth, he strode down the hall, knocked lightly on the door and entered.

To his great relief, she was lying in the bed covered by a quilt, with her face turned toward him and a swaddled bundle resting in the crook of her arm.

"Oh Will," she sighed. "Come and greet our son. He entered our world two days ago."

Gingerly, Will pulled back the linen that encircled the infant's head. He stared down at the baby's crinkled pink skin and tightly closed eyes. He stroked their son's chubby cheek with the knuckle of one finger and shook his head in wonder.

"How do you feel my love?" he asked, bending down to kiss Elisabeth on her forehead. She looked pale but her blue eyes sparkled with the love for their child.

"Sore but well gratified that we have a healthy little one, born but a day after the attack on the Mansion."

"An attack. Here?" Will asked incredulously. He had brought Elisabeth to the Ford House never thinking he would be placing her in any danger.

Elisabeth recounted the Life Guards running into her room, opening the windows and shutters and firing their muskets. She described the frigid cold and wind of the outside air, her teeth chattering until the orders were given that all was secure.[5] After the windows had been closed, Mercy brought Elisabeth two brass bed warmers and piled her own blankets on top of her.

The next morning, after what Mercy assured her was a short labor, she birthed their son, who, she added with a smile has a piercing cry when hungry.

"Loud enough to awaken General Washington, I am afraid. If he learns the source is your son, you may be demoted," she said mischievously. "Hold him Will and give me your thoughts on names."

Will took the infant in his arms, cradling the blanketed bundle in his elbow and holding him close to his chest. He readjusted the tiny knit wool cap on the baby's head so it sat lower on his wrinkled forehead.

The Raid on the Ford House

"Mercy insists we keep his head covered to protect against the cold. Last night he slept on my belly, and then nestled between Mercy and myself for more warmth."

The baby coughed and a bubble of cream-colored foam appeared in the corner of his mouth. Alarmed, Will looked to Elisabeth for an explanation.

"It is just some of my milk he has spit up. There is no cause for concern," she said reaching up for the baby while uttering soothing noises.

Will spent the afternoon, sitting on the side of the bed, watching his wife nurse the baby and then sleep herself with a sated infant nestled on her breast. When Mercy returned from hospital duties, tending to soldiers ill with camp fevers and dysentery, Will questioned her about the attack on the mansion. She had no more information than Elisabeth other than to add that three of the raiders had been killed and the rest, their number unknown had vanished into the storm.

Will went in search of Hadley and General Knox only to see the two of them, escorted by Captain Gibbs of the Life Guards, trudging along a dirty brown snow-covered path from the mansion toward the Guards' huts. He returned to Elisabeth's room. Mercy had left to obtain some warm broth for his sleeping wife. He replaced the short candle in the sconce and sat on the edge of the bed watching Elisabeth's breathing and the occasional twitching of their son. If Elisabeth agrees, he would ask General Knox to be the infant's godfather. The boy's name should be Henry after the General and perhaps Samuel as a middle name to honor both Captain Hadley and indirectly Mercy, his wife who had delivered him. He glanced around the room and determined to sleep on the floor on Elisabeth's side of the bed and wake up when she nursed. He did not want to be apart from her and the baby, not even for one minute.

He heard the heavy footsteps before he realized someone was knocking at the door. He rose to open it, and his moving from the bed awoke Elisabeth. General Knox entered and smiled benevolently at Elisabeth and the baby.

"Ah, my dear," he said in what passed for him as a whisper. "What a fine son you have borne." He reached down and gently rubbed two fleshy fingers on the baby's chest. The infant responded by making sucking noises and turned his little face with his closed eyes, trying to grasp part of his blanket in his tiny mouth.

"Your son is hungry," Knox said knowingly. "Come, Will. Let us leave Elisabeth alone to nurse. I have important matters to discuss with you." He motioned for Will to take his cape.

Will bent down, kissed Elisabeth and whispered softly, "I will be back and sleep in your room tonight."

Outside in the dark, they headed toward the Life Guard's huts, with one of the Guards leading the way with a lantern. The General walked alongside Will with one arm around his shoulder, and let the soldier walk ahead out of hearing.

"Will," Knox said. "Your friend Adam Cooper has returned. You were right not to doubt his loyalty to our cause."

"I never did," Will said somewhat defiantly, thinking of how Adam and the other Marblehead Mariners had rescued him from being tarred and feathered on the wharf in Boston. "Where is he? May I see him?"

"We go there now. I could not tell you before. It is the nature of this business."

Will wondered what business the General was speaking of but did not have to wait long for an explanation. A year ago, Knox continued, a well-known band of freed Negroes, called the Loyalist Black Brigade, were kidnapping and killing prominent Patriot leaders. Governor Livingston of New Jersey was himself the quarry of several unsuccessful attempts.[6] He wrote General Washington asking for protection.

"When your friend Private Cooper demonstrated in front of His Excellency's quarters demanding freedom for Sarah, I met with Adam while he was under guard and we reached an understanding." Knox halted and put both hands on Will's shoulders, bending down slightly. "He was to pretend to desert, join with this Black Brigade and provide intelligence on their plans to kidnap the Governor. In return, I promised, with General Washington's approval, Sarah's freedom from her master would be purchased at whatever price. The intelligence was worth it."

Will was shocked by this information. Then, he began to see how his friend would accept the offer. "Adam was incensed Reverend Penrose declared Sarah was now more valuable as his property and increased the price for her freedom. It was an amount Adam could never hope to raise," Will said, recalling his friend's anger and frustration.

Knox chuckled as they walked on. "I suspect when General Washington himself supports an offer to purchase her freedom, Reverend Penrose will be reasonable."

He stopped to stomp the wet snow from his boots. "This brutally cold winter that froze the waters between the British and us, gave rise to a plan not to kidnap the Governor but His Excellency himself. Adam alerted the few of the Life Guards who had been snow bound within the mansion for three days and thwarted the raid."

Knox pointed to a hut to their left and turned back with the Life Guard. Will clomped through the snow toward Adam's temporary quarters. His friend had saved Will's life in Boston and now, unknowingly, protected Elisabeth as well. Almost a year had passed since Adam left on his secret mission. Will wondered whether Adam had changed. It mattered not. He was still his friend. They would talk and tomorrow, he would introduce Adam to his son. Will knocked on the door and pushed it open.

Chapter 2 - Against Overwhelming Odds

Lieutenant John Stoner rode near the front of the 17th Light Dragoons, as he always did when they were not heading into battle. This part of the Army, led by General Henry Clinton himself, fresh from his conquest of Charleston- was a feint, a thrust through northern New Jersey, on the west bank of the North River, toward West Point. The plan was to lure the Rebel army out of the shelter of the Wachung Mountains. Six thousand men at Elizabethtown, led by the Hessian General 'Old Knyp,' would push through the gap in the mountains behind them, smash the small Rebel force remaining at Morristown and seize their waning supplies of gunpowder and cannon. Then, General Clinton would wheel south and trap the rebels between them.

John was certain this time the invasion of New Jersey would succeed. He had personally interrogated enough Rebel scum deserters and debriefed his Loyalist spies to know with confidence the Rebel army was disintegrating. They were reduced to fewer than three thousand starving, ill clad rabble, not worthy of being called soldiers, much less an army. In May, there had been a mutiny among the regular troops, disgruntled by the lack of food, pay, clothing and shoes.[1] Their conditions had not improved. Among the people of southern New Jersey the pendulum had swung in favor of the Crown. They were oppressed by the Rebel Governor and ready to rise up and show their true allegiance to the Crown. As proof, many of the young men had fled New Jersey and joined Loyalist Jersey Regiments and were encamped on Staten Island, waiting for the chance to return and liberate their land.

The Rebels would fly before such a mighty, disciplined force, or be cut down if they stood their ground. True, John knew, the Jersey Militia had harassed the Hessians when General Knyphausen, on his own had launched an attack in early June, and forced them to retreat to Elizabethtown. But 'Old Knyp' was capable enough of executing General Clinton's plan. This time he would not underestimate the strength of his own troops and the weakness of the Rebel scum opposing him.

The contempt the British officers had for Knyphausen's military leadership, voiced behind his back, made John recall the many instances of condescending tone and class based slights Chatsworth and others openly inflicted upon him. Stoner felt more at home among the Loyalists, military and civilian alike. They did not sneer at his Colonial accent, or his upstate New York farmer upbringing. They did not constantly chatter about the latest plays in London or their exclusive clubs and titled relatives. Yes, he thought, he was more comfortable at Black Sam's Tavern with a good Loyalist crowd, singing the latest drinking song, said to be composed by Governor William Franklin, than at some formal officer's dinner where the pompous preened and prattled on about this Lord or that Duke or Duchess. Once, in such company, he had referred to Black Sam's and a Colonel, from some Grenadier Regiment, had brought him up short with the comment – "True gentlemen refer to it as "The Queen's Head Tavern," and stared him down, daring John to challenge him. Stoner had mumbled some reply and, trapped at the dining table, averted his eyes, seething with rage at the laughter and sniggers of the others.[2]

Now, in the early morn of a glorious June day, riding with the 17th Dragoons, his thoughts turned toward his future. His original objective, had been to go to London after the war with the returning victorious army, and by virtue of his connections, obtain some well paid but not too tedious sinecure. But to live a life of being sneered at? That was not for him. John thought of himself more of a landed aristocrat, as they passed through the rolling countryside of fields of wheat and rye and orchards of blossoming rows of cherry and apple trees. He would be rewarded for his service with a large prosperous farm with a grand Georgian style house, confiscated from some rich prominent rebel. It mattered not if he were dead, in prison or exiled. Perhaps marriage to the daughter of a wealthy neighbor with the opportunity to expand his landed holdings. She did not even have to be pretty. He would have more than enough wealth to hire maidservants, young farm girls with full ripe figures who would do his bidding and satisfy his needs.

The blurred face of the buxom maid in his mind became that of Elisabeth van Hooten, when he had last seen her, in his grasp, terrified with his hand squeezing her neck before that cursed Quaker had interfered. Once the Rebel army was annihilated, he vowed to return to Philadelphia with the victorious British and search her out.

—⚜—

Two companies of Dayton's 3rd New Jersey Regiment were camped, under the warm June night sky in a cherry orchard on the outskirts of a small town. They had arrived yesterday after marching thirty-five miles in two days from the Continental Army Camp at Jockey Hollow through Hobart Gap in the Wachung Mountains.

The town itself consisted of about twenty or so houses on both sides of the main road to Morristown. Dense woods and thick low-lying bushes bordered the land cleared for pastures and orchards.

"God damn this Indian corn meal and flour. If I receive one more ration of this instead of what we were promised and are due," Private Caleb Wade said angrily waving the bayonet with which he was stirring the fire, "I will shove it down the throat of our useless sorry wretch of a quartermaster."

"No need to blaspheme, Caleb. If we starve to death, we will all see our Maker soon enough. Taking His Name in vain will not be to your advantage." Corporal James Traynor shifted his buttocks on the log near the cooking fire and looked sourly at the corn flour congealing in the iron pot over the coals. It stuck together like glue and was a starchy tasteless, barely edible pudding-like substance when cooked. Caleb was right. The men of the New Jersey Regiment all suffered from the constant companionship of hunger, an incessant gnawing in their stomachs. So did the entire army, most of whom were still starving in their cramped stinking huts back in Jockey Hollow outside Morristown.

"Those Yankee regiments from Connecticut were right to mutiny," Caleb continued.[3] "Since coming to the line we have received nothing but musty bread and a bit of stringy beef one day out of five and now this accursed Indian meal again." He was a physically imposing man with broad shoulders and big hands, who intimidated others by his size. He knew how to stir the pot. Traynor acknowledged that. Caleb would stare at an individual soldier, make it personal between the two of them, and then, having reeled in that fish, would move on to the next, building a crowd of supporters. But it was Traynor among their platoon, long-legged, lean and wiry, with his brown hair neatly tied under his tri-corn, who managed to command more respect by his quiet thoughtfulness.

Caleb stood up and paced among the men waiting for their meager meal to cook. Better to let him vent his rage and anger, James thought.

"What were the daily rations we were promised when we first signed up as Continentals?" he roared. "Come on," he beckoned to the men sitting around the fire. "We can all recite them. One pound of hard bread or soft, one quarter pound of Indian meal or one pound of flour, one pound of beef or fourteen ounces of pork."[4]

"Well. We do get our quarter pound of Indian meal," a voice said from the darkness, with a nervous laugh.

"Not every day. Not every day," Caleb shouted, repeating himself angrily.

"Those Yankees. They were the smart ones. No starving to death or waiting for the army to fall apart. No ringleaders either. They acted together so their officers could not single anyone out for flogging or worse. I say we should do the same."

There was some murmuring from the men hidden by the darkness. Traynor sensed that others around nearby fires were also listening.

Caleb continued his diatribe. "Look at me. See my shirt – more holes than cloth. My breeches worn through at the knees, stockings in tatters, a jacket with enough patches to be a quilt. A slave on a Tory farm is better clothed. And fed," he added waving his bayonet around. "While we starve, we are surrounded by God-damned farmers with fat larders and greedy merchants rich from the London trade across the bay with the British."

"You have had your say, Caleb," Traynor said quietly. He remained seated but projected his voice beyond their own campfire.

"Six months ago, our legislature gave each of us forty dollars in coin. T'was not pay but as a gift. And it was not in Continentals."

"A good thing too," someone said from the opposite side of the campfire. "One could not buy rags equal to the weight of the paper money."

"At least we could buy shirts or cloth to patch our jackets. We are Jersey men, fighting to defend our own villages, farms and homes, not only from the British but from our own cousins and brothers, who belong to Skinner's Greens."[5]

"God damn them and their mothers for birthing them," one man hissed. "They are accursed bastards, every last whores' sons of them," another shouted, at the mention of the New Jersey Loyalist Volunteers.

Traynor let the insults erupt from the darkness and when the more imaginative and venomous curses had tapered off, he dropped his voice.

"And it is we in our Regiment and the New Jersey Brigade who protect our loved ones, homes and property from the savage raids of Skinner's men, the Redcoats and the Hessian mercenaries." He let that thought sink in before continuing.

"The Yankees wanted to return to Connecticut to protect their own. Our own are here. We cannot disband or mutiny. Who will we trust to defend our families?"

"The militia will arise as soon as a signal fire is lit or an alarm cannon sounded," someone said.

"No militia has ever withstood a Redcoat or Hessian bayonet charge," another said contemptuously. "Nor their artillery," added another.

"I for one," Traynor concluded, "am content, even on an empty stomach to defend this whole county, even if the entire British army were to land at the Point and march on us."

"I would be more satisfied if the locals showed appreciation for our risking our lives by contributing from their larders to our wellbeing," Caleb replied sullenly from his place by the fire, signifying by his tone that he would argue no more. Traynor knew Caleb's sentiments were widely held and wondered whether the New Jersey brigade would hold together after a few more weeks of starvation rations. After grumbling and some more complaints about the Indian meal, the men returned to their tents, leaving the cooking fires to burn out on their own.

The next morning, before dawn, they were awakened by the dull boom of an alarm cannon in the distance, followed by the drums beating to arms. A tall beacon fire burned brightly behind them on the mountain near the gap that led to Morristown and the rest of the army. By the time Traynor and their company formed ranks, another beacon fire flared toward the east from Newark Mountain.

"They are summoning the militia," one of the men said in the early dawn. "Must mean the Hessians are moving out of Elizabethtown and coming our way," another voice suggested. "It will be a hot day for fighting," a third offered as the men sniffed the warm June air.

They left the orchard to be manned by a makeshift company of local Jersey militia with a few Continental riflemen to bolster their ranks. With Lieutenant Moses Phelps in the lead, they marched double time into the woods, crashing through the thickets and hunched down behind trees and shrubs and waited. Traynor hoped the riflemen would stiffen the militia's spine in the face of a bayonet charge. If their left flank crumbled, then his company would be in danger.

The first of the enemy troops appeared on the road coming from Elizabethtown that bisected the town of Connecticut Farms. A murmur of anger and hatred went through the ranks as they recognized the green-coats of Skinner's Jersey Volunteers. Behind them were rows of infantry also clad in green.

"Who are they?" a voice asked to Traynor's left.

"I believe they are Simcoe's Queen's Rangers," Lieutenant Phelps said, moving quietly among them. " They are men like any other. When they come up this hill at us, those in forward positions fire first on my command, then those in the second rank fire but wait for my command. Then, fire at will."

"We will give Skinner's bastards what for, Lieutenant," someone shouted as others echoed his sentiment. Traynor thought of his neighbor from Chatham, Tobias Huntington who had joined the New Jersey Loyalists. They had played together as boys, shared community chores and as young men required to serve in the militia, drilled together weekly on the Commons. After five years of war, and the destruction and looting wrought by the Loyalists in this God-forsaken county, Traynor was as ready to shoot his former neighbor as others in the company would kill their cousins and flesh and blood.

In the still humid air of the forest, there was a buzzing, not of insects but the sounds of men simultaneously urging their hated foes forward to destruction. As the green-coated Loyalists opened their ranks and began moving through the pasture up the slope toward the woods, Traynor heard himself muttering "Come on you sons of whores. Keep coming." When Skinner's Greens were within thirty yards, Phelps gave the order to fire. With a spontaneous howl of rage, Traynor and the men of his company discharged their muskets, their curses drowned out by the second volley. He hastily reloaded as the remnants of Skinner's men reached the tree line and took cover, shouting their own curses back.[6] A musket ball thudded into the tree trunk above Traynor's head. He remembered the instruction to aim low and he depressed the barrel as he fired at the torso of soldier bulging out from behind a tree. He exalted as the man fell, crying "I have been shot. Help me."

"No help for you, you God damned bastard," someone shouted. The cool of the dawn gave way to a sultry, stifling heat. Clouds of smoke hung over the woods, as the two sides fought Indian style, Skinner's troops barely gaining any ground and the Continentals dug in and holding them back. Traynor lost track of how many times he loaded, fired and reloaded, feeling the dwindling number of cartridges in his box. In the deep recesses of his mind he heard a drum, signaling retreat. Suddenly alert, he listened more carefully, reacting this time to the shouted order from Lieutenant Phelps for his company to form the rear guard. At the edge of the trees he could see the rest of the Regiment retreating through the open field, with a detachment moving off to the left to intercept the British Rangers attempting to cut them off.

Traynor stood with his company facing Skinner's Greens running toward them through the brush as the others in their company filed to toward the rear in disciplined ranks. Calmly, he waited for the order – "Make ready! Take aim! Fire!" Two solid volleys stopped the New Jersey Loyalists in their tracks. Traynor heard the screams of wounded men, mixed in with shouts of rage at being thwarted. Now it was their turn. Traynor resisted the temptation to glance over his shoulder. He quick marched, involuntarily hunching his shoulders in anticipation of a musket ball to his back. They wheeled by files and marched quick-step forty yards to the rear, passing between the earlier retreating platoons, whose muskets were now loaded and primed. By the time it was their turn to be the rearguard, they were out of musket range. Skinner's Loyalists stood in ill-disciplined clumps at the edge of the tree line shaking their fists and shouting curses that did not carry down the open fields.

—w—

Gideon Hazzard, formerly a Corporal in the all colored 1st Rhode Island Regiment, crouched behind a low stone wall and rested his musket on the moss-covered granite. He was little more than five and a half feet tall, with a solid torso and thick muscular arms from his years as a caulker in the Providence shipyards. He scratched at the three-day stubble on his face and neck and stared down at the gently sloping hill and the river below. The creases of his jowls accentuated his deep-set eyes sunk in pits darker than the rest of his face. He rarely smiled and when he opened his mouth to chew on a biscuit or salted pork, he revealed a gap between his two upper front teeth. Wide enough to hold a ramrod, one of his fellow soldiers had joked, before Hazzard had hit him hard enough to fell him to the ground with one blow.

When the all colored 1st had been disbanded, Hazzard, together with almost thirty other blacks, had joined the ranks of Colonel Angell's 2nd Rhode Islanders. He and a dozen others had been assigned to Captain Olney's Company.[7] Hazzard had been reduced in rank from Corporal to Private with no reason given. None was needed. He knew the answer. They would not have a black Corporal giving orders to white Privates. Not in this regiment.

It irritated him even though he was still respected by the other coloreds. He removed his tri-corn and wiped his forehead with his sleeve. Besides Privates Mingo Power, the mulatto, and Jeremiah Warmsley, he was the only one who could read and write. At night, in Morristown, the colored soldiers who did not have picket duty would leave their platoons and tents and wander over to sit around the cooking fires and listen to Hazzard read from the latest broadsheets or posted orders. Then, they would melt back into the darkness to rejoin their units, now composed mostly of white soldiers.

This integration into the Regiment was strange business, Hazzard thought. As an all-Negro unit they had fought alongside the 2nd at the Battle of Rhode Island and earned their grudging respect. But living with them was another matter. There was none of the easy camaraderie he had enjoyed when they were all black. Though some of the whites were better than others. Generally, those from the coast, Westerly, Tiverton, Charlestown and Scituate were more tolerant of Negroes and accepted them as brother soldiers. Those from inland where slaves worked the timber mills and the South County plantations were unfriendly if not downright hostile. Then again, some whites from the coast where slaves engaged in ship-building were like their inland cousins. The problem Hazzard thought was he never knew how a white soldier would react to his black skin. It was better to avoid them whenever he could.

No chance of that now. He scanned their position, less than three-hundred men spread out, two deep, partially up a slope from the river, hiding behind a stone wall. Below them, flax and oats, eight inches high in the June sun, rustled in the light wind.

The soldiers from his old 1st Regiment were distinguished by more than their skin color. Some still wore their original issued fringed white hunting jackets with red trimmed cuffs, although the white was now more of a dirty grey. Others had retained their high peaked headgear, black lacquered in front with a silver anchor, the symbol of Rhode Island. Hazzard himself, like many others, had obtained a serviceable blue jacket and tri-corn. He had come by his when they had camped in a barn on the march to winter camp and discovered uniforms discarded by some deserters from the Army. He still had his white breeches with knee high buttoned leggings and shoes so worn, he might as well have been barefoot. He felt the dryness in his mouth and wished he had more water in his canteen.

Sergeant Henry Gillet hid behind a part of the stone wall overgrown with thick vines and prickly Devil's Walking stick. Together with the men of Captain Olney's Company of the 2nd Rhode Island Regiment, they waited on the far side of the Rahway River, staring up the road that sloped down toward the plankless bridge before them. The soldiers of a New Jersey Regiment, identified by their color bearer, sweaty, with their faces streaked with black powder, as they pulled back from their encounter with the enemy, marched through the Rhode Islanders toward the rear.

"They look like our Negroes," Whipple said to Gillet, from his place behind the wall, gesturing to his right. Henry followed his gaze to a dozen or so blacks, formerly of the 1st Rhode Islanders, interspersed among their ranks.

"If those New Jersey men fought as well as the 1st, they would not be retreating," Henry replied. Whipple frequently disparaged the blacks in the Regiment, as if he had picked up these thoughts from Abraham Fish, killed at the Battle of Rhode Island. Henry did not understand his friend. They all had the same starvation rations, marched together in the rain, mud and baking sun, camped without tents and had not seen their pay since December.

And now, Gillet thought, we, together with the Negroes and the addition of a few riflemen, are the front line with the entire British army soon to come over the hill and down the road to the river. The boards they had torn from the bridge, leaving just the runners would not stop them. The river was only three or four feet deep at most. In the heavy summer air Gillet heard the skirling of the pipes, the high-pitched notes of fifes and the constant steady drumming, coming ever closer. He fingered the blue ribbon in his cartridge box, a piece of the dress his wife had sewn for their daughter and quickly glanced behind, as if taking his eyes from the road below for a moment would mean the British would suddenly be swarming their position.

Captain Olney was walking erect behind the low stonewall, talking quietly to the men of his company.[8] He was short of stature with a robust physique and a thick mane of hair that curled around his ears. He had calmly led them in battle before. Gillet knew him to be a brave and intelligent officer. If Henry were to die here, he would do no less than his part as a good soldier. He owed it to the Captain, Lieutenant Tew and his brother soldiers.

The lead elements of the British Army crested the hill and began their steady descent toward the river. An orderly stream of brass hatted Hessians, green-coated Jaegers and red-jacketed Scots in their kilts, marched toward them in perfectly aligned ranks, the sun glinting off their bayonets. A lone American cannon fired off to Gillet's right. The cannon ball tore a hole amidst the on-coming Scotsmen. It did not halt their advance. The river did.

Gillet waited for the order. The green-coated Jaegers had paused on the far side of the Rahway. Then, three men, their short rifles held in one hand, raced along the rails of the plankless bridge to be cut down by well-aimed fire when they made it across. Their bravery had accomplished nothing. Sporadic shots by the riflemen with the Rhode Islanders picked off a few officers before the Jaegers divided and quick marched to the right and left along the bank.

At a drum signal, the Highlanders and Hessians broke ranks and plunged into the river on either side of the useless bridge and up the muck of the far bank. They emerged, muskets held high, the breeches of the Hessians and the stocking legs of the Highlanders begrimed and dripping. Their pipers signaled them to reform and they stood in lethal order, awaiting the next command.

"Steady men," Olney said loudly. "Take aim." The Redcoats were within forty yards. "Fire." Gillet remembered to aim low and hoped his ball had gone true. Through the smoke he could see the enemy reeling back to regroup. They were still on the Rhode Islander's side of the river. They had not driven them back across the Rahway. Gillet reloaded and waited. Again, the Redcoats came on and again, the concentrated musket fire sent lead balls tearing into their flesh.

As the field below the stone wall was engulfed in the smoke from the musket volleys, Gillet heard the drum signal to form ranks. He turned and saw Captain Olney gesturing with his sword toward the company colors. Gillet stood up, oblivious to the British grape shot pinging off the stones in front of him. Lieutenant Tew shouted "Follow the Captain. By Sections of Four! To the Right! March!" Gillet repeated the order as his platoon marched in four files toward their right flank and into an apple orchard on a steep hill. There, small groups of their company took shelter behind the trees so as to concentrate their fire on the swiftly advancing Jaegers. Gillet was in the rear file of four standing behind eight men kneeling in front.

Lieutenant Tew tapped him on the shoulder. "Sergeant. Make sure your men are steady and take good aim. Concentrate your fire on any officers." A curtain of twigs, leaves and unripe apples fell on them as the musket balls of the Jaegers whipped through the branches. The Lieutenant kicked a fallen apple with his boot. "See what happens when you aim high." He laughed as the apple rolled away. "Keep those barrels low. Remember to instruct the men to leg' em, Sergeant," he barked and moved on.

Gillet nodded. He stomach tightened, as he anticipated the point of those lethal eighteen-inch British bayonets piercing his gut. He shuddered. They all knew a bayonet wound like that was fatal.

They had seen enough of their brother soldiers die an agonizing death from such gaping wounds.

Hazzard felt the Sergeant's hand on his shoulder. He turned his head but kept his musket pointed down hill. "You three men here. Fire the first round at my command. Reload and hold your fire until I give you a specific order. When they charge with their bayonets, thinking we are all reloading, I want to give them a surprise. Understand?" Hazzard nodded. It seemed like a good plan but with only four loaded muskets, counting the Sergeant's, it would not be enough to stop a concerted bayonet attack.

The Jaegers advanced at quick march crushing the waist high winter wheat before they themselves were cut down by the concentrated musket fire of the Rhode Islanders. Gillet watched them spread out amongst the first trees of the orchard and begin sniping at them from behind the trunks. Muskets balls ripped into the apple bark. He felt a tug at his hat and thought a ball had pierced his tri-corn. Time enough to examine it later, if he survived.

It was all Indian style woodland fighting, with the Jaegers having an advantage as the smoke from the Rhode Islanders' muskets rolled down hill and concealed their positions. He heard screams of agony to his left as Jaegers swarmed amongst the blue clad Rebels, slashing away with their bayonets. Gillet had lost count of the number of rounds fired. He saw the eight men in front, kneeling to reload as an equal number of green coats emerged from the gun smoke, shouting as they charged, their bayonets lowered to waist level.

He tapped each of the three men standing in front of them and rested his musket in the vee formed by a low apple branch. "Steady. Let them come closer. Aim low. Fire!" The four muskets blasted their deadly balls and three Jaegers went down. Their comrades halted their charge and bent to help the wounded.

"Charge bayonets!" Gillet shouted and leaped from behind the tree, gathering speed as he ran the ten yards or so downhill. The black Private and a few other blue jackets were on either side him. Gillet stabbed a Jaeger deep in his thigh as the man rose to counter his thrust. The Rhode Islanders viciously slashed at the few still standing as the enemy soldiers beat a hasty retreat, abandoning their wounded.

Gillet ordered the men back. The ten yards uphill seemed much longer than the ground they had covered running down, with their battle lust high. "I am shot," he heard one of his men shout in panic, as he crumpled to the ground. Gillet bent down to grab him by his shoulder, the black Private had him by the other side. Together they dragged the wounded soldier up the rest of the hill to the protection of the trees. They left him slumped against a truck, bleeding profusely from his leg.

Gillet noticed they were now positioned deeper within the orchard. The Jaegers had pushed them back and were much closer. There was less time to reload before the enemy charged forward, coming out of the smoke and screaming as they came. Lieutenant Tew, his face streaked with sweat and grime directed Gillet and his men to hold their fire. The Jaegers, thinking the Rhode Islanders were reloading, emerged out of the smoke less than ten yards away. "Aim. Fire!" Tew ordered. The concentrated blast of their several muskets tore into the Jaegers, some of whom fell screaming to the ground while the others quickly retreated.

Captain Olney, a white strip of linen bound around his left upper arm hanging uselessly at his side, limped up to Tew. "Well done Lieutenant. However, it is best to retreat. They are attempting to cut the road behind us. Detail some of the men to carry our wounded. Be quick about it."

Gillet surveyed the apple trees around him. It seemed that in every cluster of men, one or two Rhode Islanders lay dead or wounded. The easy ones to move were the ones with leg wounds or shattered arms. Those with stomach or chest wounds, screamed in agony as they were carried. Gillet knew they could not be left behind. A certain death by bayonet awaited them. However, he could not help but think the seriously wounded men would not survive being carried back.

They crossed the second bridge over a branch of the Rahway outside of Springfield, and passed through their own lines, a low stone wall midway up a steep hill. After leaving their wounded at the stone house serving as a field hospital, Gillet and the remainder of the Rhode Islanders, returned to their lines and took up their positions with their color bearer amongst New Jersey Continentals and some militia.

Captain Olney, pale and exhausted from his wound, ordered two men from each platoon to report to the New Jersey unit and return with extra cartridges to replenish their boxes. Gillet looked at their thinned ranks. His friend Oliver Whipple was not there. Maybe he was at the end of the line. Or lying seriously wounded or dead in the orchard. They were all black-faced now from the powder. Whipple would not have liked that. Involuntarily, Gillet stared at the black Private to his left. If Whipple were alive, Gillet would have to recount for him that Private's bravery in the bayonet charge and the retreat back up the hill. No shirking of duty by him.

The British had crossed the branch of the Rahway with ease and paused on the outskirts of Springfield in the river plain before assaulting the slope. There were several Regiments massed below and more coming down the road in the distance. Unbloodied, fresh troops, Gillet thought. Judging by the sun, it was close to noon. He did not like their exposed position, thinking that the British will soon bring up artillery and begin showering them with shot and shell. He took no comfort in the presence of three small field pieces in the center of the line. He knew from experience the three pounders could not win an artillery duel with the heavier British cannon. Sounds of volleys of musket fire and the occasional rumble of a cannon came from their left. Whatever fighting was going on there, Gillet thought, if the Americans retreated, then he and the rest of the troops here would be cut off.

After two hours, roasting in the blazing sun, with the exhaustion of the morning's battle beginning to take it's toll, the entire line was ordered to higher ground. They marched for a mile and a half in weary but orderly ranks up the road they had come down a few days before and took up new positions on the steep slopes overlooking it. Behind them was the pass through the Wachung Mountains. Gillet surmised that they would hold this pass at all costs until the rest of the Army arrived from Morristown. While the terrain favored them as defenders, he doubted, given their meager numbers, whether they could withstand a determined assault by fresh troops. They could see the town of Springfield, nestled in the river valley and the orchard where they had fought that morning.

Gillet walked the entire line of the 2nd Rhode Islanders, asking about his friend Whipple, while the men rested, drank, replenished their canteens and chewed slowly on stale biscuits. One soldier recalled Whipple had been with his platoon in the orchard, but after a bayonet attack they retreated and he had not seen him since. Another said he thought Whipple had taken a musket ball to the head and died instantly, but it may have been the soldier next to him who fell. It was all confusing and the damned Jaegers were always coming out of the smoke at them. Who had time to see who had fallen and who was still standing. By Gillet's rough count, almost one in four of the Rhode Islanders had been wounded or killed in the battle. He remembered the tug at his hat and looked at his tricorn. There was a ragged hole in the folded up brim, about an inch above where the hat sat over his right ear. Now that he had time to take stock of himself, he found another musket ball had pierced the part of his coat where it sat on his hip and there was a neat tear in the cuff of his right sleeve, although he did not remember parrying a bayonet thrust. With a sigh of relief, he slumped against a tree trunk and fingered the blue ribbon in his cartridge box. I would very much like to survive this afternoon's battle, he thought and write a letter to Judith. How he missed her and little Sally.

He heard a distance booming of a cannon. Only once, like a signal. Gillet hurried back to his platoon. The British would be coming soon. To their right, the men of the New Jersey Regiment were standing, shading their eyes and looking down toward Springfield. First, smoke began spiraling from one house and then a plume rose from another.

"That's the Presbyterian church they are burning," a man shouted. "There goes another. They are burning the town. They are burning the town." The cries of alarm turned into ones of rage. The New Jersey Continentals, obeying orders remained in ranks impotently waving their muskets and fists at the distant figures carrying torches from building to building. The men of the New Jersey militia, easily distinguished by their lack of uniforms and now discipline, raced pell-mell down the slopes and ran along the road toward Springfield. Gillet saw the columns of Redcoats crossing the first bridge on the far side of town, the one where the Rhode Islanders had fought that very morning. The enemy was retreating down the road toward the coast. The militia were suicidal in their anger. They would soon run into the British Army's rearguard and, Gillet thought, there would be more dead. He sat down in weary relief. His fighting for this day at least was over. He had survived and acquitted himself well.[9]

Lieutenant Tew ordered the Sergeants to form details and return to the orchard and search for any of their wounded. "Drag the dead into the open for tomorrow's burial detail." Henry arose from the rocky ground, feeling the ache in his thighs. He hoped he would find Whipple alive.

"Sergeant Gillet. Take one man to the hospital. Find Captain Olney and escort him to adequate quarters and then report to me where he is lodged."

Henry saw several men avoiding his gaze. They preferred the duty in the orchard that offered opportunities to strip dead Jaegers of their uniforms, boots and weapons. Maybe even find some silver or gold coins among the dead soldiers' belongings.

The black private stood up. "I will go sir." Gillet nodded. He pointed to the soldier who had been in Whipple's platoon in the orchard, eager to get to the battlefield before others stripped the enemy corpses first. "Look out for Oliver Whipple now. He is my friend," he said and motioned for the black private to follow him. "What is your name, Private?"

"Gideon Hazzard, Sir. From Providence."

Gillet grunted, too exhausted and thirsty from the marching, fighting and heat, to engage in a conversation.

They found their Captain sitting on the ground, resting in the shade of a broad branched tree, far enough away from the field hospital to not see the butchery going on, but within hearing of the screams of agony as the surgeon's saws did their bloody work.

"Lieutenant Tew sent us sir. We are to find you a hospitable home where you will be quartered and cared for and then report back to him."

Olney grimaced as he used his good arm to push himself to his knee and then stood wobbly, grasping the tree trunk. "The Regimental Surgeon says the ball missed the bone. Your company is welcome. I am faint from loss of blood and confess the pain makes my mind confused."

"Can you walk sir? Otherwise, we will find a barrow or cart."

"No. No." Olney said, waving his hand. "Let us seek accommodations close to the pass. I recall there were some homes along the road when we first marched past."

At the first place, a substantial two story stone house with a front porch, low barn and a small shed, the Captain slowly mounted the steps by himself and knocked on the door. A rotund man with ruddy cheeks, too well dressed to be a farmer, and too well fed to be a mechanic, stood in the doorway. "I am in need of a bed and food for a few days until I may recover from my wound," Olney said politely. The man shook his head. "There is no room for you here," he said gruffly, and furtively turned his head for a quick glance inside. He stared with ill-concealed contempt at Gillet and Hazzard, taking in their ragged uniforms, dirty, torn breeches, worn shoes and grimy faces "I have the safety of my wife and children to consider and barely enough food for their mouths. There is neither a bed nor room for you."

Olney sagged, groaned in pain and grabbed the doorframe to keep himself from falling. Henry helped him to the porch steps and lowered him carefully.

"We will rest on your porch. Bring us fresh cider to drink, some cheese and bread and then we will be on our way."

He estimated they were less than three-quarters of a mile from the battlefield and this ungrateful wretch could not put up their wounded Captain for a single night. Where would this fellow and his family be, if the Rhode Islanders had retreated and the British had come through?

The man reappeared carrying a wooden carving board that seemed larger in proportion to the small piece of bread and cheese on it. In his other hand he carried a pitcher and by the ease of the way he held it, Gillet knew it was less than half full. "May we have a mug for our Captain and ourselves," he said scowling up at the man who hovered protectively at the half closed door. He returned and begrudgingly handed all three mugs to Gillet, unwilling to pass anything directly to Hazzard. Gillet gave him the pitcher and motioned for him to attend to Olney.

Henry stomped up the steps, holding his musket loosely in one hand, the bayonet pointing carelessly in front of him.

"We have been fighting from dawn until mid-afternoon. We have been living on little more than corn meal and fire bread for weeks on end. And you, safe in your home with a full larder, deny a wounded officer help for a few days. . ." Gillet let the anger in his voice hang in the air.

"I do not have much of anything. Trade has been bad with the British occupying Elizabethtown. I cannot . . ."

Henry banged his musket stock on the porch floorboards, startling the man who jumped as if the boards under his feet had sprung him into the air.

"I will stay here with Captain Olney and send Private Hazzard to report to our Colonel. He is a fair and righteous man, slow to anger but when aroused, he is as ferocious as a bear. Captain Olney is one of the Colonel's most trusted officers and universally liked by the men in our company." He paused to give the man time to consider his words. Olney, his face pale and his teeth clenched in pain, lay with his eyes closed, his good shoulder against one of the upright beams to the porch roof.

"When Private Hazzard returns to camp, I suspect the Colonel will send the Regiment to quarter here for the next few nights while we await orders. To assure that Captain Olney receives proper care of course."

The man blanched. Gillet could see him envisioning a regiment of angry, hungry and hardened soldiers, turned loose from any restraints by their vindictive Colonel, plundering his home and property.

"If I move my young sons into one room, I suppose the Captain could have their bed. We will find food enough for him, although it may be difficult," he concluded lamely.

"Fine. It is settled. Private Hazzard and I will move our Captain into his temporary quarters. I will stay behind to ensure he is comfortably settled. The Private will be on his way to report that Captain Olney is well taken care of. Please be so kind as to give Private Hazzard some real bread, cheese and a piece of cured meat, I am certain you have hanging in your cellar."

The next morning, after sleeping beneath a quilt on the floor of the Captain's room, and a breakfast of griddle fried real bread and a thick slice of ham, Gillet left to return to camp. He was confident this merchant and his wife, motivated by the fear of losing everything, would do their best to ensure Olney healed well and quickly.[10]

Chapter 3 - The Lovesick Hessian

The three of them sat companionably close together on the worn plank seat of the empty wagon. Fourteen-year old James Kierney clicked his tongue and gently flicked the reins on Daniel's brown haunches, darker in places with patches of sweat. The horse obediently trotted away from the Quartermaster's compound. The barrels of flour they had brought from the Kierney mill stood in solid rows in one of the barns. The written promise to pay half the price for the flour, if and when sterling and hard currency were available, was tucked into Thomas Kierney's waistcoat pocket. The bag stuffed with the almost worthless Continental paper dollars for the other half, lay between his feet.

This is a good man, Georg thought. While others hoarded or traded illegally with the British for immediate payment in sterling, Thomas Kierney required the neighboring farmers who used his mill to pay in bags of flour instead of money. He then sold that flour to the American side for paper money that purchased little, or if even that paper was not available, a letter signed by the Quarter Master General's agent, acknowledging the sale and promising to pay in the future. Georg admired him for his integrity.

The sun warmed the back of their necks as they turned northeast through the green rolling hills topped by fruit trees and neatly delineated with low stone walls. The gentle clop of Daniel's hooves on the hard packed earthen road made Georg drowsy. His thoughts drifted back when he first arrived at the Kierney farm. The boy James had grown lean and strong in the three and a half years since Georg, lice ridden and suffering from dysentery, had begun his stay as a prisoner of war laborer.

The Battle of Trenton was in the distant past. Occasionally, but not as frequently as the first months sleeping alone in the Kierney's forge shed, Georg would awake frightened by his dream of helplessly holding Andreas, dying of a rifle shot to his stomach. Sweating and sitting up, he would wipe his hands, still feeling the white bits of Andreas's shattered vertebrae mixing with his friend's blood as Georg lifted him on to the wagon. No, Georg thought. He had no more desire for war, the killing and maiming, the screams of pain and the agonizing deaths.

Andreas had been right to urge Georg and Christoph to desert. Here they could own land, unlike back in Hesse whereas for the youngest sons of poor farmers, it would have been impossible. His father's small plot of land could not be divided amongst all of them. Only Konrad, his oldest brother would inherit. It was the law. The law of the Landgraf.

The soil here was good, as fertile as it was at home. No, even better. He would ask Mr. Kierney, after this war ended, how he could obtain good farmland, to work and pay the purchase price off by his labor and the sale of crops until he would own it.

James Kierney, as thin as a sapling, was now taller than his father, though still shorter than Georg by at least a head. He had the unbridled wild exuberance of a young horse. Georg's English was still rudimentary. Mrs. Kierney, Sarah and even her younger sister Rachel, now almost eight, were always correcting his pronunciation. He smiled to himself. They had finally broken him of his habit of bowing every time he entered their house for the evening meal. These were generous, spiritual people and although he had begun his stay with them as a captured Hessian soldier, over time, they had made him feel part of their family.

He wondered where the three of them would spend the night. They had left the Quartermaster's barns too late in the afternoon to make it to the Kierney farm by nightfall. Nor, he thought, was this the same road they had traveled. Georg listened to Thomas talking to his son, trying to understand the still unfamiliar English words.

"Gregory Weiser owns a clover mill. I wish to see it," Thomas said. "He plants clover hay for winter fodder." He paused, as if contemplating whether that would be a profitable crop, when James interrupted.

"But father. I have seen clover seeds. They would be crushed by the stones of our grist mill." James responded, puzzled by the concept.[1]

Thomas nodded in agreement. "If we were to plant, we would be milling fodder for the Army's horses. We could sell it to the Quartermaster's agents," he said more as a question to himself than a statement. "I wonder if it is worth beginning this endeavor?" He slammed his broad palms down on both thighs. "Ahh. I pray to God this war will be over and our independence achieved. Then there will be need for an army and no need to supply troops and horses."

James shifted nervously on his seat, undecided whether to voice what had been on his mind these past few months.

"Father," he said hesitantly. "I am almost fifteen. I am strong and a good shot with the rifle. I wish to join a Continental Regiment from Pennsylvania," he blurted out. "They are recruiting in our county," he said, as if that would convince his father. Thomas' mouth tightened in a grimace. His dark eyebrows moved closer together deepening the wrinkles on his brow, like freshly plowed furrows in springtime.

"I would not run away," James said, hastily adding "as John Langley did." He immediately regretted mentioning his friend's name who had left the neighboring Langley farm and been killed at the Battle of Brandywine. "I am hoping for your permission," James said, softening his request with a more plaintive tone.

"And if I do not grant it?" Thomas said gruffly. "Then what will you do? I need to think about this," he said dismissively, indicating their conversation was over.

Georg understood part of what had been said. He knew that old man Langley had been embittered first by the disobedience of his son and more so by his death. Langley despised all Hessians and thought of them as being responsible for his son being killed in battle. That included Georg, and his friend Christoph who worked for the Langleys, although both were prisoners of war long before Brandywine. Driven by desperation and bullying Christoph fled the Langley farm. Robert Langley came to the Kierneys hunting for him. He found Georg alone on the farm and fired at him with the Kierney's own rifle, fortunately missing him. Now it seemed that young James also wished to become a soldier. Although Thomas Kierney was a kindly man, if his son went off to war perhaps his attitude toward Georg would change.

They travelled on in silence, their mood dampened by James' talk of enlisting. He is just a boy, Georg thought, recalling the times his company had chased, surrounded and bayonetted Continentals and militia alike. He envisioned James spitted to a tree by a Hessian bayonet stuck in his gut and brought a hand to his eyes to wipe away the vision.

As dusk approached, they arrived at a cluster of substantial limestone homes along a narrow branch of a river. Something about the place reminded Georg of the wealthy farmlands he had seen as his Regiment traveled from Hesse to Holland – the neatness of the fences and stone walls, the tidy, well swept barnyards, the appearance of orderliness and prudent comfort. Further down the road, was a solid, spire-less church with its wide round wooden arched doorway framed by granite stonework, culminating in a triangular pinnacle of lighter stone. The overhanging shingled roof increased his sense of familiarity. It must be Lutheran, he thought.

Directed by his father, James drove Daniel into the yard and the three men dismounted. Georg led the horse into the barn as Mr. Kierney and James walked toward the three story stone home. He unhitched the wagon and put the horse in an empty stall. Assuming the owners would give Mr. Kierney permission to feed Daniel and perhaps not even require payment, Georg discovered a feed barrel tucked against the back wall in the shadows, filled a carved wooden scoop with oats and poured it into the rack at the back of Daniel's stall. Next, he carried two buckets of water from the well and emptied them into the trough. Sheaves of hay were neatly stacked along the wall of the narrow hay barrack. He separated two of them and as he was walking back to Daniel's stall he saw, through the open barn door, a tall young girl cross the yard. Her blond hair was tied in a thick braid that came almost to her waist.

When Georg left the barn, she was standing by the well, her back toward him. He hesitated, trying to think of how not to startle her, when she turned and saw him. She was big boned, with a pleasant face, made all the more attractive to him by the rosy plumpness of her cheeks. She quickly wiped her hands on her embroidered apron and smiled at him, revealing a full mouth of white teeth with two matching upper incisors that were slightly too long.

"Good evening," she said. "Are you with the other two gentlemen?"

Georg was struck dumb. He had not been around young women, other than the Kierney's daughters, for months on end. She was so vibrant and good looking to his eyes he was ashamed as he removed his stained round hat, revealing his rough cut hair. He was fearful his poor English would embarrass him and could only stammer a brief reply.

"Ja. Ja. I am vit dem," he said pointing toward the house. He looked down at his worn boots, the Kierney's generous neighbors had given him, and scuffed the loose dirt in the yard.

To his surprise, she responded in German. It was the most lovely sounding dialect, not gruff as his rough Hessian but to his ears, polished and refined.

"Zum zie Deutsch? Vas ist ihr namen?"

Speaking in his native language, Georg's shyness vanished. The words just tumbled out of his mouth. He told her his name was Georg Frederich Engelhard and from a small village in the principality of Hesse-Hanau, but, he blurted out quickly, he had no intention of returning. He heard himself tell her he formerly was a soldier in the Knyphausen Regiment, captured at Trenton in '76 and a laborer on Mr. Kierney's farm for the past three or more years. He said that he wished to remain in Pennsylvania after the war and own a farm. Amazingly, he realized had not even expressed this desire to the Kierneys who he regarded as his family in America. Finally, slightly embarrassed by his torrent of words, he asked her for her name.

She smiled and with a mischievous grin said, "Now, it is my turn. I am Christina Weiser. My father owns this farm. I am his youngest daughter," she said as an afterthought.

Without hesitating, as if it were the most natural act for him to do, he walked beside her toward the house, still holding his hat in his hand. Her head came slightly above his shoulder and she walked with a graceful but strong stride. That came from doing honest farm labor, he thought.

She told him about herself - how her family had arrived in 1750 from the Rhineland and settled in this fertile area of Chester County near the river. She was born in '63, the last of the girls. There were two younger brothers and five older ones, thirteen children in all. Her father, she told him, was a Major in the Chester County Militia. He commanded a battalion, in which two of her brothers served.[2]

Georg listened to the singing lilt of her voice, her pronunciation of the flat A sounds in German and thought them more beautiful than the best sung hymns.

"I have never seen the ocean. Have you?" she asked and then laughed at the silliness of her question. "Of course you must have. You do not have wings to fly over the water." She made a joke of her absurd inquiry by looking at his shoulders for wings. "My parents have told me of the miserable voyage from Portsmouth to Philadelphia when all aboard were convinced the ship would sink in a storm."

He smiled at her, enthralled by the musicality of her laughter, like tiny little bells that entered his ears and bewitched his mind. "That is true," he responded eagerly. "We also left from Portsmouth and prayed to God Almighty for fifty-eight days to save us, loudly singing Psalms in the hold while the water rose up to our ankles."

They were close to the house now. Christina pointed toward the well where they had first met, now several yards behind them and told him to wash. She waited for him as he self-consciously scrubbed his callused hands, wet his face and smoothed back his hair. He no longer cultivated the characteristic Hessian soldier's mustache and had no desire to grow one but he did wish he had grown his hair longer and tied back in the American way.

He followed her into the kitchen and from there to the dining room where

Thomas and James Kierney were seated with the man Georg assumed was Mr. Weiser.

"Father," Christina said enthusiastically in German. "This is Georg Frederich Engelhard, formerly a Hessian soldier in the Knyphausen Regiment. He works for the Kierneys."

Gregory Weiser studied Georg who out of custom, moved his heels together and bowed from the waist.

"Do not do that Georg," Mr. Kierney reprimanded him. "You do not bow to any man in America. We have no Lords and Dukes here."

Georg shrugged. "I do it out of respect," he mumbled in German to Mr. Weiser.

"Thomas is right," Mr. Weiser responded in German. "In my house, we bow only to God. Please take a seat." He gestured to a chair at the far end of the table. Aware that Christina had left the room, Georg lost his confidence and said nothing more.

He sat half listening to the conversation in English, thinking of Christina's braided hair, her voice, her laughter and her blue eyes. That night, at the dinner table filled with her brothers and sisters, Georg was diagonally across from her. True to Mr. Weiser's word, when they said Grace, they all bowed their heads. The conversation was in English, fast and clipped and Georg had trouble following along. With the noise of so many voices around the table, he understood little. He was merely thankful to be in Christina's presence.

The next day was Sunday. The entire family walked to Church, as did the others from the nearby houses. The churchyard was crowded with simple carriages and wagons of farm families from further away. The service was in German. Georg had infrequently attended church with the Kierneys. For once he understood every word and Thomas and James just nodded and rose with everyone else and sat when others did.

Christina was seated in the front pew with her family, her hair attractively done in a halo braid. Georg assumed, from the location of their seats in the Church, the Weisers were the most prominent and wealthy family in the community. How could he, a simple Hessian soldier, destined to labor for years to even own a small plot of land, aspire to marry a woman like her? How had the thought of marriage entered his mind? He had just met her yesterday and had only that one conversation. He took solace in the familiar Psalms and the words of the sermon, urging him to completely put his trust in God for all things on this earth.

It being the Sabbath, there was no farm work this day. The Weiser men and the Kierneys retired to the cool shade of the porch while the women, together with several servants toiled in the kitchen preparing the main meal for mid-afternoon. Georg noticed that Thomas and his son were not sitting next to each other. James was unusually quiet, almost morose and brooding, only responding to be polite. Georg guessed there had been more words between them and it had not gone well. He wished he could tell the boy about the reality of the war he had fought in and the horrors he had seen. When the conversation turned to inflation and the worthlessness of Continental paper, Georg rose from the table. He tapped James on the shoulder.

"Come mit me," he said gesturing toward the barn. James rose with a puzzled expression on his face, assuming Georg wanted to show him something about their horse Daniel. Georg felt Thomas Kierney's eyes on his back as they descended the porch steps. He motioned for James to wait and ducked under the low kitchen doorframe. Christina stood before a solid wooden table, scrubbing potatoes and carrots.

"Please, Christina. I need your help," he said in German, forgetting that the other women in the room understood him as well. She blushed and looked to her mother for permission. Another young woman, by her looks one of Christina's older sisters, stifled a laugh. Mrs. Weiser nodded. Georg forgot himself again and bowed to her as the woman of the household and quickly followed Christina out.

He led the way to the benches in front of the blacksmith's shed. The sight of the forge inside the open door, the tongs and hammers arrayed on the wall, and the acrid smell of old burnt charcoal were comforting to him. After all, he lived in such a shed on the Kierney farm.

Georg was overcome by the sweet smell of clove oil in Christina's hair, still done in a halo braid. The warm sun, the birds swooping from the loft of the barn and darting here and there in the nearby pastures almost distracted him from what he intended to do.

"Christina," he said in German. "I need you to translate my thoughts for James. He would like to join the Army and I wish to tell him of what I have seen and what I am ashamed I have done."

She turned to James sitting next to her and told her what Georg proposed. James shifted uncomfortably on the bench. "I am willing to listen, Georg." Perhaps because Christina was the interlocutor James added, "I am almost fifteen and there are soldiers as young as I am fighting to protect our land and women from the British and their Hessian mercenaries."

Christina relayed James' response in a flat tone but Georg knew the boy was angry and had spat out the word Hessian. He feared James would impetuously resist anything he had to say. He chose his words carefully and began slowly and unemotionally.

"I have been in many battles from when we first landed on Staten Island. I simply want to tell you of my experiences in this war." Georg described the fear he felt when discipline compelled him to stand in ranks as American cannons fired at them or when they said their prayers before climbing up the slopes of Fort Washington in the face of enemy fire. He told of the confusion of the noise and smoke of battle and how, despite the musket fire and booming of the artillery, he always heard the high-pitched screams of agony of the wounded. Of charging forward, stepping over dead or maimed Hessians, missing limbs, calling out for their mothers or for God himself, in their anguish and unbearable pain; of the blood lust that overcame him having seen their own wounded and how, because of that lust he had bayonetted those who surrendered or begged for quarter; of the smell of seared flesh, the sound of men sobbing in shock as they saw a cannon ball had severed their leg, the soft plopping sound grape shot made as it struck human flesh, the stench of dead bodies in the aftermath of a battle; of having to bury your dead in a churchyard, or leave them behind on a battlefield when ordered to retreat; of stripping the enemy dead of their clothes and boots, leaving them white and naked in the baking sun; of stomach wounds, and the gore that flowed when a bayonet pierces a man's body; of the incessant buzz of those stinking green flies drinking from pools of blood during a lull in the fighting or crows picking at eyeless sockets; of the piles of amputated limbs sawed off by the regimental surgeon and his assistants outside sheds or barns that served as field hospitals; of the agonizing death of his friend Andreas from a rifle ball to his gut; of how, after each battle, he lost a little of his humanity; and how being defeated and captured deprives a man of his sense of worth and causes some to simply give up and die of a broken spirit.

Georg sat with his shoulders hunched, haunted by the images he had conjured up.

"There is one more thing to be said about war." He paused and waited for Christina to translate. James leaned forward in anticipation.

"I will never recover from the loss of friends in my Company who have died. I will forever see them and their maimed bodies in my dreams. We were all young farm boys at the beginning. Older than you but still young. And what we have become is not for the better." He looked at James and thought the boy was like hickory wood – tough but light, not strong enough to parry a Hessian soldier's bayonet. In the close fighting he had seen, James would not survive. He could not tell James that he was just a boy, no match for soldiers who killed without mercy, whose battle experience gave them the decisive edge over new recruits like him.

James spoke slowly so Georg could better understand. "I do not want to offend you Georg, but you fought as a hired mercenary. I will be fighting for our freedom. I can withstand all of the horrors you have described because I am committed to our cause. I would be fighting to defend our land." He pointed at Georg. "You came as an invader."

Christina noticed that Georg seemed unable to follow all of James' words and translated effortlessly from English to German. "I am encouraged to know," James continued, "that even you, a veteran soldier were afraid. I too will be afraid in battle but my courage will come from knowing that even if I die, I have done so to protect our women and children from the British and Hessian soldiers who wantonly murder, rape and abuse our people and pillage the countryside."

Georg did not have to wait for Christina to tell him. He heard the anger in James' voice and knew he had failed. He nodded and simply said, "There is nothing more I can say." When Christina translated, he heard his sense of despondency mirrored in her voice.

Thomas Kierney looked at them curiously as they returned to the main house. "I must get back to my chores in the kitchen," Christina said to Georg.

"Please, Christina. One more moment." Georg climbed the porch steps and asked Thomas to meet with him and Christina. The words poured out of him so fast that Christina was barely able to keep up. Georg related how he failed to convince James not to enlist. He hated war and the killing but he loved the Kierney family more. For what they had done for him and how they had treated him kindly. The thought of young James facing death alone on a battlefield was too much for his conscience to bear. He, Georg, would enlist with James and, with God's help, protect him from death or serious injury. He would be at his side and hopefully, when the war ended, he and James would return safely to the Kierney farm.

When he finished, he saw the tears in Christina's eyes. "I thank you," Thomas Kierney said moved by Georg's offer, "but I will not permit it. If you are captured you will be shot as a deserter. I cannot have that on my conscience," he said emphatically, pounding his heart with his closed fist. As Christina translated, Thomas grasped Georg's shoulders in both of his hands and embraced him, vigorously patting him on the back. "I will talk to James. I will try and persuade him the way to help our cause is for him to remain on the farm and by his labor produce food for our Army."

It was an awkward arrangement, given the afternoon's discussion but Georg and James were to sleep in the same bed, one vacated by two of the Weiser boys to accommodate the guests. They retired early, leaving Thomas Kierney and Gregory Weiser to companionably spend time together. Georg would have enjoyed smoking the pipe that Mr. Weiser had offered Thomas who politely refused, but he lacked the audacity to ask. With the long forgotten smell of tobacco smoke following him up the stairwell, Georg decided not to say anything more to James about joining the Continental Army. They lay next to each other in the darkness, listening to the incessant buzz of the cicadas and the occasional hoot of an owl in the distance.

"I know you spoke to me of your war experiences because you have concern for me," James said. Georg absorbed his words and simply grunted. "I appreciate that. But I feel I must enlist and fight. I will do so but I wish to go with my father's blessing. That would give me comfort. He should understand it is a matter of the family's honor."

Georg said nothing. Mentally, he composed a prayer to the Almighty to give James the wisdom not to enlist and to protect him if he did. Unconsciously, he had clasped his palms together in prayerful position. In the dim moonlight that penetrated the room, James must have noticed.

James reached across and wrapped his one hand around Georg's two tented palms. "I know you mean me well."

"Ja. I do James. I do."

"I am sorry I spoke bitterly toward you," James said before turning his back away. Georg reached out and patted James on his shoulder, a gesture of acceptance of his apology. He turned over and smiled to himself. The two of them would have to disobey Mr. Kierney. Georg would not let the boy go to war without him.

Monday started off poorly for Georg. He was up at dawn hoping to encounter Christina doing her morning chores. He did not find her in the kitchen and disappointed, went to the barn to feed, water and brush Daniel. He was certain they would be leaving today, perhaps immediately after breakfast. He wanted to talk to her before they departed. Although, he knew the Kierneys thought of him as part of their family now, he still was only a prisoner of war farm hand. He did not have the freedom to travel on his own to visit Christina, and it seemed unlikely that Mr. Weiser would even allow it.

His gloomy thoughts were interrupted by Thomas Kierney greeting him from the sun-drenched barn entrance.

"Make sure Daniel has enough water," he said. "It will a hot traveling today." Kierney was in a jovial mood, perhaps Georg thought because he was returning to his farm. He sensed it was more than that, but Thomas, a man of few words did not say anything else as he checked the wagon wheels and axles. Georg was offended by his reticence. He believed he was entitled to some explanation. After all, he had made up his own mind to go with James if he went without his father's permission. Of course, he realized, Mr. Kierney does not know that. The work on the farm would be much more burdensome for him without Georg and James to share the labor. Georg knew parts of the gristmill roof needed shingling; there were stumps to pull out in the newly cleared field and a new cold cellar to be dug.

Georg entered the dining room through the foyer of the main entrance, reluctant to disturb the women in the kitchen. Gregory Weiser and a few of his sons were already seated, as were Thomas and James. When the door to the kitchen opened, Georg looked up eagerly but it was one of Christina's sisters. He was surprised their breakfast was as simple as at the Kierney's on a workday, bread, cheese and hot porridge. In an apparent gesture of hospitality toward their guests, there were small jars of different jams and a tub of butter. Despite their wealth, the Weiser household was a frugal one, he noted.

Georg hurriedly excused himself. He had to see Christina again. He walked briskly about the yard, determined she was not outside and strode toward the kitchen. "Guten Morgen" he said to

Mrs. Weiser, bowing and hoping his guttural rough German did not offend her. She responded in kind, with a slight tilt of her head and a bemused smile playing at the corners of her mouth. Christina was emptying a bucket of water into a long rectangular copper tub beneath the butcher-block table. As she left with two empty buckets, he picked up the tub that was barely full and awkwardly turned it sideways while ducking simultaneously through the kitchen door.

She was cranking the well pulley as he approached and their hands touched as Georg reached out for the smooth wooden handle. He took over and easily hauled the bucket up and poured it into the basin at her feet. When it was filled to just below the rim, Georg bent to lift it and carry it to the kitchen. They had not yet spoken a word to each other.

"Georg," she said, in German, touching his arm lightly and pronouncing his name properly with the harsh g sound. "I am pleased you asked me to help explain your thoughts to young James. It gave me insight into your heart. You are a decent man."

He shrugged and hoped he had not blushed. "I have done many terrible things in my life here in America. I have thought I must now only do the most good and hope it pleases God," he replied. She was wearing a simple linen dress with the same embroidered apron when he first saw her. He realized that was only the day before yesterday. Her blond hair, once again in a long single braid smelled fresh, like newly cut hay. He wanted to tell her how beautiful she looked to him but even speaking in his native language did not bolster his courage enough to express himself so openly. He bent down and lifted the basin. Holding it steady, he carried it into the kitchen, turning sidewise and lowering his head to avoid the lintel.

This time, Mrs. Weiser smiled at him. "We are preparing some food for your journey. Mr. Kierney is anxious to leave," she said, pointing to slices of ham and a wedge of cheese nearby. She was a handsome woman, he thought. Christina had her mother's grace and good looks.

"I must go," Georg said quickly, bowing as he left. He was disappointed in himself. He should have told Christina how much he wished to see her again. Then, he thought that would have been a foolish thing to say. The Kierney's would not be visiting the Weisers and he and James would be in a Continental Army Regiment far from this peaceful farm.

Thomas and Mr. Weiser stood talking on the porch as Georg came around the corner of the house. James came bounding down the steps whooping and yelling something about soldiering. He exuberantly danced around Georg until a word from his father sent him running toward the barn to hitch Daniel to the wagon. As Georg and Thomas climbed on to the wagon seat, with Georg on the outside this time, Christina approached with a reed basket covered with a flower-patterned cloth.

"This is food for your trip home," she said in English. "Bierbrodt," she indicated to Georg, patting the cloth. "I made it myself." And then more softly, "I hope to see you again." And with that, she stepped back from the wagon and waved as they left the road and drove past the church. She was still waving as they reached the bend in the road.

"Father. Tell Georg the good news or I shall burst from not doing it myself."

Thomas smiled and put arm around Georg's shoulder. "James will enlist in Major Weiser's Chester County Militia Regiment. He will serve ninety days, as do all other recruits." Georg slowly absorbed the English words.

"I will be trained and fighting for our independence," James said enthusiastically, leaning forward in front of his father to see Georg's reaction.

"The County Militia is required to defend Chester County. Like all our militias, they are prohibited by the Pennsylvania legislature to leave the Commonwealth," Thomas explained. Georg was puzzled. It was a strange way to fight a war against the British Army that marched from New York to New Jersey to Pennsylvania, and he had heard, sailed to the colonies far to the south. Slowly, he realized that if the British Army quartered in New York City and on Staten Island with its plentiful supplies of grain and meat, did not invade Pennsylvania, James was in no danger of going into battle.

"Gregory offered this to James instead of his joining a regiment of Continentals." Before Georg could ask why, Thomas said, "His daughter Christina told her father of your offer to enlist with James to protect him." He saw that Georg looked puzzled. "You do not need to understand all of my words. James will serve for ninety days and you will remain on the farm. There will be much for the two of us to do with James gone" he said poking Georg in the arm.

"Listen carefully," Thomas said, holding up his index finger and speaking deliberately. "You," he said as he pointed at Georg, "will drive James in our wagon to the Weiser farm where the new recruits are to assemble. I can do without the horse for three days. One day down, one day there and one day back." Kierney paused, watching Georg assimilate this new information. He leaned over and patted the reed basket. "You can return this basket and the cloth to Christina at that time. I am certain Mrs. Kierney will fill it with something appropriate to reciprocate their kindness."

Chapter 4 - The Hysterical Wife

Elisabeth held their son Henry around the waist as the little boy giggled and stared out the carriage window. He was almost eight months old, sturdy, just beginning to lose the baby fat around his thighs. His reddish brown hair, the color of his father's, now covered his entire crown although some scaly white flakes were still visible along the temples. Lucy Knox said this was normal and disappeared before a baby was a year old. Elisabeth, new to motherhood and without her own mother's advice, welcomed Lucy's experienced guidance.

When she looked at Henry's face, she saw Will's brown eyes sparkling back at her but with her features - her nose and chin and full lips that puckered after feeding. Henry had developed the endearing habit of pointing with his little crooked index finger that now was directed toward the brilliant fall foliage - the intense red and orange of the oaks, red maples, black gum and sassafras trees, the luminous yellow, and dazzling orange and scarlet of the sugar maples, and the lighter yellows of the ash and beech.

One of the troopers escorting their carriage appeared at the window to Henry's delight. The little boy smiled and gestured with his finger as if to say to his mother – "look who came just for me."

The trooper bent low in the saddle and leaned in. "Mrs. Knox. With the Lieutenant's compliments. We will rest at the Reed house for the night. From there, 'tis only a half a day's ride to West Point."

"Thank you for the information," she replied, dismissing him with a wave.

Lucy Knox shifted her rear on the cushioned seat that provided little comfort from the jarring, bouncing ride and sighed. Her gray travel cloak, which she had taken off as the day warmed, was rolled behind her as extra padding for her back. In her fleshy arms, she cradled her own son named Henry Jackson after her husband's friend.[1] Elisabeth had lost the weight she had gained during her pregnancy. Mrs. Knox seemed to have added more since the birth of their first son at the end of May. She must weigh two-hundred and a quarter at least, Elisabeth thought to herself.

Four-year old Lucy, alternately kissed her baby brother's arm extending from his linen shift and reassuringly carried on a one way conversation with him.

"Do not worry little brother. We will be with Papa soon," she cooed softly to him. "Mama and Lisbeth are here and they will care for us until then."

Lucy Knox smiled at her daughter and son. The little boy's eyes fixed on his sister's face and he arched his back and twisted his body in his mother's arms to be able to see little Lucy better. In doing so, he brushed against his mother's breast and immediately became interested in sucking. Lucy unbuttoned her bodice and put the little boy to her breast. Elisabeth had weaned Henry in early August and was glad of it. His four front teeth had hurt her, although she had to admit, she missed the overwhelming sense of amazement that her milk alone had nourished the tiny wizened infant into her hearty and healthy son.

"I was hoping for a letter from my dear Harry advising where we will be staying while the artillery is encamped near West Point." She sighed. "I do hope it will be a proper home now that we have two children to care for." She placed Henry on her knee and jounced him up and down, patting him on the back with her hand until he produced a prodigious burp. That provoked a smile from his mother who rewarded him by lowering her head and blowing on his neck.

It mattered not to Elisabeth where she lived. She would soon be with Will. Even if it were simply a small room with a bed and cradle in a crudely made wood cabin, that would be enough for her. The Army had left Morristown at the end of June and she had not seen Will for almost three months. Lucy Knox had written numerous letters to the General imploring him to reunite their family. Finally, he had relented and made arrangements for his wife and two children to come to West Point. There were Loyalist militias operating north of New York City and rumors of an imminent British attack up the Hudson River valley. "Nothing would please him more," General Knox had written to his beloved Lucy, than for his "dearest friend and their darling children," to join him but he would not risk their safety "for the most longed-for pleasure of their presence." Lucy had read the letter to Elisabeth so often she knew many of the phrases by heart. She was, of course, thankful to be traveling with the General's wife and family. The courtesies afforded Lucy Knox at the wayside inns and homes of prominent patriots redounded to her as well.

They were quite the impressive caravan – a cavalry escort, two carriages, the second one transporting Mrs. Knox's personal servant, a female cook and a nanny for the children, followed by two wagons laden down with pots and pans, a cradle for Henry and a small bed for little Lucy and trunks filled with Lucy's dresses, gowns, cloaks, other clothing and quilts and linens. Two wooden boxes held bottles of Madeira wine and brandy Lucy had obtained from friends in Philadelphia, a gift for her husband and his official family. They lay, carefully nestled in cloth and straw, to enable them to survive the journey. Four barrels of beer completed the cargo of consumables. Lucy Knox was the consummate hostess and intended to fulfill her role with foresight and graciousness.

"I remember," she said to Elisabeth, "a much different journey more than two years ago, when General Arnold escorted little Lucy and me from Hartford to the army encamped at Valley Forge. My dear Harry was much taken by the General's chivalrous nature and the attention he paid to my well being and our infant daughter."[2] She smiled at some secret and then decided to reveal it to Elisabeth. "I first met General Arnold in Cambridge where I hosted many a tea and dinner for him in our drawing room. Indeed, I introduced him to Ms. Deblois with whom he immediately became infatuated and sent her many letters expressing his affection, using me as the conduit." She clicked her tongue and wagged her finger in disapproval. "She was a beautiful young lady but her family were Tories and wished the rebels to be driven from Boston at the point of British bayonets. So, the General abandoned his courtship of the 'heavenly Ms. Debois,' and as you know, his heart was later captured by your friend, Peggy Shippen.[3] I suppose most men may be beguiled by a pretty face and deceived into believing this young girl or that one is the sole object of their heart's devotion and they would die if their affection was not reciprocated." Lucy said, musing on Arnold's prior courtship.

"And once a man has found their true love?" Elisabeth asked.

"Then both husband and wife become dearest friends with each being a part of the other, as are Harry and I, and bereft when apart." She laughed, slightly embarrassed. "My thoughts were so filled with the image of my Harry I forgot to add and you and Will as well."

Elisabeth tut-tutted to indicate the omission was nothing.

Once they were quartered near West Point, Elisabeth knew she would have to call on Peggy Shippen Arnold and Edward, her own young son, born in March barely one month after Elisabeth had given birth to Henry at the Ford Mansion. As the wife of the commanding General of the fortifications of West Point, Peggy certainly would not have shed her patronizing manner nor her sense of entitlement. Perhaps, the shared experience of being pregnant with their first born and the common fear of the dangers of childbirth followed by the joys of young motherhood would create a bond between them. Elisabeth was not sure what she dreaded most – being patronized by Peggy or being unduly pressured to be her friend.

She blamed herself for her negative thoughts. Peggy Shippen was now the wife of General Arnold, a war hero and true patriot. While Peggy certainly had enjoyed the attention of British officers in Philadelphia at many of the same soirees, dances, teas and plays Elisabeth had attended with Captain Montresor, it was in her past.

There was the usual commotion and hustle and bustle when

they arrived at the Reed house. Despite Lucy Knox's earnest protestations, the Reeds relinquished their large bed and room to her and her infant son, with little Lucy sleeping with the nanny in a loft. "My little Lucy is a sound and healthy one. However, until I am reunited with my dear Harry I am nervous for my son to sleep alone in a cradle instead of feeling him breathing in my arms," she explained, insisting that Elisabeth and Henry also share the same bed.

While Lucy spent a restful night deep asleep in the hollow of the mattress depressed by her weight, Elisabeth was kept awake by her snoring. In the early hours before dawn, just as she felt restorative sleep overcoming her, her Henry awoke and she anxiously soothed and quieted him with rocking, soft lullabies and offering him her little finger to suck. As soon as she heard the servants about in the kitchen, she went downstairs and sitting by the fire, fed Henry pap, porridge and goat's milk, still warm from the udder.

Their breakfast with the Reeds was disturbed by the arrival of a courier and a letter for Mrs. Knox. Lucy eagerly took it in her hands, immediately let out a cry of joy as she recognized her husband's handwriting and read it quickly to herself. Her face assumed a beatific smile as she folded the letter on her lap, carefully re-creasing the folds.

"I must share my good news with you my dear friend," she said nodding to Elisabeth, "as well as our kind host and hostess. My beloved Harry has rented us comfortable quarters, a fine Georgian home within an easy ride to West Point and close to General Arnold's headquarters but on the west side of the Hudson River."

Elisabeth sensed, without having seen the premises Lucy was already planning her first elegant dinner party at her new residence.

"Harry will not be there to greet us upon our arrival," she continued with a tinge of self-importance in her voice as she unfolded the letter again. She ran her finger down the page until she found the relevant part.

"I trust my Dearest Love, disappointment will not overcome you as you read the following. Instead, be proud of your Harry and my meager contribution to our Great Cause. I am to ride with His

Excellency and General Lafayette to meet with Admiral de T and Count R at an undisclosed location. Our plans, with the blessing of Providence, may see the end to this war and the final defeat of the British. I am certain My Beloved that it was Providence that guided you to my bookshop and prompted you to teach me French so that I may be of use to General Washington in these discussions. However, I doubt whether Providence approved of the many lessons where you . . .

Lucy colored, paused before completing the sentence and brought her hand to her mouth.

"My dear Elisabeth," she said quickly. "Please forgive me. In the excitement of receiving this letter, I forgot to inform you of Harry's words about Will." She hastily turned the sheet over and located the place above her husband's signature.

"Be certain to inform Elisabeth that Will remains at West Point, awaiting her arrival. I have advised him that his wife and babe may lodge with us until suitable quarters are arranged for the married officers at Fort Arnold. [4]

"It is settled," Lucy Knox said with conviction. "One of Harry's Headquarters Guards will notify your dear husband and he will fly to you as swiftly as a bird."

"Both Will and I are grateful for General Knox's interest, and yours too, in our wellbeing," Elisabeth replied, knowing the General's wife appreciated her occasionally caring for her daughter and being her traveling companion. Even though Lucy was only four years older than her, on this journey she fulfilled the roll of Elisabeth's older sisters and mother. Elisabeth felt their absence keenly, especially in need of their experience and advice in the care of her first born. She hoped that Mercy Hadley, her friend who had delivered Henry, would be at the Fort with Captain Hadley. Mercy would make her feel more secure. She worried for the health of her son. The coming cold weather and exposure to the effluvia and vapors of the camp would bring the onset of coughs and fevers. Elisabeth shuddered, recalling the death of the infant Julia Knox a year ago July, succumbing to the wracking cough that shook her frail little body. She rocked Henry in her arms, thankful that he seemed to have his father's robust health.

Two days after settling in at General Knox's home, Will arrived on Big Red. Rather, he galloped up to the house mid-morning and jumped to the ground in his eagerness to see Elisabeth and their son. The sweat on his horse's flanks and the lather from his mouth indicated it had been a full gallop for most of the way. The next three days were the most blissful she had known, filled with the contentment and knowledge that she and Will would be together while he was stationed at Fort Arnold. He was needed to help improve the positioning of the artillery and would be here through the fall. Then, she thought the artillery would move to join the army in winter quarters and perhaps the war would be over by the spring.

It was early in the morning. The cook had killed three chickens and was engaging in plucking and cleaning them. Lucy Knox was upstairs with her two children and the nanny. Elisabeth, having fed Henry and given him to Will, was cutting vegetables for the stew pot hanging from a large curved iron hook over the hearth. The white clapboard building attached to the Georgian stone home General Knox had described to his wife housed the kitchen with lofts above for the sleeping quarters for the servants. Leaving the chopping knife on the wooden kitchen table alongside the uncut carrots and onions, she wiped her hands on her apron, and left the low-ceiling kitchen to step outside.

Big Red grazed placidly in the adjacent pasture. Will, in shirt sleeves, stood nearby in the warm sun, enjoying the unusual balmy fall weather. He held Henry in the crook of his arm and ambled slowly through the field. She could not hear his words but he was talking in an animated fashion to their son, pointing with his free hand to the trees and birds above.

From their first day together, Elisabeth noticed a strangeness in her husband's behavior. When he was nearby he was attentive as always and in her heart she knew from his smile and the way he looked at her, he loved her fervently and with all his being. It struck her Will had lost some of his hearing one night when he failed to react to Henry whimpering quietly in his pine crib on the floor of their tiny bedroom. She experimented, speaking loudly at times and then softly at others. Regretfully, she concluded he indeed was unable to hear her on many of the latter occasions.

It was no matter she thought. If this was the worst that happened to her husband because of the war. . . She let the thought die in her mind as Will whistled for Big Red. The horse approached his master and lowered his head. Will stroked the horse's nose and lifted Henry sideways on the horse where the saddle would have been. He held their son in place with his hand on the baby's chest. Henry giggled with delight to be so much higher than his father and grabbed a handful of Will's hair in his little fist.

Maybe they could visit her family in Albany before the heavy winter snows set in and the river froze, It was less than one hundred miles north. Perhaps they could borrow a carriage or her father could send one of his trading vessels down the Hudson for them. She would have to write him immediately for it was almost the end of September. Although she had no idea how Big Red would get to Albany, in her mind she envisioned herself and Will and Henry, riding through the cobblestoned streets of Albany on the big horse up to her parents red-brick mansion. She imagined being greeted by them and her sisters, handing little Henry down into the outstretched arms of Agnes, the beloved servant who had been with the family for as long as Elisabeth could remember. It had been Agnes who had sat beside her when Will drove them across the frozen Hudson by sled in '75. And now, Will was a Lieutenant in General Knox's artillery, sitting so handsomely on Big Red and she, a mother with a son – a grandson for her parents to coddle and coo over.

These are the silly daydreams of a foolish young girl, she admonished herself before returning to the kitchen as she took one last loving look at Will with Henry bouncing on shoulders and Big Red walking beside them.

Will left for Fort Arnold about five, after the midday meal was over. It was getting dark. He said it was only a short five-mile ride but she worried about him nevertheless. Strange, she thought to herself how she was more anxious for his safety and wellbeing when she was in the same locality and he was merely stationed in camp,

The Hysterical Wife

than when they were separated by hundreds of miles and he was engaged in battle.

She climbed into the bed they had shared the night before. To ward off her overwhelming feeling of dread and loneliness, she reached down with one hand to gently rock Henry's cradle and imagined their quarters at the Fort. Will had assured her they would be ready by the end of the month and no later than the first week in October. Then she would join him and from there, she would arrange to call on Peggy Arnold at the Robinson House that served as the General's residence. It was on the east side of the river and required a ferry ride. She would see if Peggy as the mother of her own new born son, would recognize the necessity for Elisabeth to travel in comfort with Henry and send the General's barge instead of leaving her to cross the river by an ordinary ferry. Now, that would be arriving in style, she smiled to herself as she drifted off to sleep.

The following morning, while the nanny tended to the two Henrys, Elisabeth took little Lucy with her and showed her how to weed the vegetable garden. They picked sage and rosemary to spice the roast chicken for the dinner meal. Mrs. Knox wrote letters and when the babies were napping, invited Elisabeth for tea in the drawing room.

"I will need cakes and pies if I am to entertain properly," she said, looking askance at a small piece of bread she had smeared with raspberry jam. "Still, as Harry says, it is the company more than the food and drink that makes for a stimulating dinner party. We proved that at Valley Forge did we not?" She took a nibble of the bread and licked the jam from her lips. "I hope that Harry is able to persuade General Washington and his young officers to dine with us. You must meet Marquis de Lafayette. A more gracious gentlemen I have rarely encountered."

She was about to continue on about the courtly Frenchman's attributes when Elisabeth heard Will shouting for her by name. The two women quickly rose and from the front window saw Will swinging out of the saddle as one of the sentries grabbed the reins.

Elisabeth was barely out of the room and halfway down the steps before Will was bounding up to meet her. Mrs. Knox, for all her girth was close behind on the landing.

"Hurry, Elisabeth. Gather some clothes, leave the baby and come with me. Mrs. Arnold has lost her mind. General Knox thinks you are the one to soothe and restore her reason."

"What do you mean, lost her mind?" Lucy asked. Will shooed them back into the drawing room and closed the door. "General Arnold has betrayed us to the British. He fled on board a British sloop leaving his wife and babe behind. The poor woman has gone mad, screaming and yelling all are out to murder her and their son. This was related to me by messenger from General Knox with instructions to bring Elisabeth post haste to the Robinson house." He turned toward Elisabeth. "Now hurry to get ready. The General's barge will meet us below Fort Arnold and take us across."

"I will not leave our baby," Elisabeth said.

"He will be well taken care of by me and the nanny," Lucy said.

"I will not leave him," she repeated adamantly.

"Well and good," Will said. "This is not the time to argue. I will help you to gather up your clothes and his things as well." He turned to Lucy Knox. "I have been cautioned to tell you the betrayal by Arnold is not to be spoken of. The army itself is yet unaware."

Will stood on the mounting block and with his hands around Elisabeth's slender waist, effortlessly lifted her up to sit sidesaddle on Big Red. Then, he handed Henry up to her. The little boy was wearing a woolen cap pulled down over his ears. Elisabeth feared he would be chilled on the ride. Will, with his left foot in the stirrup, swung himself into the saddle behind her. With the reins in his hands, his arms encompassed his little family. A rolled up blanket with a few of her clothes was cinched to the back of the saddle and another linen shirt and blanket for Henry, as well as his pap spoon and wooden bowl nestled in Will's saddlebag.

Elisabeth leaned backwards, her left shoulder pressing hard into Will's chest as she clutched Henry within the folds of her cloak. For her, the ride was harrowing. Even with the mid-afternoon sun warming her face, she feared the jouncing would harm their little one.

"How is he?" Will asked bringing his lips close to her ear and peering over her shoulder. Henry peeking out from within his cloaked perch smiling and giggling, excited to be up so high.

"He will be a fine horseman someday," Will said. "See how fearless he is? Do not worry my love. Big Red is sure footed and so broad it is as if you are riding on a ship."

She smiled nervously in return and stoically maintained a cheerful manner, cooing and speaking in a high pitch singsong voice, more to calm herself than to reassure Henry. As they neared the Fort, Will turned Big Red away from the wide road leading to the gate and slowed the horse, guiding him down a narrow rocky trail that led to the river below. Elisabeth had a glimpse of a barge tied up at the end of a pier. The angle of descent was steep. Panic-stricken she leaned further back into Will's chest, closed her eyes and firmly held Henry with both hands around his waist. She felt Will's muscular forearms close in around her. When she sensed they had reached level ground she opened her eyes. The pier was before them and strong hands reached up to take the baby and then help her down. She sat on a cushioned bench under an awning near the prow. The benches in the stern had been removed. Will coaxed Big Red into position and the barge tipped wildly at the dock until the horse was centered and equilibrium was restored. Henry giggled with joy at the tumultuous rocking and seemed more perturbed when it ceased.

The river was narrow at the Point. The helmsmen and crew steered the barge around the tip of an island and across a narrow channel toward a pier on the east side. In the distance, through the trees, Elisabeth saw wisps of smoke curling up above the bright autumn foliage. Once on the eastern side of the river, they remounted. Will urged Big Red up the trail from the water on to a trail more than a road that threaded through thick woods. The incline was steep enough to require Elisabeth to lean back into Will's arms. They emerged from the trees into a wide meadow surrounded by orchards of orderly planted trees. Ahead, was the

Robinson House, a two-story building with wide windows, nestled among tall shading evergreens.

General Knox met them in the entrance way and if he was surprised to see Elisabeth had brought the baby, he did not show it.

"I would offer you some rest and sustenance if time permitted but the situation is urgent." Elisabeth caught a glimpse through an open door of several men in uniforms conferring earnestly in an adjacent room.

"Yesterday morning, when her husband fled after his dastardly treachery had been discovered, his distraught wife lost her mind. According to Colonel Varick, who was present when the poor woman first became hysterical, it was the most piteous sight he had ever witnessed. The poor distraught woman shrieked and screamed, asked the Colonel, who himself was ill with a fever, if he had ordered her child to be killed." Knox spoke in a deep whisper as if the very mention of Mrs. Arnold's condition was a source of deep sorrow.

"Then, when his Excellency arrived after his tour of the fortifications she claimed he was not General Washington but someone to assist Colonel Varick in killing her little Neddy. She clutched the wee wailing child to her breast and lamented his fate caused by the deceit of his father. This, I witnessed myself."

"And how is she now?" Elisabeth asked.

"She is more subdued but has taken neither food nor drink and frequently points to the ceiling of her bedroom and screams the spirits have taken her husband and hot irons are bedeviling her head." He shook his head in bewilderment. "Dr. Eustis from the fort has no remedy for her utter frenzy and wild madness."[5]

"Show me to her," Elisabeth said. "Will, bring me Henry's pap spoon and bowl and find some bread and fresh milk from the kitchen. Or, if there is none, a little hot water to make the bread soft."

"You are not bringing our little boy with you into her room?" Will asked incredulously.

"That is definitely my intention. We will speak to each other as two young mothers," Elisabeth replied. Her tone and facial expression left no doubt she was serious. Will retreated to the front door to retrieve his saddlebags.

While he was gone, General Knox introduced Elisabeth to Colonel Varick, one of General Arnold's aides. Varick escorted her upstairs to the bedroom Peggy had shared with her husband before his flight. He knocked twice and announced through the closed door, "I have brought you a visitor. A woman acquainted with you from Philadelphia."

There was no reply from within. Elisabeth shifted Henry to her hip and holding his bowl and spoon in one hand, turned the brass knob and entered. Peggy was sitting on the bed propped up by two pillows. Her blond tresses tumbled over one shoulder as if they had been deliberately arranged. The strap of her nightdress had fallen to the middle of her upper arm so that the curve of her breast was fully visible.

"Hello Peggy," Elisabeth said matter-of-factly as she closed the door behind her. "It has been many months since we were last together in Philadelphia." She sat down on the edge of the bed and admired the little boy nestled in Peggy's arms. "Look at us now. Both young mothers with fine infant boys. This is our son Henry. And that must be Neddy, named after your father."

Peggy looked at her slyly with what Elisabeth thought was the hint of a smirk. Elisabeth said nothing and mashed the wet bread in the bowl and gently began feeding Henry who attempted to intercept the spoon his mother held and grab it himself.

"I am so relieved to no longer be nursing. Henry has sharp little teeth and they hurt."

Peggy pulled Neddy closer to her and the little boy instinctively nuzzled the nightgown out of the way and began sucking noisily. She stroked the crown of his head and avoided making direct eye contact with Elisabeth.

"I am so in need of your presence, Elisabeth," Peggy said, her voice urgent and tight with tension. "You must help me. They are trying to kill my little Neddy and me too if they could get away with it." She looked out of the window to the distant woods. "The spirits have taken Benedict there where they are torturing him with hot irons."

Elisabeth let her run on. Although she seemed agitated, Elisabeth had the impression that Peggy was repeating the lines she had used with the Generals, Colonel Varick and others, without the hysterical behavior and mad performance of the previous day. When Peggy paused in her description of how the hot irons were piercing her brain, preventing her from sleeping or eating, Elisabeth redirected the conversation back to their babies.

"I was terrified as my time approached," she said. "I had only my friend Mercy Ford Hadley to attend me, while you must have enjoyed the care of the finest of doctors in Philadelphia. Now, when I behold my little boy, I have no clear recollection of the pain of giving birth nor the terrible fear that preceded it."

Peggy peered at Elisabeth's face as if trying to identify her, before permitting herself a slight nod of agreement. Elisabeth saw for a brief moment, a look that was more of cunning calculation as if Peggy was planning how to convincingly return to her normal self, using Elisabeth's presence to do so. She switched Neddy to her other breast.

"I was attended by Dr. Rush who is a close friend of my father's." She sighed. "I very much wish to be in the bosom of my family in Philadelphia and feel safe and secure once again." She said this in such a matter of fact way, Elisabeth at first did not realize Peggy was using her as a conduit to convey this message. As she contemplated how to reply, Henry lost interest in eating any more pap and crawled out of her arms toward Peggy and Neddy. Peggy's son, having finished sucking, squirmed in his mother's arms and propped up by her, observed Henry rocking on all fours trying to make forward progress on the soft flowered quilt. Henry lifted himself up on his knees and pointed with his crooked finger at Neddy. To both mothers' surprise, Neddy raised his small hand and with his clenched fingers aimed it at Henry. Peggy permitted herself a smile and patted Elisabeth's hand.

"You are staying here?" she asked anxiously. "I feel your presence in this house will protect me from those intending to do me harm."

Before Elisabeth could reply, there was a sharp knock at the door. Peggy pushed herself back against the headboard, gathered her son tightly in her arms and looked frantically at the door, as if demons were about to descend upon her.

"It is I, Colonel Varick. I have a letter for Mrs. Arnold. It is from the General. Her husband."

"It is a trick,' Peggy hissed, looking wildly about. "Ask him to hand the letter to you. Do not let him in."

"Watch Henry," Elisabeth said. She left her son in the middle of the bed and partially opened the door.

"She seems calmer now," she whispered, taking the letter from Colonel Varick's hand. "Leave us alone for a while longer."

There was no masking Peggy's eagerness to read her husband's message to her, nor her surprise that the letter was unopened.[6] To Elisabeth, these seemed sincere and heartfelt emotions and not disassembling behavior. Peggy scanned the letter quickly then re-read it again.

"He has asked General Washington to take me under his protection and permit me to travel to Philadelphia or to come to him in New York. And he asks me to write him one line 'to ease his anxious heart,' and for 'God Almighty to bless and protect me.'"[7]

She folded the letter into quarters and placed it between her breasts as if it were a charm hanging from a necklace. The envelope lay on the bed.

"This is all I could have hoped for," she said calmly. "Elisabeth, would you please ask my servant to come to my room." She pulled one pillow from behind her and placed the now drowsing Neddy's head on it. "And then be so kind as to inform Colonel Varick, I will require paper and pen and will be pleased to see His Excellency, General Washington by late afternoon." Gone were the ravings about iron rods in the head, murderous intentions of those around her and lamentations of the fate of her baby boy. "With General Washington's generous assistance and the arrangements he will make, I hope to leave for Philadelphia within two days."

Elisabeth grabbed Henry as he was about to fall off the edge of the high four poster bed and holding him over her shoulder moved toward the door. "I am pleased that my visit, in some small way, helped to restore your reason," she said, regretting that a hint of sarcasm crept into her voice.

"Oh, my dear Elisabeth. It was the letter from my admirable husband that has restored it. You merely served to pass the time of day. Please extend my good wishes to your handsome husband. I hope he remains as true to you as mine has to me." Her small lips pursed in the condescending expression with which Elisabeth was all too familiar.

Elisabeth's hand tightened on the brass door knob. She turned compelling herself to appear composed so as not to give Peggy the satisfaction of knowing how irritated she was by her patronizing manner. "He will be more than that and constant to our cause as well, upon his sworn oath of fidelity, an oath your husband has dishonored."

With that, she left holding Henry in one arm and closed the door gently so as not to startle the sleeping Neddy. She went down stairs to inform Colonel Varick of Peggy's demands and then to find Will.[8]

Chapter 5 - The Aftermath of Treason

The barge bobbed up and down in the middle of the river, the sails furled on its one forward mast. An anchor, attached to the oversized stern capstan held the boat in position. Captain Holmes, along with Sergeant Adam Cooper and ten soldiers stood near the bow that was pointed east toward Constitution Island.

The forged iron chain, between the rocky outcropping shown on the charts as West Point and the island, a distance of one thousand five hundred feet, loomed beneath the surface like a giant black necklace curving downstream. Fifty-foot long log rafts, at one-hundred foot intervals, enabled the chain to float high enough to tear into the hull of any British vessel attempting to pass.

Last night, general orders for the day were read to all troops at newly renamed Fort Clinton, informing them "treason of the blackest dye was yesterday discovered," and detailing the traitorous efforts of General Arnold to turn West Point over to the British.[1] All soldiers were required to perform their assigned tasks with the utmost urgency to repair and reinforce West Point's defenses neglected by the infamous traitor.

Holmes and his work party had started at first light. He selected Sergeant Adam Cooper, who had been promoted for his role in thwarting the raid on the Ford Mansion the past winter, and a platoon of ordinary soldiers from a Connecticut Regiment. They began in the middle of the river. Holmes glanced back at the soldiers feverishly working to restore the shore batteries on the west side of the river. Below Fort Clinton, swarms of them, like ants disturbed from their nest, clambered along the rocky beach, hauling stones up from the river and dragging trees trimmed of their branches, down the slopes from above. Even if the chain was in poor repair closer to the two shores, cannons would deal with any small British ships that attempted to hug the rocks. The frigates with their deeper draft would have to attempt a mid-river passage.

The massive chain was divided into fifty-three sets of ten links each, the tenth link, a clevis, a U shaped link with a large bolt pin where the sets were connected together. The log raft floats were spaced where the sections were attached by swivels to allow them to turn without twisting the chain. Holmes' orders, from Major Jean Louis de Genton, the Fort's chief engineer, were to inspect the clevis and swivels where the sets of the chains were joined to ensure they had not deteriorated due to Arnold's treasonous neglect. If a British attack was imminent, there would be no time to replace the water-logged and rotting timbers comprising the raft floats. That could be done when the chain was hauled out once the river began to freeze in early winter.[2]

It was late afternoon and they had examined eleven of the fifteen swivels. They followed the same procedure each time. Adam, a fisherman unafraid of the water, was the one who had the dangerous job of attaching the rope to the swivel. Stripped down to his canvas breeches he held the multi-braided rope in both hands. With a nod from Holmes, Adam slipped over the gunwale. The chain floated ten to twelve feet below. He surfaced, gasping for air, holding on to the rope, part still coiled on the deck, the remainder wound tight around the massive capstan. Under he went again, staying down longer this time and when he surfaced exhausted with water droplets clinging to his tightly curled hair, he hung on to the taut rope before helping hands hauled him back into the barge.

"'Tis tied, Captain. To the triangle of the swivel. Tight as can be," he said shivering in a blanket wrapped around his shoulders. He sat on the foredeck hatch cover in the remaining shaft of sunlight from the late September sun.

Water trickled in rivulets from his breeches and formed puddles around his bare feet.

"All right men," Holmes ordered. "To the capstan. Put your shoulders into it." There were four oak spokes or bars, each as thick as a man's thigh, protruding horizontally from the upright elm hub.[3] With a shout, two men to a spoke, the soldiers pushed and grunted as the capstan slowly turned. Holmes peered over the side until the set of the chain broke the surface. He signaled with a raised hand and the soldiers swiftly looped the rope around the iron cleat to prevent the rope from slipping.

Holmes, on his hands and knees peered over the side the better to see. The bottom of the triangle was seated in the middle of the large bolt pin of the clevis and the tip was snug against the figure eight link that made up the other part of the iron swivel. It was the bolt pin that he wanted to examine closely. The top ring holding this bolt in place was encased in a green slime. He stretched his arm into the water up to his elbow and scraped the slime away with a bayonet. The chain turned slowly in the current exposing the ring at the bottom of the pin. It was rusting. He used the bayonet point to scrape a few flakes from it and decided it was superficial. Sound enough to last the few months until winter. He dried his arm on his breeches and signaled for the men to give the rope a little slack.

One of the soldiers eagerly leaned over to untie the rope. Before Holmes could caution him to wait for someone to hold the link with the long pronged pole, the current slammed the chain against the side of the sloop catching the soldier's hand between the hull and the iron. The man screamed and pulled his arm out of the river, his wrist crushed and bent at an unusual angle.

Quickly Holmes ordered the anchor hoisted. Sergeant Cooper, the only other one on board with any nautical experience directed two soldiers in setting the sails as the others manned the sweeps.

Holmes held the wheel and kept his eye on the short pier jutting out from a battery redoubt. Even with dusk approaching it still teemed with soldiers hastily rebuilding and heightening its walls. A well-worn trail, a dull brown line through the brilliantly colored trees led from there up the rocky hillside and beyond to

Fort Clinton. The Connecticut Regiment was in barracks outside the Fort and he assumed their Regimental Surgeon would be there. With luck, the soldier would keep the limb if gangrene did not set in. Holmes shuddered at the thought of being a cripple with one arm for the rest of one's life.

Adam walked along the deck encouraging the inexperienced soldiers to pull the sweeps together. Satisfied they were reasonably in rhythm, sufficient at least for the short distance to shore, he went and stood behind Holmes. His gaze focused on the stone, wood and earthen massive eastern wall of Fort Clinton. Many of the gun embrasures were empty and only a few dark muzzles of twenty-four pounders peered down river where it curved just south of Constitution Island. Will and others from the artillery regiment had hurriedly been sent south to Tappan for additional cannons. Hopefully, they would arrive soon and the guns placed in the newly restored batteries before any British warships appeared on the river.

Adam's thoughts turned to his own wife, somewhere south of New York. He and Sarah had been married five months ago in March, the day after she became a free woman. He had to leave her behind in Morristown with the rest of General Washington's servants and staff, when Knox's Artillery Regiment had been ordered north. He had no idea where she was now and when he would see her again.

"Captain?" Adam asked. "How long has it been since you have seen your wife and family?" Holmes held his eyes on the approaching pier. "I visited them in Salem for two weeks in the month of June," he said wistfully. He turned and looked at Adam. "Given the time you and I have been together, from '76 in Cambridge to now, almost the end of '80, I have spent more time with you than with my wife. My first son is some three years of age and my youngest boy turned two this past July."

"I am hopeful the army will take up winter quarters to the south and Sarah and I will be reunited."

"That is a pleasing thought Adam. First, we may have to deal with the British Army and their Hessian mercenaries.

Either their army sallies forth from New York City to attack us here, or we go south to root them out."

Adam nodded. He did not want to wait until the army went into winter camp to see Sarah. Not if he could fall in battle before then. Better to be reunited sooner. He resolved to speak with General Knox. Perhaps he would know whether Washington's kitchen staff was still in Morristown. He smiled to himself, thinking of Sarah now a freewoman working in that same kitchen and earning her own wages. No portion to be paid to any master and no danger of a master selling her to someone else. He would teach their own sons to fish and they would grow up free and strong in Marblehead.

The ungainly barge was nearing the narrow pier. The soldiers had raised their sweeps. Holmes's command shattered Adam's enjoyable daydreaming. "Adam. Go forward and tie us up before another one of these inexperienced soldiers injures himself by trying to help."

He leaped nimbly ashore and after wrapping the rope around a pier post, tied it fast. The soldiers moved off the pier and as a group escorted their injured comrade up the path to their barracks and the surgeon. They disappeared amidst the work crew carting stones to an uncompleted redoubt. Suddenly, there was a shout of anger and cries of pain. Adam turned to see a French Officer flailing about him with the flat of his sword and ordering the Connecticut soldiers to return to work. The one with the injured wrist had fallen on the ground and was protecting his head with his good arm, while the Frenchman kicked him viciously in the ribs. "Get up you lazy dog. You have not been dismissed," he shouted, landing an especially hard kick on the innocent soldier's hip, knocking him on his side. The soldier cried out in pain as his smashed wrist touched the packed earth.

Adam rushed up the slight hill, holding the long pole with the iron hook at the end in his hand like a lance.

"Stay your hand," Adam yelled as he closed with the Frenchman. The officer turned and without any warning, struck at Adam with his sword. Adam parried with the shaft and brought the pole down hard on the Frenchman's sword arm. In a fury, Adam followed up with a series of blows to the shoulders and ribs beating the Frenchman to his knees. He stopped when Captain Holmes grabbed him by the shoulder and ordered him to desist.

The French officer rose slowly from the ground, swaying dizzily and glared at the two of them. Holmes addressed Major Genton who had come running down from a partially constructed redoubt further up the hill.

"I do not tolerate such brutal behavior to men under my command," Holmes said, facing Genton. "Neither from a Continental nor French officer." Adam, unsure of Major Genton's intentions toward Holmes, stood next to him, grasping the pole, intently watching the Frenchman he had thrashed who was still holding his sword in limp arm.

Genton spoke to the officer in French, and the man sheathed his weapon with his good arm.

"This is Major Jean Bernard Gauthier de Murnan of my corps of engineers. He is in command of this work party and these soldiers are obligated to respect his orders."

"Not my soldiers," Holmes shot back. "Does he not know who he commands and who are others passing from the shore to the Fort? He assaulted them without provocation."

"I will see you and this black dog of yours court-martialed," Murnan hissed, holding his injured forearm across his waist. "Or is it permissible in your ill-disciplined army to strike a superior officer?" [4]

"I have confidence in the justice of my fellow officers," Holmes replied quietly. "As for Sergeant Cooper, he was acting on my orders to protect our men. I only regret that he ran faster and reached you before I."

Holmes took Adam by the elbow and led him past the two French officers and followed the rest of the soldiers from the sloop up the incline toward the fort. Once inside, Adam had the men line up, except for the injured one and his escort, to await orders from Holmes. The parade ground was shrouded in long shadows and candles had already been lit in some of the Fort's rudimentary structures.

"Captain, Sir and Sergeant Cooper." The corporal in charge of the platoon stepped forward. "If I may, on behalf of the men, we appreciate how you gave it to that Frenchie. With your permission sir, upon your order to dismiss, we will give you three cheers."

"Corporal. You will have the men assemble here tomorrow after reveille. They should draw their rations for the day." Holmes smiled and nodded to Adam.

"Platoon dismissed," he shouted. The Corporal turned on his heels. "Platoon dismissed," he repeated and added, "Three cheers for Captain Holmes and Sergeant Cooper – Hip, Hip, Hurray. Hip, hip hurray. Hip, hip hurray."

"Let us see if General Knox is still about. I must report the incident involving Major Murnan. Then I will make my entries in the log book to record our inspections of today." He glanced at Adam walking beside him, still carrying the long hooked pole. "The last person to call you a black dog was that Hessian at the battle of Trenton when the Mariners captured their entire Regiment." Adam had struck the Hessian in the stomach with the muzzle of his musket and then, when the man doubled over, clipped him on the chin with the stock.

"And we presented the Hessian colors to General Sullivan," Adam added, grinning at the recollection of the shock and anger of the captured Hessians seeing their flags marched off by three Mariners, including Titus. Good old Titus. Dead now of a pistol shot from a British Marine. He would still be alive if he had not lost an eye in the melee with the riflemen at Cambridge, when the backwoodsmen had gone after all the blacks on sentry duty. Adam felt the anger rising within him. For him it would always be a fight for dignity.

"Will this Frenchman cause us any trouble?"

Holmes thought before replying. "There will probably be a board of inquiry. The General will stand with us. Perhaps an apology will be made to the Frenchman commanding their Corps of Engineers. That will be the end of it."

And who will apologize to me for Murnan calling me a black dog. No! This will not be the end of it. Not for him. He wished Sarah were here. By her very presence she calmed his simmering anger and led him to think better thoughts. As he and Holmes walked quickly in the gathering dark, he hoped they would find General Knox within the commandant's office. Right then and there, he would ask the General to issue orders, passes, letters or whatever was necessary to bring Sarah to West Point.

—ʍ—

I shall not die this way, Sergeant Henry Gillet thought to himself. He tried to quell the terror that was rising up within him. After the fever that nearly carried him off and all the battles I have been in, I will not die here. I cannot. He wiped his hands on his work breeches and felt his linen shirt, damp with sweat, clinging to his back. He loaded his wheelbarrow to the rim, leveled the dirt with his shovel and left the tool behind. Ahead of him was a twenty-foot high stone and earthen wall being built for a powder magazine, well back from the battery on the shore of Constitution Island. To bring his barrow to the site, Gillet would have to push it up an inclined rocky path and, at the top, cross over a deep gorge by way of two narrow, thirty foot long planks laid side by side.

This was his first load. As Sergeant, he would lead the others in crossing. Behind him the men of his platoon of the 2nd Rhode Islanders waiting nervously. They were sailors, fishermen and flat landers. There were no mountains or gorges where they came from. They knew the ebb and flow of tides, the currents and the storms at sea. If it frightened others, it did not scare them. However, the thought of crossing a sixty feet deep gorge was terrifying. If he fell from the planks, Gillet knew his body would be smashed on the rocks below.

He started up the narrow path, lined with scrub trees and low brush. His heart pounded in his chest. He kept his eyes lowered, staring at the dirt in his barrow, willing himself not to see the distance on the other side of the gorge. As he approached the wooden planks, his throat was dry, his ears rang and his vision blurred. This would not do he said to himself. He would plunge off the planks from fear and not any misstep. He needed to get control of himself. Gillet stopped at the edge of the gorge before the metal-rimmed wheel hit the planks. With his hands, he took some dirt from the barrow and pressed it down on the ground to create a small ramp between the path and the edge of the planks. He did not want to begin the perilous crossing with the slightest jolt. As he smoothed the dirt, he peered over the edge of the gorge and saw the big boulders below. Slowly and carefully, he raised himself up from his knees and held the smooth wooden handles of the barrow in his hands. He hoped the planks were made of some strong wood and the engineers had made their calculations properly as to their length and strength.

Petrified, Gillet softly offered a prayer to God to watch over him and fixed his gaze on the other side. He would not look down. There, beyond the partially completed wall of the magazine was a forest. A tall oak, probably hit by lightning, had fallen against a stouter tree to form an inverted Y. He focused on the intersection of the Y and walked steadily across the gorge. It was only thirty feet he told himself, counting his steps for encouragement. When he reached the other side, the path widened and he made his way along the five-foot thick wall. It was constructed of logs and stones. He dumped the barrow's load in between the timber framework.

Going back, he was the last to cross. There was no Y shaped fork to concentrate on. Instead, he focused on the back of the head of the private in front of him, the soldier's shirt as wet as if he had been in the river, the hair on his bare head dripping sweat on his neck. Gillet could see every wrinkle, scratch and red infected lice bite on the man's skin.

He lost count of the trips they made. The only respite from the terror of crossing the gorge was digging and filling the wheelbarrows. He had to fight an inclination to slow down the work of excavating so as to delay having to confront his fears and that terrifying gorge. He thought he was mindful of the strain on the men and set a pace that was reasonable and not motivated by his dread of that two plank bridge. There was some grumbling at the quickness of the pace but since he led the men across on every trip, it did not amount to much. It was only at the end of the day, when the last crossing had been made, the men relaxed and began to joke among themselves. That night, at their campsite near the river, where they were attacked by swarms of mosquitos, the men threw green twigs on their fires and huddled closer to the smoke. Their rations, the same since they had arrived at West Point, were salted shad and bread. The men of Gillet's platoon supplemented their dinner with eels they had caught and roasted over the fire. The oil from their elongated bodies fell on the hot stones, the hissing momentarily drowning out the buzzing of the insects.

Each man received another gill of rum and when that was gone, it loosened their tongues and they bragged about how they had bravely crossed the gorge that became deeper with each telling. Gillet kept quiet. He knew from the incomplete state of construction of the powder magazine's walls, they would have to traverse the plank bridge tomorrow and probably several days thereafter before their work was completed.

The next morning, following reveille and roll call, after a hurried breakfast, they returned with their pickaxes and shovels to the excavation site. The bravura of the night before had vanished and Gillet sensed a feeling of trepidation among his platoon. This time, another work party was first to cross the gorge. His platoon was second. The early October morning air was chilly. Yet the men stripped off their jackets and laid them with their tri-corns in neat rows and chose to work in their shirt sleeves. It felt more secure to be less encumbered.

It did not help their morale when one of the work crew preceding them stumbled on the plank bridge, apparently because his wheelbarrow load was off kilter. He collapsed on his knees on the planks as the barrow tumbled below. The poor lad crawled on all fours to the other side and lay sobbing in plain view of his fellow soldiers.

Gillet turned to his men. He surprised himself by the steadiness of his voice although his gut was churning with fear. "Make sure your loads are balanced," he said. He waited while the platoon worked the dirt in the barrows to their satisfaction. It probably made no difference he thought, but perhaps it would serve to calm them a little. Private Hazzard, three men behind gave him a gap toothed smile and flexed his knees. The gesture triggered a thought. "Keep your bodies low and your pace steady. No need to rush. 'Tis more familiar today than yesterday." Gillet said loudly. "Almost like drilling on the parade ground," one man responded. "No commands while we are on the planks 'Obliquely to the left,'" another shouted. "Or to the right," another added, as some of the soldiers laughed.

Gillet let the comments continue hoping that it would lessen his fears as well as those of the men.

Out of habit, he wiped his hands on his breeches, bent at the knees lifted the handles of the barrow and walked up the inclined path toward the planks bridging the chasm. The inverted Y greeted him like an old friend, the morning rays illuminating the slashing burn mark where the lightning had struck. With his eyes fixed upon it, he crossed the maw of the rocky gorge at a deliberate pace. As the day wore on, Gillet had to admit, while he was never without fright, he was not stricken with the uncontrollable terror that had affected him the first day. Nevertheless, each time he crossed the gorge that seemed to beckon him to the rock strewn bottom, he vowed to himself he would do everything in his power to avoid being in mountains or on rocky cliffs ever again.[5]

That evening, they ate the same meal of salted shad and bread, washed down by the usual ration of rum. The sutler's wagon with several barrels of rum arrived and the men lined up with their cups and milled expectantly about in anticipation of an extra gill. They quieted down when Captain Olney climbed on the wagon to address them. He praised them for their dangerous work. He promised their tasks would be over soon and they would return to the west side of the river. "Not soon enough," came the cry from the darkness that emboldened the man. Olney laughed. "Now there is a soldier eager to seize his musket and meet the Redcoats if they dare to attack West Point." His words were met with cheers and shouts. "Or if they will not come to us," he yelled fervently, "we will march down to New York and drive the bloody rascals into the sea." More shouts erupted. "Now men. Enjoy an extra ration of rum. The harder you work the sooner we will be off this island."

A voice called for three cheers for their stocky and beloved Captain, who removed his tri-corn and acknowledged the huzzahs. As the men drifted back to their tents, the Captain, accompanied by Lieutenant Tew, walked around chatting seriously with some and joking with others.

It was completely dark by the time he reached the dying fires of Gillet's platoon. Nevertheless, he recognized Gillet in the firelight and after talking to the men, beckoned the Sergeant to accompany him. The Lieutenant remained behind.

"Sergeant Gillet. I have a proposal for you." Gillet acknowledged by inclining his head and waited, apprehensively thinking it would be some more dangerous duty involving the fear-inducing gorge.

"General Washington has ordered the formation of a special corps to be called 'Sappers and Miners.' They will be attached to the Army's engineers. Two men are to be drawn from each Regiment," he continued. "I am prepared to recommend you."

Gillet was relieved. Still, his Yankee cautiousness dictated he learn whether as they say, he was jumping from the frying pan into the fire. "Sir. I am honored you have thought of me. What are the duties of this special corps."

"They will be instructed in the manual and mechanical aspects of fieldworks and supervise fatigue parties in their construction. They will work with mines and saps and construct approach trenches to the enemies' defenses. There are other related tasks as well," Olney concluded, placing his hand on Gillet's shoulder. "Are you willing to accept?"

This was the answer to the numerous vows he had made to himself that day. No more mountains. No more rocky gorges. It was as if Providence had heard his pleas and rewarded him for his courage.

"Yes sir. I am your man."

"Good. Good," the Captain said, clapping him on the back. "Your training will be in the best manner, according to the principles of engineering taught at a famous French military school. You will be under the command of General Louis Duportail, Chief Engineer to General Washington."[6]

"Sir?" Gillet asked. "Will there be American officers as well? I am not too keen on serving under the Frenchies. After they left us in the trenches before Newport." He thought of their rear guard action against the more numerous Hessians and Redcoats, and of Abraham Fish, his friend killed during the retreat.

Olney took his point. "I have been told it was the French Admiral and not their Generals who urged them to withdraw. Duportail is trusted by General Washington. That should be reason enough to assuage your doubts," he said abit too vehemently. "And yes," he added reassuringly, "there will be American officers in command of the companies in this new Corps." He turned back to the campfire.

"Are you game for the assignment?"

Gillet hesitated briefly before answering. "Yes sir. You have convinced me."

"Excellent. Those recommended by their officers from the different regiments will assemble at Fort Clinton, beginning tomorrow."

Henry hoped Olney would not think him brash to speak up now. "Sir. May I recommend another from our regiment to join this new one?" Olney waited for him to continue.

"Private Gideon Hazzard. You may recall he and I accompanied you after the battle of Springfield when you were wounded. He has a level head and the physique well suited for work in the trenches."

Olney frowned as if trying to recall the incident. "One of the coloreds from the 1st Rhode Islanders? A short stout fellow? If you recommend him, tell him to report with you tomorrow morning at the pier."

When Gillet returned to the platoon and relayed Olney's offer, he was surprised at Hazzard's reaction. The Private was wary, even after Henry told him Captain Olney has assured them they would be serving under Continental officers.

"I thought you would see this as an opportunity," Gillet said, as they sat on a log near the fire." Hazzard swatted at some insects, invisible in the darkness and stoked the fire with a stick. Sparks flew up into the night as the flames licked at the unburned remnants of green branches, giving off an aromatic cloud of smoke. He reached out with his hands and waved the smoke toward them.

Hazzard mulled how much should he tell Gillet. He was not yet sure of him. Where was the better chance of being promoted? No! Not promoted. Restored to his rank of Corporal. His reduction because he was black gnawed at him. Should he demand that rank in return for volunteering? It was unlikely to be met. There were many others likely to join.

"We will be learning from the Frenchies?" Hazzard asked stalling for time to respond.

"Yes. From their engineers," Gillet responded enthusiastically. "All according to the latest techniques from their military academy," he added recalling Captain Olney's words.

Hazzard sat silently thinking the situation through. In a new regiment maybe he had more of chance for promotion. He was strong and could wield a pick with the best of them. If he excelled maybe they would recognize his abilities. If Hazzard stayed with the 2nd Rhode Islanders, there was less chance of advancement.

"Remember how the Frenchies left us at Newport and we had to fight our way back to Tiverton," Hazzard said.

Gillet nodded. "I asked the same question. Captain Olney is a good Rhode Island man. He assured me this French engineering general has the trust of General Washington. I am inclined to accept our Captain's judgment on this."

"I am in," Hazzard said, a bit of reluctance more in his posture than his agreement.

"Good fellow," Gillet replied. Hazzard noted the Sergeant seemed genuinely pleased with his decision. Perhaps he was one of the white soldiers he could trust. It was hard to tell most times.

—⚏—

The hanging was over. The British spy with the French name had died bravely as close to twelve noon as the execution order required. Now the men of Lieutenant Phelps Company of the 3rd New Jersey Regiment were marching out of Tappan to West Point, forty miles to the north. Past Mabie's Tavern, with its crooked chimney and long narrow porch, where this Major Andre had spent his last night and eaten his last breakfast that very morning.[7]

The rest of the Regiment left two days after Arnold's treason was discovered. They, along with soldiers from Connecticut and New Jersey had been rushed north, in anticipation of a British attack on West Point. As Corporal, Traynor was on the end of the line, closest to the few buildings of the small town that soon gave way to rolling pastures and apple orchards, some picked clean, others waiting to be harvested.

"At least we got to see the sorry bastard swing," Private Caleb Wade said loudly. "Too bad though Gen'rl Arnold got away." Traynor glanced ahead as Lieutenant Phelps, riding at the front of their column turned in his saddle. It appeared he was inclined to tolerate their talking as long as the men were marching in disciplined ranks at the pace being set.

"If I was to capture him," Wade continued, "I would saw off the leg that took a musket ball at Saratoga and bury it with honors. Then I would hang the rest of the traitorous, bloody bastard from the nearest tree. God damn his soul."[8] Some of the men laughed. Others called out, questioning how Arnold could be a hero to their cause one day and betray it the next. Traynor held his tongue. There were three years between Saratoga, the surrender of Burgoyne's army and Arnold's treachery at West Point.

"He did it for money," a soldier called out. "I heard General Clinton promised him twenty thousand pounds in gold and silver." [9]

"And who would you have heard that from," another shouted derisively. "Do you have your nose up the British General's arse?"

The first soldier, trying to make himself heard over the laughter, yelled all the louder, "No. One of the sutlers in camp told me," he said defensively. "He heard it directly by the clerk at this hung Major's court martial."

"Twenty thousand pounds is a lot of money," Caleb said, accepting the statement as true and taking control of the conversation again. "Judas, the greatest fucking traitor in history was paid only thirty pieces of silver."

"What is that in dollars," a small voice asked tentatively.

"A lot more than you can count on all our toes and fingers. You dumb ass. What does it matter?" Caleb shouted out. "Continental dollars are not worth one of your farts." [10]

It went back and forth for a few more miles before the men became silent. Rather than give the company time to rest, Lieutenant Phelps ordered the drummer and fifers to play a march to maintain the pace. They reached a large farmhouse before dusk and halted for the night. Ahead, the mountains blended into the gathering gloom. It began to drizzle. Traynor hoped their baggage train with their tents and blankets were not too far behind. He did not relish sleeping on the wet ground. The Lieutenant, having secured his own dry quarters within the farmhouse, emerged and supervised the roll call. Surprisingly, only four or five of the entire company of eighty-two, including drummers and fife-boys, were missing. Traynor noted regretfully one of them was Caleb. Lieutenant Phelps would be sure to hold some one responsible. It probably would get back to him that Caleb was in Corporal Traynor's file. He doubted that a man as strong and robust as Caleb Wade had become tired. Unless he had misjudged him, the loud-mouthed private would not desert. Their baggage train arrived and, in the routine business of unloading the wagons and setting up tents in the farmer's fields, Traynor forgot about Caleb.

Sergeant Henderson approached their campfires just as the men had begun roasting their rations of salted shad on green twigs over the flame. Somehow it tasted better warm.

"Lieutenant Phelps has ordered the sentries out. The others got the road above and below the farm." They all knew that was the easier duty. They could light fires. "Private Wade's platoon is to take the two six hour shifts of sentry duty in the woods." The Sergeant pointed at Traynor. "Pick four men and station yourselves in the trees over there," he ordered, pointing to a grove of woods and thickets on the hill across the pasture. James surmised they had drawn the worst sentry duty because of Caleb. The Sergeant pulled Traynor aside. "Tonight, the watchword is 'Independence,' and the counter-sign 'Jersey and Brave.'" He held Traynor tightly by the elbow and brought his unshaven face closer, so close James could smell the rum on his breath and see the hairs protruding from his nostrils. "The Lieutenant told me not to lose any more men tonight. He admonished me in front of that fat assbag farmer. It irks me to be reprimanded before civilians sitting warm and snug in front of their fires while we camp in the cold out here. You can be certain Corporal, this platoon will have additional duties when we arrive at West Point." He released Traynor's elbow with none to gentle a push to move out.

Traynor led the men through the pasture more than one hundred yards from the camp. He stationed them at the far side of the woods overlooking another field and beyond that a denser darkness which was more forest. They were spaced about twenty feet apart. Anyone approaching would have to cross the open field. The light rain had stopped and although the moon had not yet risen, when it did there would be light enough. Without a fire, it would be a chilly, damp business until they were relieved.

The Sergeant was not a bad fellow, he thought. He was simply passing the Lieutenant's annoyance down the chain of command to him. Traynor was not the kind to take it out on his men. One did not gain respect by doing that. He shifted from foot to foot to keep the blood flowing in his toes and acknowledged Henderson was a brave one in battle and that commanded respect enough.

After about two hours, outside of the occasional hooting of an owl, the upward whistling notes of the whip-poor-wills on their nightly hunts for insects, and the grumbling in his empty stomach, all was still. A quarter moon had risen. He thought he detected some movement below the edge of trees at the far end of the open field. Traynor waited until he was certain it was not a deer. He moved quietly until all four sentries were in a group, bayonets fixed and firing pans primed. Three figures were coming through the field toward them, each one bent over carrying something over their shoulders. Their muskets were held loosely in their other hand, parallel to the ground. It did not appear to be a raiding party but Traynor was taking no chances.

When the three figures were about twenty yards away, Traynor challenged them. "Halt. Independence." The three froze in place.

One of them taller than the other two shouted back – "We do not know the watchword. We are stragglers from the 3rd New Jersey. Lieutenant Phelps' company. Who are you?'

"Stand and state your names," Traynor called out.

"Is that you Corporal Traynor? I thought it was your voice. It is me Caleb. Private Caleb Wade." The other two figures eagerly shouted out their names.

"Come on slowly," Traynor ordered loudly. "Keep your muskets aimed at them," he said softly to the others "until they are close enough for me to identify them."

There was no mistaking Caleb's physique. The three approached like young boys caught by a farmer fishing in his pond. He gestured to the other sentries. The three shirkers hesitated at the loud sound of four hammers clicking slowly against the firing pans.

"Holy fucking Judas," Caleb bellowed. "You were primed to shoot us."

"We are on sentry duty," Traynor replied. "Stragglers come by the road, following their unit. And without sacks," he said pointing at the lumpy bags the three had placed on the ground. "I have to report all those entering the camp without knowing the watchword. I will go back with you and then return after informing to Sergeant Henderson."

"Wait, Corporal," Wade said quickly. "It is true we are stragglers. We were fatigued by the bloody flux and needed to rest. When we recovered, we followed the road as you said but found ourselves in need of water to revive ourselves." He warmed to the tale, knowing they all were curious as to what was in the sacks. "We approached this house, hidden from general view of the road and politely asked for some refreshment. The man of the house had a temper, did he not?" he asked the others. The two men hastily confirmed that this was true with a chorus of "Yes, sir. He sure did." Caleb added, "He cursed us as rebel scum and much worse."

Traynor doubted there was much worse in the way of cursing Caleb had heard from the farmer.

"Well. He showing himself to be bloody loyalist through and through, and casting such aspersions on Continentals like you and me," he said including the sentries by his gestures, "his property was fair game. We took only victuals – a nice cured ham or two, a wheel of cheese, some bread, not the stale stuff we have been eating, a few jugs of cider and fresh picked apples from the cold cellar. Also a few bottles of rum we found in this Tory rascal's cupboard." Traynor felt his stomach contract at the thought of real food. He knew where Caleb was heading but had to let the man make his proposal first.

"So you see, Corporal. We have enough food and drink to share amongst the men of our platoon and theirs too," he added pointing to the other two men. "That is if you do not report us." He shook his head in mock bewilderment at the concept. "Otherwise, it is certain that all of these victuals and drink will be taken by our Lieutenant and wasted among the officers who are well provided for at every welcoming farm house. Is that not true? Am I misstating how our fellow soldiers fare versus the officers?" He stared at each of the sentries challenging them to deny his words.

"Private Wade." Traynor said, remembering Sergeant Henderson's description of their Lieutenant snug before the fireplace down below. "I will accept your word that the contents of your sacks came from a loyalist household. However, if you have lied and contrary to General Washington's clear orders looted and plundered the farm of an honest Patriot, you will hang for it. Do you understand?"

"Yes sir, I do. I guarantee you no complaint will be filed." Traynor caught a note of ominous certainty in Wade's voice that made him think the worst. Best not to ask, he thought, looking at the other two stragglers who nervously stared at the ground. "There is no doubt, sir. The man was a foul-mouthed loyalist," Wade reiterated loudly.

"Very well then," Traynor said. "You," he said pointing at one of the sentries. "Escort the three of them back to camp through the field. The rest of us will remain here on sentry duty." He stepped closer to Private Wade. "None of the men are awake now. You will store your sacks and ensure they remain untouched until tomorrow's evening meal. Then, the food and drink will be shared equally." Caleb nodded he understood, grinning for getting away with what both of them knew was desertion, leaving the line of march to carry out some private procuring and perhaps looting a Whig farmer's winter food supplies in the bargain. It was a fact they were and had been starving for a long time and far too few farmers were willing to provide food to the men of the Army protecting them. Loyalist or Whig, Traynor thought, it was a rough sort of justice.

"One more task, Private Wade." Caleb's face froze as he tried to ascertain what additional condition Traynor intended to impose and how much of his loot he would lose.

"First thing tomorrow, after reveille and before roll-call. Find Sergeant Henderson and present him with one full bottle of rum. Full mind you," he emphasized, staring up at Caleb. "Tell him you were stragglers, took the rum from a Tory home and the sentries let you pass once you identified yourselves." Traynor was certain the Sergeant, in return, would report all present and, if questioned by Lieutenant Phelps, simply report the stragglers made it back to camp after the previous evening's roll call. Sergeant Henderson's liking for rum would ensure it would all go smoothly.

Chapter 6 - Of Balls, Teas and Dinner Parties

The elegant New York City residence of newly appointed Brigadier General Benedict Arnold was all aglow. Candles shone from every window of the handsome three story Georgian building, located only two doors away from General Sir Henry Clinton's house on lower Broadway. Tall street lamps illuminated the wide sidewalk dissipating the dreary early December darkness. Carriages clattered down the cobblestone street, halting across from the wrought iron fence and leafless trees of Bowling Green to discharge their passengers. It was the first ball and entertainment the Arnolds were hosting, since Peggy Shippen Arnold's arrival in New York City in the middle of November.[1]

Lieutenant John Stoner, resplendent in his new uniform, expertly tailored to hide his pudgy figure arrived on foot, slightly out of breath from the exertion of walking the few blocks to the Arnolds' mansion. Once inside, he unhooked the clasp holding his cloak, waited impatiently for a doorman to take it and strode into the crowded ballroom. Black servants circulated among the guests with trays offering wine, beer, and sweet punch for the ladies. From the look of the expensive floor to ceiling dark velvet curtains, the colorful lace and ribbon decorations cleverly folded to appear like spring flowers, the numerous tables piled high with sweetmeats, cakes and delicacies, the Arnolds had spared no expense. That was to be expected. He knew from accounts of Peggy Shippen's dinners, soirees and dances in Philadelphia she would make a grand impression for this, her first foray into British society in New York.

John took it all in and congratulated himself on having arrived. The room was crowded with high-ranking British officers, included General Clinton surrounded by his staff, each officer's powdered wig whiter than the next one's; "Old Knyp," with his flushed face and the old sabre scar running from his eye to jaw, attended by tall, mustached Hessian Grenadiers; Peggy Shippen Arnold, her hair done up in an elaborate pillar that added two feet to her height, holding court amongst a dashing group of Cavalry officers, whose knee length boots glistened like the blackest onyx, with their young ladies, hair also piled high on their heads in the latest English fashion, dress sleeves well off their milk-white shoulders, hanging attractively and languorously on their arms, like so many exotic birds.

It was all due to a seemingly accidental encounter with General Arnold near Fort George at the tip of Manhattan, when the General was feeling vulnerable. John knew Arnold would be inspecting the Fort and contrived to be between the Fort and Broadway. He had hailed him as the General was limping back toward his temporary quarters, the Royal Governor's Mansion. It was the end of September and Arnold, having just arrived on *The Vulture*, was unsure about the fate of his wife and child. Nor was he in General Clinton's good graces. Major Andre, Clinton's Deputy, was being tried as a spy and his fate was yet to be determined. There were rumors of a Rebel offer to trade Andre for Arnold and the coolness of some of the senior British officers toward him, many of them friends of Major Andre, gave Arnold reason to suspect they supported such an exchange.[2]

John, by his knowledge and earnestness had impressed upon Arnold the dangers of abduction, kidnapping or even assassination. There were many Rebel deserters about in the city as well as people from the countryside, any of whom may be part of a ring of spies or sympathizers. Numerous farmers daily entered the city also selling all manner of produce to the British quartermasters.

Invited into the General's quarters, John suggested to General Arnold that he needed special security. The British either did not understand this or perhaps may even wish him ill. He, Lieutenant John Stoner of General Ruggles Loyalist Associators, could be trusted. His unique position as an aide to Major Pritchard, charged with ensuring the security of the British General Staff, enabled him to be of such service. He already had an extensive network of his own informants and yet could operate independently of the British.

Arnold accepted but quickly added he was in no position to pay him. With a show of restrained indignation John protested that his offer was not conditioned on payment. It was out of his sense of duty to General Arnold, a known military strategist and a man of proven courage who would cause large numbers of soldiers to desert the American Army.[3]

And now, he, John Stoner was reaping the benefits of his service to General Arnold. To Lieutenant Chatsworth's chagrin, the invitation, delivered by an orderly to the quarters they shared with other officers of the 17th Dragoons, was for John, not for Chatsworth. John feigned surprise, even outrage at the omission. Secretly, he reveled in Chatsworth's discomfort, who looked down on John's lack of breeding, made snide remarks about his accent and lack of culture, and even encouraged the other troopers to question his courage. Chatsworth wrangled an invitation from someone he knew on General Clinton's staff. But his mere act of having to beg someone for a favor, gave John satisfaction. John reveled in the prestige of being admitted to the best circles of New York society. It was almost better than accumulating more wealth. Although he conceded he was doing quite handsomely by his surreptitious sale of permits and exceptions to merchants and shippers of dubious reputation.

The few civilians, in their elegant black tailed coats and frilly white shirts, stood out in the sea of uniforms, mostly red with some smattering of green of Colonel Simcoe's Queen's Rangers. John noticed Judge Thomas and his wife standing near the seated General Arnold, his bad leg resting on a low stool. He seized the opportunity and approached the Judge certain it would bring praise for his courage from Mrs. Thomas. He was not disappointed. She launched into her account of the night Rebel raiders had attacked their home on the Island, greatly embellishing John's role in protecting her and the Judge from the vile brutes who had been armed to the teeth with cutlasses, pistols and the like. John affected modesty but knew the story had enhanced his reputation with General Arnold. After appraising John, the General leaned forward and gestured with his cane for guests to move out of his line of vision. His gaze fixed on his petite young wife, floating across the dance floor with a tall officer, the captivating couple graceful and erect, knowing that they were the center of attention.

John left the General and roamed the edges of the dance floor, appraising the women. He became intoxicated by the sweet collective smells of their perfumes, the display of the flawless flesh of their necks, shoulders and the curves of the tops of their bosoms, pushed up and out by the stays beneath. It was time he mused, for him to pluck one of these society flowers, while continuing to satisfy himself with the occasional serving girl, maid or cook that came within his purview.

A corporal, dragooned into service as a servant for the General's event, touched his elbow and whispered in John's ear.

"General Arnold requests your presence in the library."

Stoner took another glass of Madeira from a passing tray and followed the Corporal upstairs. He found Arnold sitting alone near the fire, his lame leg as usual resting on a cushioned stool, a half empty brandy snifter in his hand. He motioned for John to be seated next to him where Arnold could see his face. There were some books on a few shelves, hardly enough to warrant calling it a library. The desk near the window, overlooking Bowling Green was clearly the General's with its two inkwells, a stack of quills, sheaves of paper and a cut glass pitcher with what appeared to be brandy inside.

"My wife enjoys these balls more than I do," he said, patting his raised leg. "The ball that shattered this ended my dancing days." He stared into the fire. "However, I can still ride and lead men into battle. I will do so shortly and that is why I have summoned for you. I have been impressed by your courage."

John cursed his impulse to have the Thomas's regale Arnold with their highly exaggerated version of events. He could feel the sweat beginning to form on his brow. Pretending he was too close to the fire, he pushed his chair back. Damn, he thought. Arnold is about to offer me a commission and take me off to battle where I will get my horse shot out from under me or be blown out of the saddle by some scummy Rebel rifleman. Wildly, he began to think of pretexts to refuse. That Major Pritchard has just entrusted him with a mission that John cannot reveal, even to General Arnold. Or that the 17th Dragoons were to be sent north toward West Point and he could not abandon his fellow troopers when they faced danger. No, he realized in desperation. Arnold could verify or disprove any claim relating to military assignments. He was at a loss, his mind seized with a vision of himself at the front of a charge against a fixed position, with General Arnold riding alongside urging John on.

"I tell you this in the strictest confidence, John. Once again, duty requires me to quit domestic happiness for the perils of the field," Arnold said eloquently. "In a few days, I am to lead my American Legion, Simcoe's Queen's Rangers, some Hessians and Highlanders - sixteen hundred troops in all - into Virginia."[4] He paused relishing the importance of his first command as a British Brigadier General. "Sir Henry has given me orders to attack Rebel bases and capture or destroy their supplies. I also intend to bag Jefferson either in the Governor's office in Richmond or in his mountain top lair."

John had visions of himself, weak and seasick after the voyage from New York, that is if the French fleet did not intercept their convoy and sink his ship. The swampy Virginia lowlands and wooded country would be swarming not only with militias that would receive the alarm as soon as Arnold landed, but with backwoods riflemen picking off the officers at a distance.

"I was prepared to offer you a Captain's commission in my Legion. I am a good judge of men. I know you are the sort of officer I could rely on." He held up his hand to prevent John from responding.

"Although I must leave behind those most dear to me, my beloved wife Peggy and our precious son Neddy, my conscience calls upon me, nay my husbandly duty requires, that I do my utmost to protect them. Information has come to me," he said vaguely, "that those who harbor such malice against me are willing to strike at my own cherished family. I turn to you John to protect them while I am in the field."

John stifled a sob of relief in his throat as if he were so effected by the General's trust in him, he was overcome by emotion. He took a sip of wine to regain his composure.

"Sir. I am honored by the confidence you place in me. I will take every precaution and measure to ensure their safety." He was so relieved to learn that he was not being sent off to battle, the words spilled from him in a gushing torrent. "I will be as vigilant as if you, yourself were in this house," he said, with fervent sincerity. "I will double my watchfulness and that of my agents. The smallest innocent bird will not be able to perch on Mrs. Arnold's windowsill without my knowing of it."

"Neither she nor I are concerned with innocent birds," Arnold said acerbically, frowning at John's effusiveness. "However, I was certain you would understand. While I cannot offer you a commission, know that your most valuable contribution to my peace of mind will not go unrewarded."

John rose, a little unsteadily on his feet from the wine or relief or both. "Thank you sir," and caught himself before saying it was unnecessary. Let the General reward him. There were rumors that in his brief stay in New York, Arnold was already involved in some shady deals with merchants who purchased goods from prize ships at reduced prices and resold them for a handsome profit.

"I will inform my wife of your duties so her mind will be eased as well. Feel free to call upon her from time to time and appraise her of your efforts," Arnold said in parting.

I will definitely do that, John thought as he closed the door. Being able to visit with Mrs. Peggy Shippen Arnold would enhance his reputation among the ladies of society in the city and would further make Chatsworth jealous.

Of Balls, Teas and Dinner Parties 119

The next evening, close to midnight, wearing a dark cloak to ward off the chill as well as for concealment, John prowled the rocky shore between the Hudson and lower Broadway. Several locations offered possibilities for beaching a small boat. It was less than twenty yards to the rear of the elegant homes on lower Broadway. One of Stoner's agents had reported General Arnold was in the habit of strolling in his garden for a while before ending with a visit to the outhouse and retiring to bed. There was a fenced alley between Arnold's elegant townhouse and garden and that of his neighbor's to the north. John approached from the river and proceeded up the alley keeping to the dark shadows cast by the house. This could be a possible route for kidnappers or assassins. It would be well, he thought, to station a few men here from midnight to dawn to thwart such a plot. And when the General was in Virginia to protect Mrs. Arnold as well.

John froze as a shadow ahead of him rose from a crouching position and took the shape of a man. He could vaguely make out a uniform as the shadow leaned his head against the fence that separated Arnold's garden from the alley. He was tall and somewhat familiar to him. Unarmed, John remained motionless. He did not relish any confrontation with the mysterious soldier. The shadow stood for a long time observing something inside the garden. There was the creak of a door opening, then closing and another smoother sound of a door shutting with finality. John surmised the General had finished his business in the outhouse and retired to bed. He wondered where he could hide if the man proceeded back down the alley. Instead, the soldier turned and sauntered off as if his being there was perfectly normal.

As he emerged onto Broadway, John recognized the uniform. It was Sergeant Major John Champe, a deserter from the Continental Army Arnold had recruited for his Legion.[5] At first, John was irritated that Arnold had established multiple layers of security and not informed him that Champe was also charged with such duties. Upon reflection, he admired the General's sagacity and thoroughness. He would talk privately with the Sergeant Major and they would coordinate their efforts.

He slept late into the morning, fatigued by his late night activities. When he chanced to pass Arnold's headquarters just before the evening gun, he learned that the General, his staff, horses, baggage, supplies and sixteen hundred men had embarked that day for Virginia. John waited an appropriate time before having his orderly deliver a note to Mrs. Arnold, asking if he could call on her at her convenience. He did not conceal his glee when Chatsworth was present when her written response arrived, delivered by someone all knew to be one of Mrs. Arnold's manservants.

The day he was to have tea with Mrs. Arnold and a few of her lady friends, John paid special attention to his appearance. He hired a barber to shave him and powder his wig. He gave the man a few shillings extra to brush his uniform and polish his boots. He wished his brass buttons were emblazoned with the design of a prestigious unit like the 17th Dragoons instead of Ruggles' Loyalist Associators but there was no changing that.

When he was announced and ushered into Peggy Arnold's elegantly furnished parlor, he was conscious of the admiring looks of the young ladies and the curious gaze of the three British officers present, a Colonel and two Majors. Their expressions reflected their confusion as to why such a lowly ranked colonial Officer had been invited. Peggy Arnold added to their consternation by immediately jumping to her feet, which caused them as gentlemen to also stand, and rapidly crossed the room in a rustle of petticoats to greet John almost at the door.

"May I introduce you to Lieutenant John Stoner who enjoys the implicit trust of my husband," she said extending her arm. John bowed, feeling the buttons of his waistcoat strain, and kissed the back of her hand. It smelled of lavender. She was wearing a blue gown, with a modest bodice of lace that matched the trim on her sleeves. Her blond tresses, instead of piled high as he had seen her the night of the ball, was artfully tousled to fall coquettishly on her shoulders. She took his hand and led him to the plush embroidered banquette, motioning for one of the Majors to move over and make a place for John. Basking in her attention, he barely heard the introductions, caught the name of the Colonel, Henry Johnson, and

Of Balls, Teas and Dinner Parties 121

immediately forgot those of the Majors. As Peggy presented him to the five young ladies he recognized their family names. They were the daughters of wealthy and prominent merchants. One, Becky Franks from Philadelphia who had recently arrived from that city, acknowledged him with a warm smile and a nod of her head. The talk was of the coming New Year's Eve ball, to be hosted by General Clinton and the shortage of good Madeira wine in the city. John sat in what he hoped was a nonchalant pose, enjoying his closeness to the beautiful Mrs. Arnold.

"I am certain His Excellency's ball will be lavish, but lacking the discerning eye for décor and detail that you, Mrs. Arnold, brought to your extraordinary event of this last week, it will pale by comparison," Colonel Johnson said. Although older than John by ten years, his erect posture revealed there was no bulge of fat hidden by a well-tailored waistcoat. "A woman's touch is needed to raise such occasions to the grandest levels," he concluded, inclining his bewigged head gently toward Peggy.

"Perhaps, I will offer my services to Sir Henry," she responded gaily. "However, sir, you underestimate the talents of some members of your sex in this regard," she admonished the Colonel playfully wagging her finger at him. "The grandest extravanza ever, the Mischianza to celebrate the achievements of General Howe before his departure to England was planned, designed and executed in the minutest detail by Major John Andre."

The frivolous atmosphere immediately changed to one of gloom at the mention of Major Andre, hanged less than three months ago for his part in Arnold's failed plan to surrender West Point, and Peggy's innocent use of the word, "executed." Becky Franks attempted to recover by describing the celebratory crowds lining the shores of the Schuykill for the Mischianza, the pageantry of the mock jousting of the two groups of costumed knights, one led by Major Andre himself, the mirrored dining room, illuminated by more than three hundred tapers, the brilliant fireworks display following a lavish dinner and the dancing and gambling until dawn.[6] "Peggy and I, and two of her sisters along with ten others wore costumes made of gauze and silk with sashes spangled and fringed with gold or silver and tasseled with pearls, all designed by Major Andre," she added.

"I recall how lovely you looked," Colonel Johnson said, "and regretted that I was not the knight chosen to seek your favor that evening. All of the ladies glittered that evening with a special beauty." Becky beamed at the compliment.

Peggy regained her composure and resumed her role as hostess and center of the gathering. "As gay as the dances and teas, dinners and plays were, all became drab once the Rebels occupied the city. My husband tried to treat all in Philadelphia with justice and fairness but was thwarted by those radical Whigs, Joseph Reed foremost among them. They accused him of every manner of evil and corruption. None of it true, of course," she added emphatically.

Becky forcefully supported her friend. "The parade of General Arnold's effigy through Philadelphia, followed by it being burned was particularly despicable," Becky said. "I myself saw it from the window of our home.[7] It was this Reed's false accusations and maliciousness that led Peggy's husband to understand the corruptness and moral bankruptcy of these Whigs." She tossed her head contemptuously. "Not to mention their financial bankruptcy as well. Their congress of rascals cannot manage their accounts well enough to pay neither their officers nor their soldiers."

"Most of these Rebels effect the airs of officers and gentlemen and yet are no more than country bumpkins – farmers, mechanics, even teamsters, can be found among their officers," Peggy said. "Very few are real military men like my husband."

Becky gave an unladylike snort of derision. "Can you imagine, Colonel Johnson? At one of the dinners given by General Arnold, a Rebel officer appeared wearing a scarlet uniform. He was naturally infatuated with me," she said matter of factly, "and audaciously stated he was wearing the colors of the British Army to better secure a more courteous reception from me." She straightened her back in righteous indignation. "I turned to the people around me. Peggy was there and will remember what I responded -'How the ass glories in the lion's skin.'" [8]

Colonel Robinson guffawed in appreciation. "Well said,

Madam. Well said, indeed."

"Very witty," John added, feeling uncomfortable as Becky gave him a condescending, inquisitive look. She studied his features and then turned to Peggy.

"Do you remember that young Rebel Lieutenant in the Artillery? Very dashing on his big horse."

Colonel Johnson chuckled. "That is why, my dear, we men pay particular attention to our mounts." Two of the other young ladies giggled at his remark. Becky smiled and continued with her thought.

"Was not his name Stoner? The same as the Lieutenant here?"

John felt himself flushing. He sensed that Becky knew the answer and was deftly seeking to embarrass him. He tightened his jaw in anticipation, unable to escape her intent look. He heard Peggy Arnold rustle next to him.

"Oh. I do recall. His name was Will Stoner. He married that young thing from Albany who sometimes attended our soirees. Elisabeth Van Hooten. She was on the arm of Captain Montresor until she reverted to her upbringing and cast her eye to the Rebel side. John. Perhaps he is a relative of yours?" It was more of a statement than a question but John was too flabbergasted to detect the nuance.

He had suspected Will was still alive. But married to that Dutch bitch. The Rebel spy. It was beyond his remotest thoughts. And now it became clear. All the while she was in Philadelphia, pretending to be infatuated with Captain Montresor she was bound to the Rebel cause through his own brother.

He was aware they were staring at him, waiting for an answer. "Stoner is a common name in New York," he stammered. "He may be a distant cousin. I do not know him" he replied trying to appear nonchalant yet knowing he was not being very convincing.

"Pardon my confusion," John rushed on. "I am taken aback to hear about this Elisabeth Van Hooten. She is someone I long suspected of being a Rebel spy," he said, struggling to reclaim the initiative. "When I was in Philadelphia on Superintendent Galloway's staff it was my special responsibility to ferret out spies within our midst. As well as to ensure the security of the General

Staff," he added self-importantly. "The marriage to this Willem Stoner confirms my suspicions about her were correct." He noticed the Colonel staring at him and realized he had slipped. Damn he thought. Peggy had called him Will not Willem. "Well," he said breezily although he felt trapped. "They are beyond our reach until we put an end to this wretched rebellion. Then, those who committed treason and rebelled against the King will receive their just desserts."

"We will receive the sweetness of victory while the Rebels will taste the bitterness of defeat," the Colonel said smiling at his cleverness and looking to Becky for approval.

The remainder of the afternoon, shut in the close quarters of Peggy Arnold's parlor, was agony for John. Once he was outside, he breathed easier. He crossed Broadway and with his head down against the chill wind and not wanting any company, particularly not that of Chatsworth and his fellow officers, he strolled into Bowling Green. He passed a few of the remaining open market stalls and tried to clear his head. The Dutch bitch was married to his brother. How could he get revenge for her making a fool of him? Driven by an irrational thirst for revenge, he turned over in his mind numerous improbable schemes to kill his brother and make Elisabeth a widow. A chance encounter on a battlefield? Unlikely. He intended to stay as far away from the dangers of war as possible. Have others do his dirty work for him, perhaps pay some Loyalist militia men or deserters, to do what? Attack his artillery regiment? Not possible. Apprehend him when his brother was alone and have him murdered? It left too much to a chance encounter. On the other hand, it may be easier to apprehend the Dutch bitch and have her executed as a spy.

Unsure of how to proceed and still lacking even the outline of a plausible plan, John crossed the cobblestoned street. He was still in Peggy Arnold's good graces. She may know where Elisabeth is. Perhaps, he could even prevail upon her to open up a correspondence with her to pinpoint her location. Once he knew where she was, he could devise a plan to strike at the bitch and his brother.

Of Balls, Teas and Dinner Parties

Sarah hurried the short distance between their small cabin and the kitchen of General Knox's stone headquarters building. Letting herself in through the side door, she removed her cloak and hummed softly as she stirred the porridge that had been cooking all night over the embers in the hearth. She was the only one in the kitchen a few hours before dawn and she enjoyed the solitude. She prodded the remnants of the logs in the hearth oven and was pleased they no longer glowed a hot, reddish orange. Next, she plunged the long handled hearth broom into a bucket of water, thankful that she did not have to go outside to the well this cold December morn. Smiling at the memory of leaving Adam sleeping in their narrow bed in the rough plank sided cabin, she swept the ashes from the oven floor, reached into her apron and scattered corn meal on the stones. She scrutinized the tiny granules as they turned an even brown that indicated the oven was ready. She mixed and kneaded the dough and, with the confidence of experience, she placed a loaf of unbaked bread, on the flat paddle shaped shovel and inserted it into the oven. She repeated the process with four other loaves, careful to put the denser ones made of rye in the center and the lighter ones of wheat toward the front.

Sarah had come to General Knox's headquarters by carriage from New Windsor, a distance of ten miles or so, leaving Isaac Till and the rest of General Washington's kitchen servants behind. Mrs. Knox had personally requested her services and General Washington had acquiesced. Although she was a free woman now and married as well, she would not even have thought to leave General Washington's service without his consent. Servants did not do that and besides, it was an honor to be working in his kitchen. She smiled to herself recalling she had been addressed by the driver of the carriage as Mrs. Sarah Cooper. It had taken her awhile to become accustomed to it, although she certainly had no desire to be called by the name of her former master.

Once the fear of a British attack on West Point had receded, the Knoxes dined with General Washington and Mrs. Knox praised the pastries they were served. Sarah was introduced to them as the person responsible. Mrs. Knox was now planning an intimate little dinner for visiting French officers and her husband's staff and charmed General Washington into sending Sarah to bake for her.

Adam had only been able to visit her twice at New Windsor but now, as a Sergeant on General Knox's staff, he resided at headquarters. Not in the main building where the General and the officers stayed, but in a small cabin adjacent to the kitchen. She appreciated the privacy as compared to the cramped servants' quarters in the low ceiling lofts at New Windsor. The joy of being together was tempered by her sense of Adam's angry disposition. Not toward his friends and not toward her of course. With others he manifested a pride that was easily bruised and a hostile testiness that could erupt on a moment's notice. In his eagerness to protect her status as his wife and a free woman, he assumed insults where none were intended and saw slights when none had been made. Sarah knew she had a calming influence on him, and sometimes, all it would take would be for her to gently touch his arm and she could feel his anger subside.

Sarah found the eggs, delivered yesterday midday, in a basket lined with straw. She and Mrs. Knox had decided appropriate desserts for the dinner party would be baked wine custards and layer cakes. She would make the wine custards first and chill them outside the kitchen on window racks. The layer cake could be made later, after she helped with the preparation of the stews and roasted vegetables. This afternoon, when the French officers arrived, she looked forward to surprising them by speaking their language. The Marquis de Lafayette himself had remarked on how adept she was in learning French when she had been a servant in his kitchen at Valley Forge.

By two in the afternoon, with the activity in the kitchen at a frenzied pitch, Major General Francois-Jean de Beauvoir, Chevalier de Chastellux, and his entourage of officers arrived at Knox's headquarters. Veal, venison and beef roasted on spits in the hearth. Stews of chicken and vegetables bubbled away in iron pots, kidney, sheep's tongue and quail pies cooked in the one oven, as Sarah tended to her cakes baking in flat tin pans in the other. She had improvised, adding a little ground cinnamon to the flour when there had not been enough sugar. Dinner, to be served around four was for twenty people, the General and Mrs. Knox, the Chevalier and ten of his officers, and some of General Knox's staff, Colonel Sargent and a Lieutenant Colonel she did not know, Captains Holmes and Hadley, Mrs. Hadley and Adam's friend, Lieutenant Stoner and his wife Elisabeth.

At the appropriate time, under the direction of the Knox's very harried chief cook, a man whose girth indicated he enjoyed eating as much as cooking, everyone helped carry the food in tureens, bowls, platters and dishes into the crowded, noisy dining room. The table, now extended thirty feet, with the original walnut leaves and hastily fashioned additional ones of pine, filled the entire room. Sarah placed a flat platter of sliced roast beef, swimming in a dark mushroom gravy, at Mrs. Knox's end of the long table, careful not to tilt it and spill the gravy on to the white linen table cloth. The French officers, interspersed on both sides of the long table were resplendent in their rich deep blue uniforms, trimmed with golden thread at the collar and front of their jackets, with ruffles of lace at their throats and cuffs and brightly polished gold buttons. She heard General Knox, seated at the head, describing in French, to a group of officers, the deplorable condition of West Point when he and General Washington had returned from their September meeting with French General Rochambeau. Mrs. Knox was engaged in conversation with the Chevalier and the American officers, translating for the Americans seated nearby.[9]

"This is the young lady, I was telling you about," Mrs. Knox said to Chastellux in French, as Sarah passed by. "She learned her French from the Marquis de Lafayette himself."

"Enchante, Madam," the Chevalier said, affecting a slight nod of his head. He had a long face dominated by a narrow nose and dark arched eyebrows The creases surrounding his eyes gave him a wise, penetrating look. He was not wearing a wig and his hair was streaked with strands of grey.

"Madame Knox," he said continuing in French, "informs me you have baked some delicious desserts for us. I will most assuredly not partake too much of the foods being served so as to be able to sample each of them."

Sarah curtsied slightly. "I hope you will find them to your liking," she replied in French.

"Your accent is very good. Much better than mine in your language," he replied switching to English.

"You are too modest," Lucy Knox said. "My Harry tells me he has heard you translate General Rochambeau's conversations on General Washington's behalf. You yield to no one in your ability and competence of English."

"Thank you Madame. Your husband's French also serves His Excellency, General Washington well. And yours is as refined as that heard at any of the salons of Paris."

"You are most kind," Lucy said beaming at the compliment. She was interrupted by shouting and a commotion from outside the dining room. Henry Knox turned his head as one of the doors flew inward. Sarah screamed. Adam was crumpled at the orderly's desk, blood flowing from his head on to the entry log. A French officer, a satisfied smirk on his face, his cloak furled over one arm, his sword unsheathed in the other advanced into the room.

"What is the meaning of this?" Henry Knox bellowed, rising from his chair. His loud voice stopped the French officer at the doorway. He was no more than five feet away from the General. Will, three chairs down from Knox, jumped up and rushed forward to interpose himself between the armed French officer and General Knox.

"I bear an urgent letter for Mon General," the officer said, pointing with his sword to Chastellux.

"Sheath your sword immediately Major Murnan," Chastellux barked in French.

"Very well, Mon General. I only needed it to teach that black dog a lesson," he replied in English as a way of explaining his actions.

As he said this, Will slammed him against the wooden door, one hand grasping the Major's sword arm, the other around his throat. Sarah and Captain Hadley's wife, Mercy rushed out into the hall and bent over Adam, as two sentries, confused by the scene stood in the main entrance uncertain what to do.

"Lieutenant Stoner. Release the Major." Will took one step back.

"Major Murnan," Knox commanded. "Give Lieutenant Stoner the letter for General Chastellux." Murnan looked to his General and fellow officers for support and when none was forthcoming, reached inside his waistcoat and slapped the envelope contemptuously into Will's outstretched hand.

Without waiting for an order, Will turned and walked the length of the table and presented it to Chastellux. Knox his face red with rage turned toward Murnan. "Sir," he said in French. "You have assaulted a member of my headquarters staff who was conducting his duties. You are under arrest. I will consult with General Chastellux and we will decide as to whether you face a court martial by a court of American or French officers."

Knox motioned for the two sentries to step forward. Murnan looked down the table to General Chastellux. "Surrender your sword Major and submit immediately."

Murnan smirked. "As you command Mon General," he replied, bowing from the waist.

"Sir. May I go to Adam," Will asked Knox.

"Of course. Report back to me on his condition."

"I would like to go too sir," Captain Holmes said. Knox motioned for him to join Will.

Will found his friend, lying on a couch in the orderlies' room, Sarah kneeling beside him and holding his hand, as Mercy washed the long gash above his forehead from a bowl brought from the kitchen. "It is deep and I will have to sew it up. Fortunately, it did not pierce the bone."

Adam's eyes were open. He looked up at Will and Nat. "This mad Major should have been court-martialed in September when he attacked the Connecticut Continentals," he said. "And now this. What do you say, Captain?" Adam asked bitterly. "Will nothing be done again?"

Holmes hesitated before answering. Will spoke first. "Adam. General Knox will treat this as an assault on one his own. You are part of his headquarters staff," he said earnestly. "You were on duty. He will see that this French Major will be punished."

Adam looked at Nat. "That is what Captain Holmes said after that Frenchie beat some Continentals at West Point." Sarah wiped the blood seeping through the compress away from her husband's eyes.

"We were all Marblehead Mariners once," Nat said softly, searching for the right words of comfort. "We are still together fighting this war as brothers. General Knox will see this man is punished. I am confident it will be done."

"I doubt it," Adam said, lifting his head to take a drink of brandy from the cup Sarah held, before Mercy began stitching him up. He gritted his teeth, both in anticipation of the needle and in his anger there would be no justice. No matter. He vowed if he ever encountered the French Major again, he would kill him.

Chapter 7 - Mutiny

Morristown, 17 January 1781

My Dearest Samuel: I will not trouble you with an account of my journey from Fort Clinton to my mother's home in Morristown. It was arduous enough but I arrived in good health and spirits to find our home far less crowded than when His Excellency and Staff shared our Premises the past winter. There are several Officers lodging with us still and to my consternation, quite a few of them sick with various ailments. Mother insisted they be removed to their Regimental Hospital. We turned out their bedding into the snow and left their rooms vacant for two days, despite the protestations of those Officers living in more cramped quarters and the chill from the open windows that pervaded the rest of our home.

Mother and I, and my sisters M. and A. have been attending at the Hospital everyday but one since my return. I need not describe to you the suffering of the men from putrid fever, bloody flux, throat distemper, and scabies. Mother has an ample supply of sulphur ointment for the latter although the soldiers in their agony of constant scratching of open sores, implore her for more generous latherings. One soldier horribly scalded his right arm and hand in a cooking accident. I devised a linen glove with a high sleeve that he wore and kept saturated with olive oil and snow water and within a week, new skin had formed and the sore was well on the way to healing. I write this to you if you should have need among your men injured in a similar way. I suppose, in the absence of olive oil, liquified lard or butter, would suffice.[1]

I must now inform you of the Most Terrifying and Unusual Occurrence this New Year's Day past. The Pennsylvania Line, housed in the huts on Mt. Kemble you are well familiar with, Mutinied. As I write these lines, I am appalled and filled with dread to see these words on paper. The Mutineers declared their intention to march on Philadelphia for redress as to their pay and clothing allotments. However, I have it from Colonel S. of General W.'s staff these soldiers claimed they had enlisted for three years beginning in 1777 while their officers were of the opinion it was for the duration of the war. General W. tried unsuccessfully to dissuade them from their course of action and later expressed concern the men would "turn Arnold" and march to New York City. Fortunately, surely by the Hand of Providence, the Mutiny was peacefully resolved. The Mutineers marched to Princeton and Negotiations with General W. and Mr. R. from Congress lasted for several days. The end result was satisfactory to all sides with the soldiers' enlistments being individually reviewed and those who were eligible being discharged. The men were also to receive proper uniforms and promises for their back-pay as soon as Pennsylvania could raise the money. This all from Colonel S. who participated in the discussions. As I write this letter, almost One Thousand soldiers have received their discharges, reducing the Pennsylvania Line to half its strength and those who remained have been given shirts, blankets, woolen overalls and one month's pay. No one was punished even though a Captain resisting the mutineers was killed and many other Officers were wounded.[2]

My dearest husband, I am fearful for your safety if these thoughts spread to the rest of the army. Were this disease to infect others, then I truly fear for the cause you and I so ardently support. Let us pray that Congress and the States will come to their senses and provide our soldiers with the clothing, rations and pay promised and to which they are Eminently entitled.

I am cognizant of your tender concern for my condition and critical of my continuing my usual activities. I promise not to undertake any task or labor that places our unborn child in jeopardy. I urge you to recognize with my experience of birthing others' babes, I am less filled with trepidation and apprehension and more joyful at the approaching event. I wish you were present to be the first to view our child after its arrival and I will send you a letter by the fastest post once I am delivered. I hope that you will gaze upon Will and Elisabeth and their young son and smile at the thought we will soon enjoy the presence of our own little one. Please convey to me your Thoughts on names although you may wish to wait until you learn whether we have a Son or Daughter.

In your next letter advise me of the recovery of Sergeant Cooper. His wound should have healed properly and I pray he has already returned to the service of General K.

My dearest Husband. I await your letter and anticipate our reunion at the end of Winter. Our Separation is made easier for me by the knowledge that we are aiding our Noble Cause, each in our own Way and hastening, with the aid of Providence, the time when we shall see Independence and Peace.

Your loving wife,

Mercy

The men of the 3rd New Jersey Regiment stood on the parade ground awaiting the arrival of their Colonel. It was mid-morning and they had been summoned out from their tents in the fields surrounding the small town of Chatham. Puzzled, because they had already performed their marching drills after roll call and had been dismissed, they waited in the cold, under a bleak, grey January sky that threatened snow. Corporal James Traynor of Lieutenant Phelps' Company listened to the murmurings of the men, loosely lined up in ranks. Some thought they would be marching to better winter quarters, perhaps back to Morristown beyond the Wachung Mountains. Others argued they were being sent back up to West Point to reinforce the troops there.

"Your brains came out your ass when you last had the bloody flux, you stupid bastard," Private Caleb Wade bellowed at one who had opined they would head north. "The Redcoats are warming their asses before roaring fires in New York City and you think their Officers will leave the warmth and comfort of their whores to march to the Point? There is less of a chance of that happening than we poor soldiers getting the pay we are owed for the past seven months."

As usual Wade was stirring the pot with nothing to be gained, other than to make himself a spokesman for the men's grievances, Corporal Traynor thought. As far as Traynor was concerned, the State Legislature would provide them with their pay when they had the money to do so. They were not withholding what was their due from malice but rather from lack of funds. He stomped his feet to warm his toes in his thin boots. Better to have warm woolen overalls and socks than the worthless Continental dollars that bought nothing. Perhaps the Colonel would announce a wagon train of clothing and beef on the hoof were coming from Trenton.

The murmuring stopped as Colonel Dayton, accompanied by their Lieutenant Colonel, the two Regimental Captains, their Lieutenants and even the Regimental Chaplain rode slowly up the road from Chatham's tavern. They drew up in a line and the Lieutenants trotted their horses forward to face their companies. From their grim expressions, Traynor thought whatever this was about, it was not for the best.

Colonel Dayton sat motionless on his dappled grey mare, his long dark blue cloak draped over his shoulders, his tri-corn pushed back on his head to reveal his wispy, long white hair. He surveyed the three hundred or so men in orderly ranks before him, his mouth grim and unsmiling, his eyes fixing on the lines of men in the front, as if recognizing each and every one, knowing what county they came from, and recalling what he knew of their families. He took his time and yet not a single man shifted or stirred. With a soft click and an almost imperceptible nudge of his heels in the long stirrups, he urged his mount a step or two forward.

"Soldiers of the New Jersey 3rd. Together we have endured the fatigues of the march over rough and mountainous roads, frequently made near impassable by snows, through bitter cold, rain, hail and snow and during our summer campaigns, in blistering heat." The Colonel spoke slowly and distinctly, in a voice loud enough to be heard in the rear ranks. Traynor in the first file in the company to the Colonel's left also was able to see Dayton's serious expression and thought to himself, there will be no announcement of the arrival of food or clothing.

"Together we have fought the British, their mercenaries and those traitors from our own State who have abandoned our cause and the fight for Independence. We stood as one against the best of the Crown's army at Monmouth and again this past year at Springfield. Between battles and campaigns, I know you have suffered the constant pangs of hunger, nay almost to the point of starvation, shivered in clothes worn through, and slept under blankets barely worthy of that name." He stood up in his stirrups, the better to be heard. "Know this, that I, on my honor as a veteran of the French-Indian War, and as your Colonel, I have exerted every power of persuasion, every fiber of my being, every talent God has given me to secure from our State government the rations, clothing, and pay you are entitled to."

The men spontaneously broke out into cheers for their Colonel. He let them have their moment, sitting back in the saddle and waiting for their huzzahs to subside.

"I now come before you on a most grave matter." Traynor was close enough to see Dayton take a deep breath as if to speak further required a great effort. "In a despicable departure from what they owed to you, their brother soldiers, and to their country, to their officers, to their oaths and to themselves, some of the New Jersey Line at Pompton have mutinied."

Traynor reacted as the other men did with a shocked gasp and involuntary cries of surprise. Pompton was only twenty miles away. If the mutineers intended to proceed to the State capital at Trenton and demand redress they would have to pass through Chatham.

The Colonel waited for the soldiers to become silent. "Due to the pernicious advice of a few, who are probably in the pay of the Redcoats to betray you, their fellow soldiers, these mutineers have ignored the orders of their officers, elected the ringleaders to command them and are marching south from Pompton." He gestured to the north as if the mutinous men were just around the bend. "Behind them come steadfast Continentals in pursuit who will bring these betrayers of their oaths and our trust to speedy justice."

Dayton let the threat of those words hang in the silence before continuing.

"I know you will not betray your own sacred oaths nor stain the honor of American soldiery. I leave the decision to you. I intend to poll the proud New Jersey 3rd as to whether on one hand, you intend to join this pernicious mutiny or on the other, continue to endure with patience and virtue, the sufferings I am straining to alleviate, and to aspire to the noble distinction of a patriot army. The choice is yours. Choose honor and patriotism in the service of our cause, or dishonor and ignominy if you join the mutineers." [3]

The men erupted in shouts of "No! No!" and "We are with you, Colonel."

Dayton again waited for the shouting to die down. "You will be polled by Company. I hope you will see fit to do your duty."

Traynor realized, with some consternation, their company would be the first. Lieutenant Phelps stopped his horse ten or so paces in front of their ranks. "By Company. Those who choose honor and patriotism and reject mutiny take two steps forward." The entire company stepped forward, although Traynor noticed Caleb Wade glanced around to see if others would remain in place before aligning himself in the file. A cheer went up from the rest of the regiment and the men of Phelps' Company permitted themselves to grin, satisfied and proud of themselves. The same was true for each of the following companies. Not a single man expressed any desire to be part of the mutiny. When the last company had been polled, the soldiers broke into a spontaneous cheer, first of their Colonel, then their Captains by name and finally for the New Jersey 3rd.

Colonel Dayton, now looking less grim stood up in the stirrups again. "Your actions are the strongest proof of your fidelity to our common service in our cause and your sense of abhorrence of the conduct of the mutineers. Detailed orders of the day will be read to you. In sum, they provide those who have homes within two days march will be furloughed for ten days. Those who do not, will march to Springfield and to better quarters than we enjoy in Chatham, where I have been assured, more ample food supplies are waiting." [4]

That afternoon, when the orders were read to their company by Sergeant Henderson, Traynor discovered his platoon and two others, except for the men being furloughed, were to remain behind in Chatham with Colonel Dayton. The extra gill of rum issued to them did nothing to assuage Private Caleb Wade's anger at being deprived of better quarters and provisions at Springfield.

"God damn it," he grumbled loudly sitting by the cooking fire, petulantly stirring the week old potatoes in the pot on the tripod. "Springfield is only four miles away. You would think our good Colonel, who says he has done everything to help us get our due, would send a fucking wagon to get us the food the others will enjoy." He pointed over his shoulder at the empty huts behind them. "Better quarters for us mean less crowded, drafty huts. That is not worth the hind tit of a pig."

"Perhaps a wagon will come tomorrow," Traynor said quietly to mollify him and head off the kind of angry talk he anticipated from Caleb.

Wade ignored him. "Those Pennsylvania boys who raised a ruckus last month, they got what they demanded – a review of their enlistments, warm clothing and food and promise of pay. What is wrong with that?" he shouted standing up. Angrily, he kicked a log further into the fire, almost upsetting the tripod.

"Careful, Caleb," one of the privates said. "That kind of talk can mean trouble for all of us."

"If you do not like my talk, you can burn in hell," Caleb replied but lowered his voice. "The Colonel has not been able to help us. Maybe those wealthy dickweasels in Trenton, sitting safe in their warm homes, need to see some angry starving soldiers with bayonets to move them off their fat asses."

Wade's outburst was followed by silence and there was none of the usual banter around the fires that evening. "What do you think will happen tomorrow Corporal?" one of the men asked him as the others began to return to their quarters.

Traynor shrugged. "The Colonel said there were troops pursuing the mutineers. 'Tis my feeling this mutiny will not end peacefully. Best to obey orders and keep your mouth shut. The Colonel is a good man and will do right by us." He rose to head to the latrine, hoping this soldier and the others would not have second thoughts about voting not to join the mutiny.

The next morning dawned cold and crisp, grey with overcast skies and the sense of snow in the air. There were no drills this morning, following reveille and roll call. The twenty-five or so men remaining in Chatham kept to the fires in their cabins until mid-morning. Traynor heard the sound of drums and halooing and emerged from his hut and joined the others from the two platoons left behind. The mutineers, two regiments of them totaling almost four hundred men, marching in good order with fixed bayonets arrived at the parade ground and stood in loose ranks. Two Sergeants and a Sergeant Major stood at their fore, as if they were officers. They seemed surprised to see so few soldiers about and looked confused as to what to do next. Their faces broke into smiles as Colonel Dayton, accompanied by one Captain and Lieutenant Phelps, rode up from the Chatham tavern. After some discussion the Sergeants shouted to their men they would be negotiating on their behalf at the tavern and dismissed their men until they reported back.

As soon as the mutineers broke ranks, Traynor saw Caleb approaching several of them. Tall as he was, he stood out in the small group that crowded around him, talking and gesturing, and frequently patting Wade on the back. After taking a long drink from a wooden canteen one of the mutineers had offered him, Wade led a small contingent of them to the men of his platoon and began haranguing them to join in the mutiny.

"They want what we want. Review of our enlistments and proper discharges of those who swear they signed up for three years in '77, and the pay due us," he shouted. "For those who remain in service, better food and the clothing we are entitled to." He threw his arms wide open. "Can anyone disagree with those demands? Is this not our due?"

No one answered. Some of the men looked down, avoiding Caleb's gaze.

"We gave our word of honor twice now," Traynor said quietly, as Sergeant Henderson joined the group. "Once, when we took the oath to enlist and then yesterday to our Colonel. I counsel you not to join these men. If they negotiate a settlement, the New Jersey legislature will have to provide what is agreed to and we will benefit as well. There is no need to mutiny and taint our honor in the process."

"We have not tainted our honor," one of the mutineers said angrily, taking a few steps toward Traynor. "We are only asking for what was promised to us." Another one shouted that if Traynor lacked the courage to fight for what was his, he was a disgrace to his regiment and the mutineers did not want him to join them. There was much shouting back and forth until Sergeant Henderson called for them to quiet down.

"Their leaders and our Colonel are meeting now. None of you men," he said gesturing to those of the 3rd, "need to do anything. We have been in battle together. Let us stay together now as we voted to do yesterday and see what happens."

Caleb was having none of it. "The French pox on all you mealy mouthed dickweasels." He glared at Traynor and Henderson. "The only language those fat assed legislators understand is the threat of brave soldiers who have suffered enough. They betrayed us. We are not betraying anyone but ourselves if we do nothing. Now! Who is with me to join our brother soldiers and take what is our due?" He looked around the group.

"I am with you," one said. It was Private Mathias Vose, one of Wade's drinking companions. They were joined by two others who shuffled forward somewhat reluctantly. Wade grabbed Vose's hand and shook it and heartily clapped the other two on their backs. "Anyone else?" he demanded. When no one else joined them, he scowled and raised his fist. "Shit on all you cowards. You have less guts than a whorehouse of poxy snatches," he said, turning on his heel and leaving his former comrades sullen and quiet.

"Let them go," Traynor said, worried that any confrontation would lead to violence.

Late in the afternoon, the Sergeants returned from the tavern. The men lined up in ranks with Wade and the other three from the 3rd integrated into one of their files.

"The New Jersey legislature is striving to improve our conditions. We discussed our grievances over pay, rations and clothing. We believe the assurances from Colonel Dayton the legislators will respond appropriately. There are full pardons for all if we immediately return to our duty, conduct ourselves in a soldierly manner and end the mutiny," the Sergeant Major announced.

"And if we do not?" someone cried.

"Then the Colonel informs us we can expect the reward due to such obstinate villainy."

"Which means what?" another mutineer asked. One of the Sergeants shrugged his shoulders and none of the others responded. After an ominous silence, the soldiers took up the chant "Vote! Vote! Vote."

The proposal as offered by Colonel Dayton was read out loud by the Sergeant Major. He waited a moment and then called, "All those in favor signify by shouting 'Huzzah.'" There were three loud cheers of assent and the men disbursed to take their equipment from their baggage wagons and move into the empty huts.

That night, Lieutenant Phelps came to the campfires of the two platoons of the men of his company. The men were greatly subdued as compared to the boisterously celebrating mutineers, buoyed by the successful negotiations and the rum they had brought with them. "Tomorrow morning there will be no reveille nor roll call for you. You are to remain in your huts until given an order to emerge. It is for your own safety."

"Why Lieutenant? Are we prisoners in our own camp?"

"No. Not all," Phelps replied quickly as he looked away from the man who asked the question and fixed his gaze on Sergeant Henderson. "Sergeant," he snapped. "Make certain these men follow my orders and all will be well." He softened his tone. "Colonel Dayton asked me to reassure you all. I can say no more." Hurriedly, he strode into the darkness, avoiding the noisy mutineers on his way back to the tavern.

"What in God's name is that about?" one of the men asked Henderson as they sat watching the embers of the cooking fire.

The Sergeant shook his head. "I do not know. Lieutenant 'Nuthatch' did not confide in me."

A few of the men chuckled at the use of Phelps' nickname, apt because his upper lip protruded enough over his lower one to

Mutiny 143

resemble the beak of the small brown capped bird carrying a seed.

"Sleep under arms tonight with bayonets fixed. Make your trips to the latrine before dawn. And make them quick." He smiled trying to ease the men's anxiety.

"Armed for what?" a soldier asked. No one spoke waiting for Henderson's response. The drunken din and singing from the mutineers' campfires continued unabated.

"Damn. I could use a gill of rum right now." The Sergeant looked wistfully across to the mutineers' huts. "It could be they plan seize our Colonel to make sure they get their way."

"They had better not try or we will answer them with the hottest fire they have ever seen," a soldier said. "A lot worse than we gave Skinner's Greens last June," another added.

"I have faith in Colonel Dayton," Henderson said, standing up. "He has been with us in every battle. If you need more reassurance and unfortunately there is no rum for it, then pray to Providence that tomorrow we will see this thing through together."

Traynor, along with the nine men in their hut primed their muskets and lay down with their arms alongside them, the flames from the hearth at the far end reflecting on their bayonets. Soon, he heard the usual snores, coughs and farts of those who were asleep. He finally drowsed off somewhere in between a state of solid sleep and restiveness, waking in fits and starts, listening to the hooting of owls in the distance and the occasional drunken shouts of a few of the mutineers still engaged in celebrating. He thought he recognized Caleb's voice but was not certain.

He awoke and lay still, his eyes fixed on the one window of the hut, trying to assess the time. Traynor guessed it was around six in the morning. Normally, he would have welcomed the absence of reveille and roll call. Several crows loudly cawed to each other warning of something they could see but he could not. It was cold in the hut. The fire had almost burned out and their quarters smelled as usual of men's bodies and foul air. He heard the sound of running feet and wondered whether the mutineers were pouring out of their cabins to seize Colonel Dayton and the few soldiers of the New Jersey 3rd as well. He sat up tense, his musket across his knees, staring at the thick wooden bar on the door. The other men in the hut were awake now, jumpy and alert, anxious as to what was transpiring outside.

From outside the other huts, they heard shouted commands of "Come out unarmed and assemble at the parade field," followed by musket stocks beating on closed doors. "Quick March! Move! Move along!"

There were muffled cries of "No conditions. Better to die here!" followed by a few musket shots and then silence. The sound of feet crunching through the frost covered ground resumed, along with orders to march and move along.

Traynor jumped at the knock on their door before he realized it was a hand and not a musket butt.

"Corporal Traynor. It is Lieutenant Phelps. Come out. Bring your weapons and line up immediately."

The men filed out of the hut, grateful for the cold, crisp winter air, their breath forming small puffs before their lips, as they moved their sleep stiffened limbs to get the blood flowing.

"Look smart now, men," Phelps said. "Do Colonel Dayton proud and show these Yankee troops from Connecticut and Massachusetts that the New Jersey 3rd are as good as they."

"Better," one of the men responded, drawing grunts of approval. They marched in quick time, keeping their ranks properly aligned to the parade ground. There, they found a regiment sized force forming a square around the field. Several officers sat silently on their horses in their dark blue winter cloaks grimly watching the unarmed mutineers. Motionless and mounted beneath a dull grey sky, they appeared to Traynor as avenging angels of death. The mutineers to their credit, despite their late night carousing, were arrayed in fairly orderly lines with their three Sergeants standing in front as if on parade.

With a nod from the Major General in command, four officers approached the mutineers, consulted amongst themselves and dismounted. They ordered the three Sergeants to step forward. The lead officer, who identified himself in a loud clear voice as Lt. Colonel Ebenezer Sprout of the Seventh Massachusetts Regiment, declared they were conducting a court martial. The three men were accused of mutiny, disobeying orders and assaulting superiors. How did they plead? he asked. Each Sergeant responded in voices too low to be heard by any but the first two lines of mutineers, who stood with bowed heads. When they were finished, Sprout consulted with the three officers at his side. He then declared the Board found all three guilty as charged and sentenced them to death by firing squad, the sentence to be carried out immediately. The entire court martial could not have taken more than ten minutes. A collective moan arose from the now docile mutineers as their three Sergeants were led off by an armed guard.

Sprout now moved up and down the ranks of the prisoners, many of whom actually cringed as he approached. He selected six from among those unfortunate enough to be close to him. They were ordered to step out of the line and escorted off under armed guard. Traynor saw the tall figure of Caleb Wade among them and was going to yell this man was not one of those who mutinied but had only joined last night for the rum. If Wade was selected for execution, Traynor vowed that regardless of the consequences, he would speak up on Wade's behalf.

The troops on the far side of the parade ground moved aside and the mutineers were marched forward toward an open field. They lined up three deep with the middle line taking a half step to the right and the third line a step beyond so that all had a clear view of the field before them.

The three Sergeants were escorted out, their hands tied behind their backs, with the Yankee regimental drummers beating the Rogue's March. To Traynor's dismay, they were followed by Caleb and the other five men chosen, now armed with muskets and escorted by ten armed troops with bayonets fixed.

The first Sergeant was led into the field, blindfolded and forced to kneel. His executioners, the six mutineers were then marched forward until they were no more than twenty feet away and ordered to load their muskets. Traynor could see the tears streaming down Caleb's face, his big hands shaking as he primed the pan.

"Forward three kneel! Aim for the heart. Back line remain standing! Aim for the head!"

Caleb, in the back line was bawling and babbling, "No! No! I cannot do this. I cannot."

Lt. Colonel Sprout dismounted from his horse, drew his pistol and pulling the hammer back put the muzzle to Caleb's temple. "Either you agree to perform your duty or I will blow your brains out here and now." Wade bowed his head, wiped a huge dripping gob of snot from his nose with his sleeve and slowly nodded in agreement.

"Ready! Aim! Fire!"

The Sergeant's body flew backwards, his blood and brains staining the snowy ground around him.

The second Sergeant was led out, forced to kneel a few paces from the first one's body. This time, as the firing squad loaded their muskets, all six men were visibly crying. However, there was no hesitation in carrying out the order. They fired and the Sergeant's body lay lifeless next to his companion's.

The Sergeant Major was led out, hands tied but not yet blindfolded. Lt. Colonel Sprout, now remounted, rose in his stirrups. "I have been convinced by the New Jersey Officers of this line, that Sergeant Major Grant, a dedicated and long serving soldier, was coerced into becoming a spokesman for this despicable mutiny. The Court unanimously pardons him and demotes him to the rank of Sergeant."

Normally, the men would have cheered, but the mutineers, having witnessed the execution of two of their leaders, could only stand mute with their eyes downcast. The Sergeant Major however, fell to his knees and as his hands were untied, raised them toward heaven in a grateful gesture.[5]

Lieutenant Phelps dismissed them and Traynor marched his platoon back to their huts. No one felt much like cooking but they did start some fires for warmth and broke out their meager rations of cornmeal flour, more out of habit than hunger.

"I hope they improve our rations and give us our pay," one of the men said. "To mutiny was wrong but it should have scared those legislators into action."

"We may see some benefit yet of this," said another.

"I have no quarrel with my enlistment in '77. It was for the duration not three years like some of those claim," he said gesturing with his hand toward the parade ground. "Remember, in '77 they promised us rations down to the ounce and look at what we have to eat. Next to nothing. They broke their promises to us while we continued to serve."

Traynor agreed with the argument. The fact that more troops had not mutinied was surprising to him, not that he would ever do so.

As they talked they did not notice Private Caleb Wade approaching. The conversation stopped as he stood by the fire, swaying back and forth like a man in a trance. His red-rimmed eyes were unfocused and his large hands hung limply at his sides.

Traynor rose from squatting, put his hand on Wade's elbow and gently guided him into the hut and shut the door. Together, they sat side by side on one of the cots. Wade's tri-corn fell off as he leaned over and began sobbing uncontrollably, his shoulders shaking. Tears and snot mixed on his upper lip and dribbled down his chin. Traynor put his arms around the big man and began to rock him, softly shushing as a mother does for her babe who awakes from a nightmare.

Chapter 8 - Madness on the March

The faster he dug the more dirt there was to move. He clawed barehanded at the loose brown soil in front of him, inching forward on his knees, never appearing to make any progress. The rocky ceiling of the dark tunnel seemed to press down on him. The rough points of large protruding boulders jabbed into his back and shoulders when he raised himself too high. Where was his shovel and that short handled pick he had? Why was he alone? Where were the others? Frenetically, he raked at the soil with his fingers, shoving the dirt between his legs, like a dog digging for a bone.

Bones. That was it. He had never given the hung militiamen a decent Christian burial. But, he could not have, a quiet voice inside his head reasoned. There were twelve of them. It was getting dark. It would have taken too long to dig their graves. The British cavalry may have returned and killed him. Nonsense, a deeper voice said. You are a coward. You hid up in that tree while your friends were hung. Those troopers were looking for you. If you had come down, the voice said, your friends definitely would have been spared. That is why you are digging now. You must find their bones the voice harshly commanded him. Dig on.

He noticed his fingers had become longer with curved hooked nails, like talons. He thought his mouth had changed and he could dig with his teeth like a burrowing badger. His elongated fingers grasped what he thought was a tree root. It broke off. He stared down at a long slim arm bone attached to skeletal white knobby fingers clutched around a rotting piece of rope. He tried to scream but his mouth was full of dirt. All he could do was emit a stifled moan.

 Bant abruptly sat up, sweating and gasping for breath. It was dark. Above him, through the branches of the tall trees and wispy clouds he saw the stars and a hazy late July half moon. The men around him, dark prone shapes wrapped in blankets were still sleeping. He felt for his rifle and held it in his hands, stroking the length of the cold barrel, reassuring himself that it was only a nightmare and he was alive. Gradually, he calmed down, reassured by the normal night sounds of leaves rustling in a light breeze, horses neighing off in the distance and the occasional call of a night hawk.

 It was all that talk the night before of quickly taking the redoubts and then the sappers and miners digging trenches toward the British held forts in preparation for an infantry assault. He knew little of what the sappers and miners did and his imagination had added to the campfire talk of the coming battle for New York. He did not want to fight in shallow trenches or narrow tunnels like the one in his nightmare. He preferred to be in the open where is skill with a rifle gave him the advantage. He had endured the long and inactive winter. Except for the occasional foraging party and a chance to hunt Loyalist militias in the area south of Tappan, he had seen little action. There had been much marching here and there as if they were going into battle but nothing to show for it.

 This time felt different. As part of a light infantry unit of New Jersey Riflemen, they had marched from West Point first to Peekskill on the east side of the Hudson and then, forty miles in two days to camp near a place called King's Bridge. New York City was fifteen miles to the south. The rumors and gossip had all been about capturing the British forts and taking the city from the north. Bant knew nothing of strategy. Only that there were French troops as part of their advancing army and it looked like this time there would be a fight. After the months of inactivity he wanted nothing more than to kill British officers.

 Bant had not yet made up his mind about the French soldiers

who were camped less than a mile away. He observed them at a distance and thought their uniforms peculiar looking. They were made of white linen, useless he thought for hiding in the woods and shrubbery or for night patrols. Their short-tailed coats with buttons all over had red facing on the lapels, cuffs and pockets. In a battle with the smoke of gunpowder obscuring one's vision, a glimpse of the red could draw fire from the Americans. As for their headgear, the Continentals laughed out loud at the sight of the four-cornered black hat with plumes sticking upright like the ass feathers of a rooster.

In turn, the Frenchies ridiculed the Continentals in their frayed and mismatched uniforms, some wearing hunting shirts, others regular issued dark blue coats, some with boots, others shoeless or with rags bound around their dirty feet. They mocked the lack of consistent appearance of companies and regiments. The Continental troops were marked by disparities of age and height with young boys of sixteen marching alongside grown men some as old as sixty, as well as the mix of blacks, mulattos and whites in the same unit.

In the pre-dawn darkness, McNeil awoke and saw Bant hunched in a sitting position, his long rifle across his knees. He yawned and feigned indifference, knowing from experience his friend had been seized by his demons again.

"I am of a mind to volunteer for whatever duty will get me into battle the soonest," Bant said after a while. "Are you with me?"

McNeil rubbed his eyes with the knuckles of his first two fingers. "I am with you Bant," he replied. "Though I need to clear my head and empty my gut before doing anything else." He pushed his tall lanky frame up from the ground and disappeared in the darkness of the woods.

After a hurried cold breakfast of bread and salted shad, the riflemen filled their canteens half with water half with rum and were issued thirty cartridges each. Then, they were ordered to support troops of the Connecticut line that had moved into forward positions before a British redoubt. The rocky bottom of the ravine slowed their progress. Bant with his short legs struggled up the embankment and fell behind the rest of the riflemen. Eager not to be left, he scrambled anxiously through the sparse brush, grabbing at the thin trunks of young beech trees to make it up the far side.

More than three hundred yards ahead of him and slightly uphill was the British redoubt, a five-foot high earthen wall. The field between the ravine and the redoubt had been stripped of trees, chopped down to a foot above the ground, with some of the stumps obscured by tall grasses. Some bushes, here and there were waist high, too thin to provide adequate cover. The four hundred or so Connecticut troops had taken up their positions a third of the way up the field. They cheered the arrival of the riflemen who dispersed along their lines. McNeil motioned for Bant to join him. The two of them knelt on the rocky ground side by side.

McNeil pointed to the redoubt. "It is ditched and well abbattied," he said rubbing his prominent chin thoughtfully. Bant stared ahead. It was getting warm and the bees, flies and gnats had begun to harass them. He could see, beyond what appeared to be a deep ditch that ran the length of the redoubt, the sharpened ends of tree trunks like spears jutting out from the earthen lattice composed of branches, mud and rocks.

It would be a difficult assault and he knew that past this redoubt, lay the forts the men had been talking about. He looked for any of the sappers and miners he had heard about but could see only soldiers with muskets.

A large force of infantry sallied forth from the redoubt together with several officers on horseback in the lead. The British came toward them downhill to the slow cadence of a drumbeat. McNeil nodded at the mounted officers. "We have orders to fire at them at will," he said. Bant knelt and steadied the rifle with his elbow to his knee. He sighted on the one on the dark horse, resplendent in his red coat, close to three hundred yards away. He debated whether to aim for the head or chest, decided at that distance best to target the body, slowed his breathing, steadied his hand and fired. He waited for the officer to crumple forward in the saddle and slide to the ground. Nothing happened.

"Bant. You missed," McNeil said incredulously as the British troops quickened their step, rapidly closing the distance to the Americans. Bant reloaded as he heard the crack of McNeil's rifle. How could he have missed? He never wasted a ball. He had hit men at greater distances than this. Was it a defective cartridge with an improper load? Had his hand quivered? A shouted order to fire interrupted his analysis of what had gone wrong. The roar of the musket volley echoed in his ears. Through the smoke, Bant saw the British line buckle and hesitate. A second volley drove them back up the hill, leaving a thin line of skirmishers to protect their retreat. Bant sighted on one of the rearguard crouching behind a bush, under two hundred yards away. Overcome by his lack of confidence, he aimed for the soldier's chest instead of the head. He saw the man fall on his back. He thought it seemed as if he had been hit by several balls. Perhaps he had missed again. This time he did not reload. He would wait until he could be certain no one else was aiming at his target and then prove to himself his aim was still true.

The British re-emerged from the redoubt with two three pounders and began to shell their positions. Normally, Bant would have targeted the gunnery officer but this time, he felt uncertain enough not to try. They retreated with the Connecticut troops and took shelter in the ravine. After a while, the British stopped attempting to lob shells over the rim and down into the gully and their cannons fell silent. It was past mid-morning. Overcome by thirst, the soldiers lay against the cool earth in the shady part of the ravine and drank from their canteens. Bant took one pull from his but the rum tasted bitter to him. He poured its contents on the ground and scrambled down the slope to the narrow creek at the bottom and filled it with plain water. When he returned, McNeil looked at him peculiarly.

"For all the years we have been together, I have never known you to miss. And now you pour good rum in the dirt. You could have offered it to me you know," he said somewhat petulantly. "What is ailing you?"

Bant debated whether to tell McNeil about his nightmare. He decided against doing so, ashamed to reveal the uncontrollable thoughts that disturbed his brain.

"'Tis your demons again?" McNeil asked. Bant nodded quietly. He felt helpless. From past experience he knew killing Redcoats, and particularly cavalry officers helped to keep his demons at bay. If he could no longer do that then what good was he? And if he could not overcome his demons, then it would be better to die than to live a life of torment.

McNeil touched his arm. "It is probably the cartridges. Here, take some of mine and give me yours."

"Do you think so?" Bant said, eager to grasp at the thought that he had not lost his ability or confidence.

"As I said, this is the first time I have seen your aim be off. Nothing has changed in you. You have had this demon trouble before." He held out his palm with ten cartridges. Bant took them, placed them in the top rack of his cartridge box and counted out the same number for McNeil.

A Lieutenant for the Connecticut troops walked among his men calling for volunteers to scout and harass the Redcoats again. Two platoons clambered up the stony incline and disappeared over the lip. McNeil stood up. "Come on Bant. We will join them and see if we can pick off an officer or two."

Bant followed his long legged friend. He resolved if he missed again, he would simply stand up and walk toward the enemy until their musket fire cut him down and ended his incessant struggling with his demons.[1]

The soldiers of the 3rd New Jersey Regiment, like the rest of the entire Continental Army moving south, arose as the drums sounded reveille at 2:30 a.m., assembled at 3 and were on the road by 3:15 in the morning. It was to reduce marching in the August heat. They routinely stopped by mid-afternoon. Their baggage trains with their tents, bedding and cooking kettles usually arrived by no later than four or so, in time to set up camp. It had been this way since they left Dobbs Ferry, crossing the Hudson and on into New Jersey. They were now encamped at Chatham, from where they had left in late February to reinforce the troops north of New York. With the heat of the summer making the air seem as if it was thick enough to part, they set up their tents in the open fields, choosing the fresh air to the stinking confinement of the now empty huts of their winter quarters. Around them were the other regiments of Continentals, and a short distance away, the camps of the French.

Traynor sensed an increased anxiety and moodiness in Private Wade, the closer they got to Chatham. Caleb was a changed man after being forced to execute the two mutinous Sergeants. He kept to himself mostly and on the dry dusty roads, no longer initiated any banter or called out the others for what in the past he would have been quick to condemn as their stupidity or ignorance. Because he was physically imposing, the men tended to avoid him, seemingly more fearful of him, silent and withdrawn, than when he was a blustering bully.

Once they were settled in Chatham, Wade seized every excuse to avoid the field beyond the parade ground where the Sergeants had been shot. He volunteered for any dirty duty from digging latrines to burning offal. He would return stinking and grimy, his lips tight and his eyes downcast with a look of worry as to how he would escape proximity to the killing field the next day. His apprehension intensified, as it became apparent they would remain here for weeks until there were sufficient boats available to ferry them across to attack Staten Island and then on to New York City.

This afternoon, rather than lying around waiting for their meager rations to be issued for the dinner meal, someone suggested they amble a few miles down the road to the French encampment and enjoy the spectacle. "What is there to see?" a soldier asked.

"Those Frenchies have a set manner once they establish camp."

About twenty of their company left the others to lounge in the minimal shade provided by truncated fruit trees, chopped down during the British retreat from Springfield the year before. With Sergeant Henderson in the lead, they walked in small groups down the road, choking on the dust raised by the occasional courier galloping up from Trenton.

They arrived as the some of the French troops were preparing for their evening meal, while others were re-digging a circular hole cooking area. It appeared that each "mess" of eight contributed two soldiers for the digging, who stripped off their buttoned white jackets, hung them on the musket racks and hacked away at the soil with flat bladed picks. Others came from the woods pushing wheelbarrows filled with freshly cut logs.

"They are like a hive of termites," Caleb said, almost the first words he had uttered since they had left Chatham. "What is the purpose of this circular hole, Sergeant?" he asked with genuine curiosity.

"Watch what those others are doing and you will see," Henderson replied. It was late afternoon. The gnats and mosquitos buzzed around the soldiers' heads, seeking to bite and draw blood. The frenetic waving of tri-corns temporarily chased them away before they returned like bees harvesting pollen.

With the arrival of those bearing the firewood, more of the Frenchies took up tools and began repairing a circular ditch around the center hole. In no time at all, they had improved the structure of a wheel, with the central hole as the hub, and covered tunnels like spokes running to the circumference. At the junction of each tunnel and the rim, they enlarged a smaller hole and set up their cooking kettles over each hole. A large fire was burning at the hub and the heat emanated down the spokes to the individual pots, placed on low iron tripods, over a few small burning logs.

"Their kettles are smaller than our nine quart ones," Caleb observed.

"Yes," Traynor replied, "and yet our mess is six men and theirs are eight."

"The difference," Caleb said, as the French lined up to receive their rations, "is they receive their allotted victuals and we do not. Nine quarts of nothing is still nothing." He said it without bitterness and softly enough so that only Traynor heard him.

Ever since Wade had been part of the firing squad, he omitted the usual curses and blasphemies that had peppered his speech. No longer did he do his best to rile up others in the platoon It was strange to hear him talk so calmly. The huge physique was the same but it was as if the body was inhabited by a different person.

"I wonder what they get for rations?" one of the Jersey men asked.

"I do not speak their jargon but I will wander over and find out." And with that Caleb left their group and approached the nearest Frenchie who was stirring one of the kettles. He bent down to peer in and the soldier dipped a large ladle in and brought it up to Wade's nose. The American gestured to ask for a taste and the Frenchman offered him the ladle. After taking a noisy slurp, Caleb's face broke into a broad smile. Turning back to the Jersey men, he yelled, "pea soup with chunks of real ham and turnips." As the brew bubbled away in the kettles, loaves of freshly baked bread, long and thin with a dark appetizing crust arrived in wheelbarrows and were divided up among each mess. The Frenchie, who had given Caleb a taste of the soup, offered him a loaf, indicating he should share it with his fellow Continentals. Uncharacteristically, Caleb removed the worn red cockade from his tri-corn and offered it to the Frenchie in friendship.[2]

The shared small portions of the bread reminded the men of Traynor's platoon of their own hunger and their meager mess awaiting them a few miles back at Chatham. They had not noticed the gathering of the dark clouds and the first heavy drops of rain caught them by surprise. With Sergeant Henderson in the lead they broke into an undisciplined run up the road. As they passed a churchyard, the double doors of the white clapboard building were opened by a Reverend, his closely cropped grey hair framing his gaunt face.

"Come in, my brave soldiers," he called "and seek the shelter and protection of the Lord." While some hesitated, Caleb Wade immediately veered off the road and dashed through the yard, up the three wooden steps and disappeared inside. Others, without awaiting orders from Sergeant Henderson, needed little encouragement to follow, as solid sheets of rain pelted them.

Inside, the men sat on the wooden pews, dripping puddles of water on to the pine board floor. The rain drummed incessantly on the peaked roof. The Minister lit the half burned candles in the wall sconces and turned to face the New Jersey men.

"I am Reverend Israel Avery. Welcome to my church, you ragged Davids on the road to battle the red-coated Goliaths. Remember, the Lord saith he who is not with Me is against Me, and he that gathereth not with Me, I shall scattereth abroad." He held his arms out wide, parting his worn black jacket to reveal a frayed black waistcoat with plain buttons. "Welcome I say to one and all, even the Popish French who have joined us in our just war against the tyranny of the Crown." In the dim candlelight, his pinched cheeks and pursed thin lips gave him a frail aged appearance, heightened by his slight frame and the greyish unkempt curls of thin hair barely covering his skull. Yet his voice was strong and carried over the sound of rain on the church roof.

"I have been minister here since '74 and in all my sermons given to the brave soldiers who have passed through Chatham I have implored the Lord to give our people the courage and perseverance to overcome their enemies." Avery had left the floor in front of the pews and mounted the pulpit. "'Tis not Sunday and I will not preach a sermon now. However, before you return to your encampment and then march on to meet our accursed enemies, know this essential truth." His sunken eyes stared at the ranks of the soldiers in the pews. Wade leaned forward in expectation.

"Our war has been shewn to be the cause of God. Our cause is the cause of truth against error and falsehood – the cause of pure and undefiled religion against oppression and tyranny – in short, it is the cause of Heaven against hell."

As he uttered the last phrase he emphatically brought down his two raised arms and pointed with his long bony right arm to the underworld far beneath the church's floor. There was a crash of nearby thunder. Some of the soldiers started and looked around fearfully, but Wade leaned forward even further, lost in the Reverend's words.

"It is the kind parent of the Universe against the prince of darkness and the destroyer of the human race."

Avery's eyes scanned the pews and his gaze came to rest on Wade who was transfixed by the Reverend. "No matter what you have done in the heat of battle, anger or weakness, if you remain true to our cause and wage this war to your utmost, the Lord is with you." It now seemed as if this was a conversation between the Reverend and Private Wade, so intense was Avery's look and so enthralled was the expression on Caleb's face. "The Lord saith a defensive war in a just cause is without sin. You must believe that with every part of your body and soul and adhere to it in the battles to come." He opened his arms as if in benediction.

"The rain has ceased. Let the spirit of patriotism fire your every breath. Return to your encampment secure in the knowledge that our cause is just and the Lord is with you." [3] Caleb was the first to utter a loud "Amen," and the last to leave the church. Traynor waited for him outside and they walked in silence through the steamy heat toward Princeton.

"I feel as if I have been purged of some sickness and am well again," Wade said as he turned to look at the church one more time. "I thank you for the kindness you showed me when I was afflicted. I will not forget it." Traynor grunted in acknowledgment. He thought it best to say nothing.

Four days later, contrary to all expectations of an assault on New York, they marched south. They reached Trenton by mid-afternoon the following day and did not stop to wait for their baggage train. The soldiers of the 3rd New Jersey Regiment immediately embarked on Durham boats, a few small fishing skiffs and dories and were ferried across the Delaware to Pennsylvania. Then, in the heat of the afternoon, they marched inland for a few miles and made camp in a wood adjacent to the Trenton-Philadelphia road. This would be the first night since leaving Dobbs Ferry two weeks earlier they would sleep on the ground without tents. The fatigue, heat and humidity, as well as the thought of dinner being whatever remained of their rations, made the soldiers irritable. The talk amongst them turned angry bordering on open insurrection.

"Had we stayed in Trenton, some would have had roofs over our heads and the rest our tents and cots," a soldier said loudly. "And the good people of that town would have offered us provisions for our dinner," another proposed, which drew derisive laughter from those around.

"When was the last time any civilian voluntarily gave us even a drink of water from their well, let alone something to eat?" another asked.

"All those fat asses do is profit off of this war and ignore our misery," a soldier said as he stood, rubbing his back against a tree trunk to satisfy his itching. "If it were up to me, when we reach Philadelphia and parade before all those well-clothed, well-fed cockshafers, we should sit down in the middle of that cobblestoned street and not take one step more until we are properly fed and clothed."

"Do not forget our pay," another shouted. "We have not seen a dollar in a year, not that the Continentals would do us any good."

Traynor sensed it was time to intervene. He started to get up and felt Caleb Wade's thickly callused hand on his shoulder, restraining him. This is the beginning of a mutiny, he thought as he looked around to see if Sergeant Henderson was nearby. Caleb released his grip and took a few steps forward moving out of the shade into a sunny grassy area in front of the trees.

"This is not the talk of New Jersey men. This is the devil speaking." He paused, certain of their attention. "A fortnight ago, I would be among the first of you to complain about our rations, our clothing and our pay."

"And now?" one of the soldiers shouted, challenging him. "You think we deserve to be marching shoeless and in rags? And starving tonight? For what?"

Traynor expected Caleb to search out the soldier in the woods and beat him senseless for daring to speak to him like that. Instead, he watched in amazement as Wade simply shrugged and held up his hands whether asking for silence or in supplication, he did not know.

"You all know me. I was a blasphemer, a drunkard, a man who avoided the Sunday sermons, ready to beat anyone up who slighted me. I was a liar and a braggart with no brains." Traynor wondered whether Wade's lying included that night near West Point when he and two others had returned to their lines laden down with provisions taken by force, they said, from a Loyalist.

"No more," he said once loudly and repeated the words in a whisper. "I believe that Reverend some of us heard the other day. The Lord is with us. We can all see it. We have fought shoeless, in rags, starving, unpaid and sick since '77 when we first signed up." He held out his arm and pointed at the men who now stood in a semi-circle around him. "Look at us. We have beaten the Redcoats and their Hessians. How? Because the Lord is indeed with us."

The soldiers murmured among themselves, not certain what to make of Caleb and fearful that if they challenged him, he would revert to the Caleb of old and bash their brains in. None had noticed Sergeant Henderson had come from the road and joined them.

"Lieutenant Phelps says to fall in. There is a depot down the road with salted beef, bread and cider. They have no wagons to haul the provisions here so we will march to our dinner. Form by ranks," he bellowed. "Be quick about it," he added although the men were already eagerly on their feet.

Corporal Traynor marched next to Wade's file as they tromped down the road.

"Why would there be a depot on this road?" one of the other privates asked. Before Traynor could respond that with the army on the move and the route known, the Quartermaster's Corps would have pre-positioned supplies for the troops, he heard Wade's deep voice answer "Because the Lord is with us." [4]

The shock on the part of the civilians and the sullenness from the ranks of the Continentals was palpable. For the good citizens of Philadelphia, after having cheered the gaudily clothed French soldiers and their officers, festooned in all manner of gold braid and uniformly clad and equipped, the sight of the ragged ranks of their army caused gasps of astonishment and then shocked silence.

Lieutenant Will Stoner, mounted on Big Red with a polished brass twelve-pounder in tow, could feel the resentment of the troops ahead of him. Many were shoeless with dirt-encrusted feet wearily plodding over the smooth cobblestones. None had a complete uniform that corresponded to another. There was a mismatch of coats, jackets and shirts, some had stockings with holes, others had none. Instead of clean white pants, the predominant color of their torn and dirty breeches was ash grey. Unlike the French who had preceded them, with their hair neatly curled beneath their cumbersome four-cornered hat, the Continental soldiers' unkempt hair straggled out from under stained dark blue tri-corns in the manner of wild backwoodsmen. Those who had their hair tied back in a knot were few and far between. As a group, the Continentals were lean to the point of starvation.

From the soldiers point of view, the pale, well dressed and obviously well fed Philadelphians who crowded Market Street and stood on the steps of prominent public buildings, were proof of the merchants who profited from the war by selling their merchandise to the enemy for British sterling and shunned providing foodstuffs to the American Quartermasters for paper. A few women waved from the windows of well-appointed homes, the soldiers catching glimpses of polished chandeliers and richly colored draperies inside.

Will could sympathize with the rank and file soldiers. From the vantage point of horseback scanning the crowd, outside of the few Quakers in their sensible and somber clothing, most of the civilians were clad in brightly colored shawls and fashionable dress, the men's coats cut just so and the women's day dresses adorned with luxurious amounts of lace and frills. As a group, he was hard pressed to find a thin person in the crowd, while the gaunt and sunburned soldiers, barely a step ahead of starvation, looked like a pack of wolves on the prowl.

The artillery assembled on the Common. Will thought he would seek out his old friends, Mary and Edward Lewis, and give them news of Elisabeth and Henry. He had left them at West Point, with the assurance once the army had cleared New Jersey, his wife would travel with Mrs. Knox and her children to Philadelphia. Lucy was again pregnant and expecting by the end of year. She would get better care in the capital city than in the wilderness of upstate New York.

He would have to hurry if he wished to see the Lewises. His orders were that by three in the morning he must be on the road

Madness on the March

to Chester. Beyond was Christiana. There, they would join the flotilla of boats carrying the heavier cannons from Trenton down the Delaware.

After seeing that Big Red was fed and watered, Will headed to the Pennsylvania State House using it as a landmark to orient himself to the Lewis's street. The sidewalks were crowded and amongst the people ahead of him, he recognized Captain Hadley. He called his name and Samuel stopped and waited as people flowed around him.

"I am seeking out an acquaintance of Mercy's in Philadelphia," he explained. "A member of the Congress from New Jersey. He may have received a letter from my wife." Will knew she had returned to the Ford family mansion in Morristown and their first child was due imminently.

"I pray that your news will be good," Will replied. They walked side by side, with Hadley holding Will by the elbow so they could stay together.

"They say, we are bound for Virginia to engage Cornwallis and his army," Will began hesitantly. "I know the route only so far as Christiana where we are to meet up with the main body of our artillery." Will took off his battered tri-corn and wiped the sweat from his forehead with his sleeve. The afternoon sun beat down on his shoulders and he wished he had not worn his jacket.

"Cornwallis has established a base at Yorktown, a place on the coast where the Chesapeake Bay meets the ocean," Hadley explained. "We will go overland from Christiana to the head of the Bay and then board ships for Yorktown. We are then to lay siege from the land while the French fleet blockades him from the seaward." He smiled and slapped Will on his arm. "That is the plan and if it succeeds, we will capture their entire army or annihilate them should they not surrender."

Will grinned back at him thankful for the information. "I confess, now that I am a husband and father, I am more concerned to know details of the future than I was before. When I write to Elisabeth, I believe such information gives her comfort as well, rather than her relying on rumors and exaggerations."

They turned on to Chestnut Street from Seventh. Ahead, in front of the tiered brick tower topped by its white spire, were at least three regiments of Continentals, shouting and milling about. At first Will thought they were about to assault the Congress within and hold them captive until their demands were met. As he and Hadley approached, they saw, beneath the three tall entrance windows, a rough, hastily raised platform on which there were planked tables with ledgers and behind that several upright barrels. They arrived just as an officer, resplendent in a clean dark blue uniform cupped his hands and called for quiet. The six or seven hundred soldiers formed ranks to hear him out. Making a great show of it, the officer shouted that as Paymaster General of the Continental Army, he was pleased to announce all soldiers would receive one month's pay in hard specie. And with that, he dramatically stove in the top of one of the barrels with a hatchet and tipped it over so that silver and gold coins spilled out on to the platform. A deafening, spontaneous shout erupted from the men, along with huzzahs for the Continental Congress and the Paymaster General. The Regimental Clerks took their seats at the tables and the soldiers, grinning broadly and chattering among themselves, lined up in orderly ranks to receive the pay long denied them.[5]

With this crowd of eager soldiers blocking the south entrance, Hadley parted company with Will and skirted around the Hall trying to find a side entrance. Will, now properly oriented, found his way to the Quaker neighborhood "north of Market." When he knocked on the door, modest, short little Mary Lewis, opened it and almost tipped him down the two front stairs with her vigorous hug. Sitting in her kitchen, the very room where he had taught Elizabeth how to make invisible ink and use a book code, he answered her barrage of questions about Elisabeth and Henry while she bustled about serving him tea and some freshly baked ginger cookies. He waited as long as he could into the waning afternoon and when Edward had not yet returned from the warehouses on the wharf, Will left the woman who had been his wife's confidante and one could reasonably say, a co-conspirator in her spying endeavor and walked back to the Commons.

The area was crowded now with the arrival of the remnants of their artillery regiment that had been unable to board boats at Trenton. There were the recently hired wagoneers with their teams of oxen and shaggy, heavy footed draft horses, impressed from Loyalist farms in New Jersey.[6] The wagons were hauling heavy shot, side boxes, rammers, sponges and buckets. Those for the Artificers Regiment were full of tools of blacksmiths, carpenters, farriers and harness makers and anvils, spokes, iron rims, axles, and cured leather. With all of these animals in need of forage and oats, Will quickly walked to the temporary sheds housing the artillery horses to make certain the quarter bag of oats set aside for Big Red would not be purloined. It was here that Captain Hadley found him and from the jubilant expression on his face, Will knew he brought good news.

"I have a son," he shouted to Will in the now darkening shed, waving a letter in his hand. "Mercy writes that he was born eleven days ago, a healthy dark haired little boy whom she says favors my looks." He shook his head. "Perhaps a bit early to tell. Do you not think so Will?"

"Mercy is the best judge of that. I am glad for you," Will replied, thinking of the last time he had seen Henry, in his mother's arms, waving his plump little hand as he had ridden away.

"Once we smash Cornwallis' army at Yorktown, we can look forward to the day our sons will play together in peace," Hadley said.

And, Will thought, we will no longer be separated from our wives and apprehensively fret about the evil that has happened but of which we have not yet been informed.

—ᨆ—

Gillet sat on a round keg of gunpowder in the hold of a small schooner carrying most of the Sappers and Miners Regiment. The vessel tossed about on the rough waters of the Delaware, attempting to make headway in the teeth of a thunderstorm. His haversack, stuffed with two new linen shirts and two pairs of silk and oakum stockings was beside him. His month's pay, issued in hard coin, the first wages they had seen since '76 was in his pocketbook in his waistcoat, along with the strip of blue cloth from his wife. The gold coins, which their French officers said were borrowed from good General Rochambeau's treasury, would do none of them any good if lightning struck. For three days before embarking from Philadelphia, their Regiment of Sappers and Miners, some sixty strong, had been laboring in the stifling heat of the warehouses lining the piers, packing shot and shell and barrels of gunpowder, most of which were now tightly wedged in the very hold in which they were sitting. With each clap of thunder, the men looked anxiously at each other, the whites of their terrified eyes clearly visible in the darkened hold. Outside of Private Gideon Hazzard and one or two of the others he knew were coastal men from Connecticut, the others had been farmers and mechanics. They were torn between being more frightened of drowning in the murky waters below or being blown sky high by the explosives around them.

The schooner rocked viciously and Gillet clenched his eyes closed, fighting down the acidic taste of fear in his throat. As heavily loaded as it was, there was strong likelihood the boat could be swamped. At least he would have a chance in the water. If it were to be struck by lightning, his life would be over in a moment.

From the diminishing frequency of the thunderclaps, he sensed the storm abating. Hazzard caught his gaze and made a gently rocking motion with his hands. Gillet noticed the swaying was less severe. He touched his waistcoat, not for the bulge of the pocketbook within but for his fingers to be closer to his blue ribbon talisman.

The next day, when the tide permitted they renewed their journey southward on a narrow river. In the calm waters, the ship rode low, less than a foot below the gunnels but steady. The river twisted and turned until Gillet lost all sense of direction. The schooner's captain from Philadelphia, a man full of himself with an ample stomach barely contained by a deep violet waistcoat with obviously fake gold buttons, stood proudly erect at the wheel as if he were steering a seventy-four gun, ship of the line. Gillet, Hazzard and the others were up on deck, glad to be out of the dank hold, even though the air was thick and humid. He was idly watching the dragon flies skimming the water when the schooner scraped a mud bank and ran aground. The captain made much of looking over the sides and loudly berating a few of the sailors for failing to take more numerous soundings. It is all noise and bombast, Gillet concluded. There was nothing else for it but to lighten the load.

Within a minute, on orders from their Lieutenant, they stripped off their shirts, stockings and shoes, and in their old ragged coveralls, formed a line in descending order of height in the mud and muck from the gunnels to the shore and beyond. Those less fortunate, passed the heavy barrels of gunpowder up from the dank hold to those on deck and then, to the waiting hands of the men waist deep in the water. It seemed to Gillet that every insect in this part of the river had converged upon the bare-chested soldiers to feast on their flesh and suck their blood. It was worse when he hoisted a barrel with both hands, helpless to swat away the swarms of buzzing pests that targeted his face and neck and particularly his eyes. As if participating in a formal dance, each man would reach to his left, grab a barrel with both hands, hoist it over his head to the right, and then, when his hands were momentarily free, wave them wildly about his head and slap his neck, before once again turning to the left to seize the next barrel. Occasionally, the rhythm would be broken by one in the line jumping in agitation as something unknown slithered in the muddy ooze around his toes or ankles.

After an hour of hard labor in the burning sun, with the tide rising to their armpits, the schooner floated free and made for shore. The reloading of the cargo was quicker and once they were underway, the men sat on deck, with lighted twigs, burning the leeches off their legs.

"We should save the leeches for the surgeons who will need them when we come down with the fevers," Gillet said, to scare the farmboys amongst them. Hazzard caught his eye and smiled in appreciation of the macabre joke, as he threw another of the slimy tapered brown worms overboard.

When they finally docked at the river's end, they left the unloading to other troops and marched overland to Head of Elk, followed by wagoneers hired and paid with French gold, to bring the powder, shot and shell with them.

They tramped along a narrow road, lined by dense forests of oak and ramrod straight pines and broader branched tulip poplars, sweating and swatting as they walked, kicking up dust that clogged their nostrils and coated their lips and tongues. Suddenly, ahead through the trees they could see the broad flat expanse of Chesapeake Bay with a line of white clouds in the distance lying low to the water as if they were snow capped mountains. They followed a winding path along chalk white cliffs a hundred feet above the shore and descended to a rocky beach, strewn with seaweed and driftwood. To Gillet's experienced eye, the sloops, schooners and fat bottomed merchant vessels gently riding the waves in the sheltered inlet looked barely seaworthy. There certainly were not enough of them to transport the troops that had paraded through Philadelphia.

"Can you smell the ocean?" Gillet asked Hazzard, a broad grin on his face. He took a deep breath and pointing exuberantly to the gulls and the occasional eagle soaring overheard.

When they were dismissed, the men left their haversacks well up on shore, stripped down to their breeches and waded into the warm water. Gillet clutched in his hand the bar of hard lye soap he had purchased from a farmer's wife beyond Chester. With his two dirty linen shirts and grimy coveralls, he settled himself in the shallows and scrubbed his clothes first and then his upper body and hair. The sores and open bites stung more from the strong soap than the salt water but he felt clean. He tossed the bar to Hazzard who had waded out in the water up to his waist, his broad black back glistening in the late afternoon sun.

Their mess had determined to share the essentials they now could afford to buy. After all, their rations were supposed to include one pound of good common soap for six men per week. Hazzard had used some of his pay to purchase vinegar that he stored in two extra canteens. It would be for purifying water, when the rum or cider ran out. A splash of it on a lice comb also helped to kill the little buggers that remained in one's hair. Another in their squad had cheese, another a jar of preserves, and one a pot of butter. Most importantly, each of them had almost four pieces of eight left, to buy stockings, shoe leather or more food that suited their fancy, although Gillet suspected some of them would waste it on rum and wine if given the chance. The camp followers always managed to have extra rum to sell.

Gillet sat on the warm rocks, his clothes drying in the mid-afternoon sun and took in the expanse of the bay. By now, everyone knew they were heading further south toward Cornwallis' base on the York River. For those from New England, the southern colonies were the place of mysterious swamp fevers and maladies that sapped the strength of the strongest soldiers. Gillet was thankful their Regiment was going by water for most of the way instead of being compelled to march overland through the sulphurous air. Less chance of getting a fever on board ship, he thought, turning his clothing over. Once they arrived and saw the lay of the land would be time enough to dwell on the dangers of digging trenches close to the British defenses.

Part Two
Yorktown

Chapter 9 - Small Pox, Fever and Dangerous Night Duty

For the third straight day, the men of the old 3rd New Jersey Regiment, now combined with the 2nd, were in the forests, at six a.m. a few miles from Yorktown. The entire Brigade, some fourteen hundred men under the command of Colonel Elias Dayton were on fatigue duty. They were chopping down the tall straight yellow poplars, broad sassafras trees with their aromatic twigs and branches, low scrubby pines and the occasional hardwood willow oak. Their muskets neatly racked back at camp, they were armed only with axes, hatchets, and bill hooks, a wide-bladed machete like tool that curved upward at the end to a point. It was good for splitting thick branches into strips to make the bundles of fascines and the basket frames for the gabions. The early morning mist had dissipated and the sun, rising behind Yorktown to the east, already made their work warm.

Corporal Traynor signaled his work party to take a rest. The soldiers put down their tools and lay on the soft soil or sat on the newly cut tree stumps. If their orders were the same as the previous two days, they would be at this until five p.m. Here and there, a few men had set fire to piles of green brush. The smoke blowing in a light breeze temporarily helped to keep the hordes of mosquitos away and mingled with the clean smell of fresh wood chips and pine branches. Several wagons, loaded with fascines and gabion frames made their way across a field and down to the road toward the American's camp and beyond that, the British fortifications at Yorktown.[1]

"I hear the Redcoats are attacked whenever they venture out for forage or wood," a soldier said, picked at his teeth with a reed stalk. " 'Tis a blessing to do our work in peace."

"Those fascines and gabions have a purpose," Private Caleb Wade said. "Soon we will be digging trenches and throwing up earthen works close to the enemy lines. Then it will be a hot and heavy fire."

The men were silent, thinking of entrenching in the dark of night with British patrols roaming about and cannon fire overhead. One of the soldiers let loose a loud fart as he rose and headed for the brush to relieve himself. "Hope we are never so close to the British so as to hear their sentries fart," someone said. "Or worse, to be able to smell their foul English gas," another added.

Caleb let the snickers die down. "I meant what I said about their fire being hot and heavy. Once the siege begins, there may be no time for regular services. I urge you all to be at peace with your Maker."

"What has come over you, Caleb," Private Mathias Vose complained. He was one of Wade's former drinking companions, always ready for another gill of rum, and sometimes unable to stand for roll call. He had followed Wade and joined the mutineers at Chatham. Vose was considerably shorter than Caleb, but as he stood up, he pulled an axe from a tree stump and leaned on it casually, blade side resting on the ground. "Every time you open your mouth it is 'the Lord this', or 'our Maker that,'" he said contemptuously. "If you believe the Lord will provide, keep it to yourself. Spare us your new found religious poppycock."

"There are those amongst us who may find comfort in my words. It is for them to decide," Caleb responded simply. "When you are in the trenches, you will not be able to find relief in rum, Mathias."

The soldier who had gone to relieve himself came running out of the low shrubs, wildly waving his arms and frantically looking behind to see if he was being pursued. Several men stood up at his alarm and grabbed their axes.

"Sergeant," the man called running up to Henderson, catching his breath. "There are men in the woods. Negroes. Terribly sick with the pox." He panted heavily in the heat. "They are really bad off. Some may be dead already." At the word pox, several men backed away as if the bringer of the bad news was himself infected.

"Let me find Lieutenant Phelps. The rest of you get back to work."

Traynor led the work crew back to the tree line. Vose made a point of removing his jacket and flexing his muscles, stretching with the axe over his head and turning this way and that. Traynor stationed himself at a thick straight tulip poplar between Vose and Wade. His axe made a satisfying whack as the blade bit out a large chip of pale white wood.

Henderson returned with their Lieutenant and the two went from one group to the next, talking quietly before moving on. "Who amongst you have been inoculated against small pox," Phelps inquired of Traynor and the men around him.

"I have, Sir." Traynor replied. "I have also," Wade answered.

"Anyone else," Henderson prompted them.

"You have, Mathias," Caleb said. "You told me so yourself."

"Shut your lying mouth, Wade. I never said no such a thing because I never was nockulated."

The big man shrugged and ignored Vose's insult.

"Those of you who have been inoculated, go with Sergeant Henderson. You will be issued shovels and canteens. You will bury the dead Negroes, give the living ones the canteens and load them on the wagon. They will be driven to the special camp for those with the pox." He looked sternly at each of them. "If any of you have lied to me about being inoculated to avoid work duty, say so now. There will be no punishment. We cannot allow the spread of the pox to our men. General Washington's direct orders." The men selected shook their heads. "All right Sergeant Henderson. Take them with you and get this terrible business over with." [2]

The small pox party returned late in the afternoon. The soldiers who remained on the work detail wavered between their fear of being exposed to the disease and their curiosity to learn what had happened. Their fear increased as they realized they would be sharing their cooking pots and quarters with those who had been with the afflicted Negroes.

They gathered around their cooking kettles, the air seemingly cleansed by the addition of aromatic sassafras branches that also served to keep away the mosquitos.

"Tell us, Corporal. Who were they? What was it like?"

Traynor sighed, unwilling to recall their afternoon's work but recognizing the need to satisfy the men's curiosity and more importantly, put to rest their fears.

"They were poor, poxie Negro laborers from Yorktown whom the British threw out with the arrival of our army. Too many extra mouths to feed and limited food supplies, I suppose." He paused, staring at the fire and the circle of faces around him. "They were in rags and as best as I could understand them, had been without food or water for a few days,. Some had pieces of burnt Indian corn in their mouths, even those that were dead."

"How many were dead?" a voice blurted out.

"Eleven of them and half of the rest of them are likely to die." Traynor lowered his voice. "They were that far gone. When I was inoculated, the surgeon said I can no longer get the pox. You cannot catch it from us," he said gesturing to Wade and himself. "That is why our soldiers with the pox are isolated. Enough of this talk. It was a dirty business and I will say no more about it."

Wade shifted his weight on the stump he used as a stool. "I have never seen such wretched human beings in my life." He pointed to the flames burning in the pit before them. "It was a scene from the devil's own domain," he muttered, signaling that he, too, was through talking.

The following day, after reveille, the entire brigade had no responsibilities, except for the invalids who were given camp duty. In the late afternoon the regiment assembled on the parade ground, canteens filled, their haversacks left behind. They could hear the constant heavy fire of the British artillery harassing the American engineers working in the flat field before the enemy's redoubts and defensive line. At seven p.m. with their muskets loaded and bayonets fixed, the regiment marched out of camp by company and into the gloom and mist of the night. They were assigned patrol duty, at least one hundred yards beyond the work parties that followed them and dug the first of the siege trenches. There was no moon and a light rain was falling. The men were ordered to keep silent. There was none of the usual banter to cloak their fear.

Awaiting orders, Traynor lay on the wet earth, his cartridge box swiveled around to be on his hip, neither touching the ground nor catching the rain from above either. He hoped the powder would remain dry. Ahead and to his left, he could see the muzzle flashes from the British artillery and the occasional rocket illuminating soldiers building a redoubt. That was the French part of the line. Seeking shelter in the rain soaked earth would dirty their white uniforms, he thought. He counted about thirty cannon shots in the space of fifteen or so minutes and hoped the Redcoats would not unleash a similar heavy bombardment on the Continentals' part of the line. The enemy certainly was not hoarding their powder tonight.

Sergeant Henderson moved quietly among the squad of twelve men, although the roar of the cannons blasting away at the French was enough to cover any spoken words but the loudest communal shout.

"'Tis our company's turn. The watchword is 'Lafayette.' The counter is 'Grand Alliance.' If we meet with any Redcoats, I will call out the challenge and the rest of you drop to the ground. Note their muzzle flashes and then charge with your bayonets."

They crept forward from their advanced positions, closer to the British, sheltered behind their earthen walls. Incongruously, in between the cannon fire and the occasional volley of muskets, Traynor heard dogs barking in the distance. The British kept dogs to sound the alarm but he judged them to be nearer to the French than the American positions. When Henderson deemed their position to be far enough in advance of their lines and the work parties, he touched the man next to him and signaled for him to crouch down to make a lower profile. Each man tapped the one next to him until there was a thin line of soldiers, spread out over ten yards, with Corporal Traynor at the far right and Henderson anchoring the left. Past him in the gloom, the rest of Lieutenant Phelps' company was strung well ahead of the white pine branches, laid down by the engineers as the line for the trench to be dug.

Traynor hoped there were Continentals to his right. He was frightened that he might be at the very end, like hanging at the edge of cliff. He was reasonably certain the British would not attempt an attack in force and turn the American's flank. It would just be a clashing of patrols and pickets in the blackness. Traynor and the others in his squad and company waited, each soldier on one knee, peering into the inky darkness, seeking out any sign of movement, listening for the squish of a footstep on the wet grass.

"Halt and state the watchword," he heard Henderson shout. He was answered by a disciplined musket volley. As Traynor fell forward, he saw two muskets discharge, one slightly to his right, the other directly in front of him. Hoping that other Redcoats further to the right had not held their fire, he rose up and charged silently forward until he could see two dark shapes crouched before him. One was sliding his ramrod down the muzzle. Traynor caught him with his arm raised high and plunged his bayonet into his exposed chest. The man let out a cry of surprise and slumped backwards. Traynor turned to attack the other soldier. He was no longer there. Henderson shouted – "Charge and drive them back." Traynor ran forward, conscious there were others alongside him, until a line of muzzle flashes seared the night darkness from a raised earthen works and harmlessly passed overhead.

On the order to retreat, Traynor turned his back on the British works. Masked by the darkness there was little danger of being picked off by a rifleman. He was surprised by the sharp bang of a field cannon followed by the whistling of grape canister scything through the air. Again, the gunner's aim was too high. Traynor's foot caught on something soft. He tripped over the body of a dead Redcoat and fell headlong on the grass, his face parallel to the dead man's head and sightless eyes. Hastily, Traynor got back on his feet and found his position at the end of their line. For another hour they remained on patrol before marching in file back to their own lines, answering the challenge of their sentries before passing through.

At the place they entered their lines, the trench was already five feet deep and about three feet wide. Hundreds of men dug rhythmically with shovels and pickaxes, filling bags with the rain-softened earth and hoisting them up to the rim. Fascines and gabions were being passed forward over the heads of the line of men that extended back and disappeared in the darkness until they reached the diggers up front. There, the three foot high gabions were positioned a little forward of the rim of the trench and soil and stones shoveled into their woven wooden frames. Already they were part of a protective earthen wall, to be topped off by fascines horizontal to the trench. The soldiers labored efficiently in silence, soaked by the continuing light rain.

Traynor and his company clambered out of the trench and trudged across the flat land about fifty yards to rest briefly in the open, until they were again sent out on picket duty. By the time they were finally relieved just before dawn, this section of the trench was almost ten feet wide. The sandbags, gabions and fascines formed a solid earthen wall that was tested before the New Jersey men were clear of the trench.

As it became light, the British found themselves confronted by a two thousand yard long trench, a mere eight hundred yards away, that snaked from the Hampton Road on their right to as far as the York River on their left. Overcoming their initial shock, they fired a few ranging shots and then began an intense bombardment.[3] Cannon balls slammed into the newly installed reinforced wall of gabions and fascines, harmlessly sticking in the mass of earth, stones and branches. Other British cannons, elevated to arc higher in their trajectory fell beyond the trench line, plopping into the sandy soil.

"We have not a single piece in place to reply and blow those Redcoat gunners to bits," Vose said, his voice angry but also betraying a fear of being struck by a wayward cannon ball.

"We will soon have batteries in place," Traynor said, waiting for the order to clamber up the ladders and over the rear rim of the trench and return to camp. He was soaked through. His shirt clung to his back like a wet rag. The day dawned cloudy and he shivered in the cool morning breeze, longing for the warmth of the sun or a cooking fire. Tonight, it would be more of the same, either constructing palisaded redoubts to defend against British sallies on the siege line or patrolling the area between themselves and the enemy's defenses. Either way, it meant a battle would soon begin in earnest. He was confident it would end with the Continentals and Frenchies triumphant. Then, he expected the Army would winter in New Jersey and he would be furloughed and return to his home.

Home, he thought bitterly, patting his sister's letter in the pocket of his jacket. It was worn from his constant folding and refolding and stained with his tears when he first read it. His beloved wife Polly had "sukumbed to a fever," two days after having given birth to a tiny baby girl "who neither breathed nor moved when brought forth." The midwife had placed her mouth to its lips and "forcibly blew into its lungs and thus saved the babe." [4] His sister Catherine was caring for his daughter, who was now, "thanks be to Providence, a healthy little soul," and had named her after his deceased wife. So now he had a little Polly he had never seen and would never see his wife again. His sister's letter dated 3 August, 1781 had reached him the second week of September brought by one of the furloughed officers returning to their Regiment. His wife Polly had been dead for more than a month by then and as far as he knew, little Polly may now be dead as well.

—⚜—

"Take my horses and oxen!" the owner shouted, his face red with rage as he stomped down the three steps from his porch. His overseer, a leathery faced lanky man joined him, a knobby stick tucked under his arm. Lieutenant Will Stoner leaned down from the saddle and pointed toward the barn.

"And wagons," Will added. "Those are my orders, sir. From General Henry Knox."

"This is my tobacco farm. You cannot come here and seize my property," the man snarled, looking to his overseer for confirmation. "I may as well let you have my slaves. Then you can dress them up in uniforms like that black monkey there," he yelled, pointing at Adam who sat on the wagon seat, with twelve soldiers on benches behind him.

"Sergeant Cooper," Will called, over his shoulder.

"Yes Lieutenant."

"Have the men form up and fix bayonets."

At Adam's command, the twelve men did as ordered. The owner stared in shock at the white soldiers taking orders from a black man. There was a murmur of astonishment from a group of sweaty, barefoot negroes who had been unloading a wagon of tobacco leaves in the barnyard.

"Cyrus," the man ordered his overseer. "Do your job and get those negrahs back inside the barn." He waved his hand in the negroes' direction. They cowered and moved behind the wagon as if by doing so they would be better protected from his wrath. Two black female house servants stood bewildered on the porch, their hands tightly clutching their aprons. "Get back to the kitchen or whatever you were doing," the man yelled in exasperation. The two women, their eyes wide with amazement, hustled back inside.

"I am authorized to leave you a receipt for impressing your property which will either be returned to you or compensation will be paid when funds are available," Will said calmly. The owner sputtered in indignation, unable to find the words to respond to the loss of his property in exchange for a piece of paper.

They left the tobacco plantation with three horses, each pulling a wagon loaded with fodder and six oxen plodding along behind. They followed the road back toward the James River, and the anchorage where the artillery had been unloaded awaiting overland transportation to Yorktown. The success of the campaign depended on bringing the heavy guns to besiege Cornwallis and moving them in turn depended on having enough horses and oxen to pull them the six or so miles over flat and sandy marshlands to the artillery park at Yorktown. Heavy, thick hoofed farm horses, worn out oxen and wagons, hired, bought or confiscated in Maryland and southern Pennsylvania had arrived over the past few days.

Will had left Yorktown four days ago, with Nat Holmes and one hundred twenty soldiers of their one hundred and sixty man regiment, the others sick with fever or invalided. Since arriving at Trebell's Creek where it flowed into the James, they had been scouring the countryside for animals, forage and wagons.

There were already other soldiers at the landing, unloading the sloops and schooners that had come down the bay, low in the water with their cargo of gun carriages, shot and shell, rammers and sponges, canister and grape shot and barrels of nails. Many wagons carrying these supplies had already left for the artillery park, travelling over roads where construction crews had reinforced bridges for the far heavier cannons to come.[5]

Holmes had remained at the creek, with some of the artillerymen, supervising the construction of "A" frames of block and tackle for moving the guns from the ships that were expected within a day or so. Some of mortars could be carried by wagon but the big guns - the eighteen and twenty-four pounders - would have to be pulled through the sandy, swampy ground.

That night, after a late dinner with Colonel Lamb and the other officers of the Second Continental Artillery Regiment, Will walked through the camp until he found Adam, worried that his friend's volatile nature had erupted into open anger. He was relieved to find him in his tent, seated on his cot, a candle at his feet, mending his worn canvas breeches and joking amiably with Sergeant Isaiah Chandler and Corporal Levi Tyler. They were the only two left from the old gun crew who had fought together in Brooklyn, and at Brandywine, Germantown and Monmouth. Will sat down and waited until Adam finished his task, comfortable to relax among friends.

Once outside, he and Adam walked away from the camp.

"You should have reprimanded that slave holder for calling me a black monkey in uniform," Adam said angrily.

"I thought it best to demonstrate your authority, not only to him but to his overseer and slaves as well."

Small Pox, Fever and Dangerous Night Duty 183

Adam who had kept himself under control since the afternoon was seething. Will's answer did nothing to calm him. "If I could raise a band of free blacks as did Colonel Tye in New Jersey, I would sweep through this area setting fire to every plantation in sight," he said loudly.

"You forget Adam," Will replied, speaking softly, "that tobacco farmer supports our cause, as do most around Jamestown. This Colonel Tye you have told me about was in the service of the Crown and raided only patriot homes."

Adam shook his head in exasperation. "Will, do you not see with your own eyes the misery of these enslaved people?" He waved his arms at the dark countryside around them. "My Sarah is from around here. Her former master may not be a loyalist but he is a slave owner. He abused her mother and may still be doing so. He sold Sarah to another, separating her from her family." He waved his finger in Will's face. "My poor Sarah does not even know if her mother and sisters are alive. What if my Sarah comes to Virginia to work as a free woman at General Knox's headquarters? Can you imagine the indignities she will suffer?"

"I can," Will replied. His composed reasoned manner served to stoke Adam's anger even further.

"Do you, now?" he said, stopping and placing his hands on his hips. "Do you feel my anger when I am called a black monkey by that slave owner who has not taken up arms to fight for our cause?" Adam retorted. "Or when that Frenchman attacked me in the General's own home?"

Will put up his hands in a gesture of cooling his friend's anger. "I have been informed that Major Murnan was court-martialed and dismissed from service with the Continental Army's Regiment of Engineers."

"Well," Adam retorted, waving his finger at Will. "Your information is not up to date. General Washington overruled the decision and Murnan, the very one who gave me this," Adam said pointing at the white line that emerged from his dark curly hair and ran midway to his forehead, "now is at Yorktown with our engineers." [6]

"I did not know that," Will said taking a step backwards.

"Upon my oath I will make sure our paths do indeed cross. Then, I will kill him."

"I urge you as a friend, not to seek him out. No good will come of it, Adam."

Adam turned away angrily and strode back toward the camp. "The good that will result is the Frenchman being dead and my honor, like that of any other man, will have been restored," he shouted over his shoulder.

Over the next few days, the ships carrying the guns down the Chesapeake arrived and the activity at the landing site became even more hectic. Before the unloading could begin, all the gunpowder had to be placed on wagons and moved or stored well away from the beach. Illuminated by large torches burning tar and pitch, the soldiers worked in shifts through the night, hoisting the cannons from the ships, lowering them on to flat scows and then once on land, lashing them onto wagon beds or settling them on gun carriages or two wheeled limbers.

With some of the ordinance ready, Colonel Lamb ordered a lead contingent to set out on the six-mile overland trek to Yorktown. They started in the relative cool of the early morning. Will was in the middle of the column, the better to supervise its progress, with Big Red pulling a twelve pounder by himself. Behind him, teams of the big-boned, thick hooved draft horses and oxen, struggled with the eighteen and twenty-four pounders. The howitzers and mortars came last.

The men from the artillery regiment walked in the marshy soft ground leading up from the beach, and, where necessary, pushed the wagons or gun carriages through the soft loamy surface. The flat land was interspersed with clumps of swamp grasses and tall reeds, marking the course of slow-moving tidal creeks. A work detail lingered by the side of the road at the first bridge over a small tributary. Will rode Big Red across, the horse's hooves clomping on the wooden slats. He draped the reins over the saddle's pommel and dismounted. He wanted to see how the reinforced beams held as a twenty-four pounder approached.

Will felt a sudden dizziness and for a moment, steadied himself, leaning against the gun barrel. He withdrew his hand quickly. The brass was already searing from the morning sun. Taking off his tri-corn, he wiped his brow and took a long drink of warm cider from his canteen. Cautiously, unsure of his balance, he sidled down the small ravine to inspect the underpinning of the bridge. Several new, rough-hewn beams, evenly spaced along the length had been added to support the worn frame of the bridge over the stream. Satisfied with what he saw, Will emerged from the cool shadow of the bridge and into the broiling sun. He watched as a team of four oxen lumbered on the bridge pulling a limber attached to the gun carriage of the twenty-four pounder. The four wheels rumbled across as the planks creaked under the weight. The beams did not buckle and held firm. Still feeling weak, he staggered up the side of the ravine and stood holding on to the saddle before, with great effort, raising his foot to the stirrup and mounting Big Red.

The rest of the journey was agony. Despite the heat of the day, he felt cold and was unnerved when he realized his teeth were chattering. He stared ahead and was unclear whether he was seeing a heat mirage or his vision had blurred. To his right, first one then two white herons, disturbed by the passing column, rose slowly from a small tributary and banked to the east, their long black legs trailing behind them. Will wiped his eyes and now saw only one heron. He shook his head in confusion.

By the time he reached the artillery park, he was slumped in his saddle and Big Red, familiar with the route went down Warwick Road, past General Knox's headquarters and into the artillery park. Fortunately for Will, a few of the men of his old gun crew were returning from duty at the ammunition magazine and helped him down and into his tent where he collapsed on his cot.

In the morning, when he awoke, his head hurt as if it would explode, his lips were parched and his shoulder joints and knees ached, as if the bones were rubbing together. Through his blurred vision he saw Captain Hadley, deep concern on his face, wringing a wet cloth out in a basin.

"Samuel. You are back," Will croaked, hearing his own voice in the distance like another person was speaking.

"We returned two days ago, down the Chesapeake from Somerset. Our cargo of oak planks now lie in the artillery park waiting to be fashioned into gun platforms." He lay the cloth to Will's forehead. "You are burning up with fever. They have sent for Dr. Thaxter. He will be here soon."

Alarmed, Will tried to sit up and groaned in agony as the pounding in his head increased in intensity. Gasping in pain, he fell back on his cot. He grabbed Hadley's hand. "Samuel," he rasped desperately. "Please. Do not let him send me to the hospital in Williamsburg. I must do my duty and man a cannon at the siege."

"Bleeding is the usual treatment for ague," Hadley said, patting Will's hand. "It will cure you. I am confident you will be on the siege line with us."

Hearing these words, Will thought back to what he had told the feverish Rhode Island soldier at the hospital at Princeton, reassuring him as to the usefulness of being bled to cure the fever. He never knew whether that soldier survived or not. And now he was the patient. He doubted the usefulness of bleeding and was fearful that loss of blood would enfeeble him.[7]

"Samuel," he croaked. "Do not let them bleed me more than once. Promise me that."

"Will. This fever has confused your mind and defeated your reason. You must trust the doctor."

Will bit his lip from the awful mind numbing pain in his head and the miserable thought he would never see Elisabeth and their son again. Hadley bent over and placed his hand on Will's forehead. Will looked at his friend's face, close to his and the feverish curtain lifted temporarily.

"Samuel," he said, his voice weak and trembling. "Remember you implored me, when you were shot in the arm, not to let the surgeons amputate it. I beg you, for our friendship and what I have done on your behalf, do not let the doctor bleed me more than once." Desperately, he reached up and grasped Hadley's arm. "Promise as you begged me after Brandywine. Promise you will not let them do so and weaken me more." Hadley nodded. "I promise you." Exhausted by his efforts and relieved by Samuel's assurance, Will grimaced as he lay back and fell into an exhausted and fitful sleep.

Despite Doctor Thaxter's strong misgivings, he agreed to bleed Will only this time, although he grumbled that there were no other treatments he could propose. "Perhaps you think he is young and strong and will overcome the fever," Thaxter said. "Let me tell you Captain, I have seen stronger men die and weaker ones survive. If he is not to be sent to Williamsburg, and I agree the journey by wagon may worsen his condition, the person attending must keep him warm when the chills set in, cool when the fever rages and feed him broth and sassafras tea. As much as he will take." Sergeant Isaiah Chandler of Will's old gun crew grunted that he understood the doctor's instructions and agreed to watch over Will.

Hadley hurried by the artificers' work sheds and engineers' depots that had been established beyond the rows of the Regiment's tents. Rectangular in shape, the entire artillery park was seven hundred yards long and lay just off the Warwick Road. The cannons were lined up at the far end, closest to the siege line. Behind them were the gun carriages, limbers and ammunition wagons. Hadley held his nose as he passed the line of latrines laid out, as ordered, two hundred or so feet behind the tents.

In the field where the lumber had been stacked, soldiers sawed and hammered together three-inch thick oak planks forming gun platforms, twelve to eighteen feet in length.[8] Fourteen of the twenty-two platforms were already completed. They would support the heavy siege cannons and prevent them from sinking into the sandy ground. Since there was still some daylight, Hadley determined to move as many of them as possible to forward positions near the siege line. When night fell they would be sited in the redoubts. He ordered teams of oxen brought forward and hitched up to strong ropes attached to the extended crossbeams.

Hadley rode up and down the line of oxen, plodding along the road, urging the drivers, standing on the front edge of the gun platforms like they were riding a sled, to keep their animals moving. The weight of the platforms smoothed the dirt, making it easier for those following behind. A secondary road led down a broad hollow and to the trench on the American side. At the bottom, the lead teams snorted and pulled in their traces at the consistent booming of British cannon.

"Control your oxen," Hadley shouted to a driver struggling as his lead team, the animals' eyes wide with fear, tried to pull in different directions, The soldier grimaced and applied his long whip vigorously to no avail. The first few teams panicked and attempted to turn back. Quickly, Hadley made the decision to let the animals go and use manpower instead. The oxen, once unhitched abandoned their usual plodding pace and swiftly trotted up the secondary road to the safety of the staging area.

"Stupid dumb beasts," Hadley muttered, passing the oxen and the drivers, running alongside them, as he rode back to the staging area.

After conferring hastily with Colonel Lamb, Hadley led almost four hundred of the newly assigned auxiliary troops from Virginia and Delaware Regiments, armed with drag chains, strong ropes and hand spikes to the beginning of the American trenches.[9] Two chains were attached to the foremost cross pieces on either side of the platforms. This done, the men grasped the chains over their shoulders and hauled the heavy platforms into the trench. Relief teams of soldiers walked behind the assembled planks and used their handspikes to pry the platforms over any obstacles. It was laborious, slow work. The freshly dug works smelled pleasantly of newly turned earth. Here and there, teams of soldiers continued digging out the rear walls of the trench paralleling the British lines and filling barrels with the soil as a protective barrier in case mortar shells landed in the trench. Eventually, the British cannonade abated, as if the enemy gunners were waiting for the moon to rise before raining their deadly barrage down on the soldiers busily throwing up redoubts and strengthening the parallel.

Hadley cursed under his breath as he saw stacks of fascines and gabion frames blocking their passage up ahead. Impatiently, he jumped from platform to platform. Soldiers were scrambling like ants down the parallel, loading up with fascines and gabion frames and disappearing into the murky darkness of the trench ahead. Since they could not proceed until the trench was cleared, Hadley ordered the relief teams forward to help with moving the fascines and frames. When the path was cleared, Hadley led the way as the men wrestled the platforms through the wide trench, protected by the seven-foot high walls facing the enemy. The going was easier because the trench floor was smooth and compact, having been tramped down by the feet of the fatigue parties and soldiers moving through for picket duty.

They had gone about four hundred yards in when Hadley signaled for them to halt. Captain Holmes and another officer were squatting in front of freshly dug short wide trench that ran forward from the parallel toward the enemy lines.

"This is the place the engineers have designated for the eighteen-pounders," Holmes said pointing at the soldiers, still filling the gabions and topping off the parapet. "How many?" Hadley asked.

"Four. Each to be placed no less than fifteen and no more than twenty feet apart. The locations are marked by white pine strips," Holmes replied.

A rocket soared into the dark sky from the British lines, illuminating the parallel before it spiraled slowly downward.

"Shot," someone on the parapet shouted as a warning, having seen a lighted torch being applied to the touchhole of a British cannon. With an ominous, familiar whooshing sound, the ball flew over the trench and landed in a field beyond. There were screams of pain and shock from those unfortunate to be resting or assembling there, indicating there were some casualties.

The first two platforms were the shorter ones for mortars. The men pulled them further down the main trench while others labored to move the eighteen- foot platforms into the one leading to the battery.

"Whoever directed the digging failed to round off the angle," Hadley said in exasperation as the first platform stuck on the left side wall of the battery trench. Several soldiers grabbed shovels and picks and began hacking away at the obstructing wall. Another flare burst further down the parallel, followed by a barrage of cannon fire.

"Hurry, men," Hadley said softly. "We do not want to keep the British gunners waiting." A few chuckled at his comment as they maneuvered the last of the four platforms into position. The men coiled their chains and ropes at the intersection of the battery trench and the parallel and moved down it approximately another three hundred yards. Here, their work was easier but more dangerous. A large palisaded redoubt had been erected, jutting out from the parallel in a sharp triangle. An earthen ramp at the back of the trench led to a flat field and a low earthen wall. One of the engineers instructed them to place the howitzer platforms there.

The men pulled the shorter platforms up the ramp. They moved more quickly here fearful of being exposed for too long. The weight of the wood crushed the reeds and grass and made enough noise to attract the enemy's attention.

"Shell!" someone called out. Instantly, Hadley and the men dropped their ropes and burrowed into the ground. There was a hissing sound that increased in intensity before the mortar bomb harmlessly exploded above them. Too short a fuse, Hadley thought. Before the men could stand up, a cannon ball ploughed into the newly constructed wall with a soft plop.

"Quickly now." Hadley ordered. "Line the platforms up on the white strips."

"Shell!" They fell down again but this bomb arced beyond their position.

"Now! Men! Pull to!"

Once the last platform was in position, the men raced back to the relative safety of the parallel. Hadley was the last to walk down the ramp, having made certain that all of his men were accounted for.

Tired as they were, there were still more platforms waiting for them back at the staging area. Hadley hoped that the Colonel had designated another officer to bring them as far forward as the secondary road. He and his men would take it from there.

He squatted down next to Captain Holmes and accepted the proffered canteen.

"Well, Nat. We have a few hours of darkness left. Where do the other platoons go?"

"There is the last battery. It is also the farthest from the British lines, maybe over one thousand two hundred yards because the two redoubts the British hold opposite are in advance of their lines." Holmes paused and finished off the cider in his canteen.

"The General wants seven eighteen pounders and two twenty-fours in the battery. Can you bring the platforms there before dawn?"

"All of us have been exposed to artillery fire in broad daylight," Hadley said. "I, for one, prefer to avoid that experience if possible and complete our work in darkness. Tomorrow night we bring in our guns and at dawn the day after, the British will have our answer to their bombardment."

He rose and gave quiet orders for the men to return to the staging area and start hauling the platforms down. Half way back up the trench he was pleasantly surprised to see soldiers pulling the platforms toward him. Quickly, he turned his men around and led them down the darkened trench to the newly constructed battery bordering the York River. The cannons' nine positions had been marked by white pine lathes. Hadley inspected the parapet and conferred briefly with an Officer of the Engineers. The British cannon and mortar fire seemed to be concentrated further down the line. He hoped it would remain there. Without being ordered, the men began filling the barrels at the rear of the battery with sand. A mortar bomb landing now would wreak havoc. He saw Holmes coming down the straight trench, in the lead of the soldiers pulling the platforms. Hadley guessed it was around three a.m. Time enough to complete the work and get back to the relative safety of the ravine before daylight.

Just before dawn, with a pale remnant of the moon low in the sky and a heavy dew on the grass, Hadley returned to the Artillery Park. Chandler was seated on a camp stool next to Will's cot. His jacket was draped over Will's torso. A thin wisp of smoke lazily rose from the lantern. The Sergeant must have just extinguished it. Hadley noticed that Will's breathing was shallow. Occasionally, he moaned softly.

"'Tis not gone well," Chandler said shaking his head. "He was delirious for some of the night, calling for Elisabeth and even trying to reach out for her as if she were here in his tent. Worse, he has vomited out everything I have encouraged him to drink or eat." He pointed at Will as he tossed and moved about, as if trying to ease some pain. "This is the most peaceful he has been since you left."

Hadley sat down on the end of his cot and pulled off his boots. "Let us pray it will not get worse." He wished Mercy were here. She knew the herbs and treatments for every kind of fever. He trusted her more than the doctors who always advised bleeding. Like most soldiers, who had seen their share of blood and gore caused by musket balls, grape shot or bayonet, he had an aversion to bleeding as a cure. It seemed illogical that to make one whole again one must lose more blood. He lay down exhausted, hearing Chandler from far away say he would stay awake and watch over Will.

Chapter 10 – The Fate of Officers

Bant considered himself lucky. Instead of laboring with a fatigue party, foregoing his rifle for a shovel or pickaxe, he was part of a company of riflemen ferried across the York River to stiffen a Virginia militia unit, under French Command. Their mission was to contain the British within their fortifications at Gloucester Point. They camped almost fifteen miles away from the British positions. Occasionally, Bant, along with McNeil and other riflemen, supported by a small force of militia would sneak close enough to snipe at British sentries foolish enough to show their heads about their ramparts.

Today, however promised to be different. Early in the morning they moved out in force, with French cavalry well in the lead, looking for British foraging parties. Bant thought such parties were likely to be protected by British Cavalry. On the infrequent forays to the enemy lines, he had seen numerous horses grazing under guard - too many to be the mounts only for officers, and too well muscled for ceremonial use. They were cavalry horses. He was sure of it. And it was cavalry officers on whom he sought revenge and to assuage his demons.

They marched by fields stripped of Indian corn by British foragers and empty barnyards devoid of the usual pigs and poultry.

"I think we are merely one step behind the Redcoats," McNeil said and before he could continue, they heard the sounds of musket fire. The Virginia militia were ordered forward and deployed in a field of broken, dry corn stalks. Ahead, the road they had been on joined another and stretched off toward Gloucester Point on the York River. The French Cavalry returned at a gallop, leaping over the low wooden fence bordering the field and reformed behind the protective infantry line. The militia were spread out in a ranks three deep. Bant and McNeil found themselves at the far end of the line, where the field met the junction of the two roads. The fence ended a few yards behind them.

It was cool and overcast. Bant was overcome with a sense of absolute calm. He belonged at this place at this time. He was sure something momentous was about to happen. The French Cavalry had engaged the enemy's horsemen. That seemed clear to him. Eagerly, he scanned the woods to his left on the far side of the road. He thought he detected some movement there. Looking to his rear, he saw French infantry take up positions along the fence line. The British troopers were foreclosed from attacking in that direction. No. They would come at the Virginia militia straight on, attempting to break through and then crush the Frenchies from behind.

McNeil clicked his tongue and gestured with his chin. A column of red-coated dragoons trotted out of the woods and spread out across most of the field. They were followed by green clad troopers who extended the rest of the line of horsemen up to the trees. When they faced the militia, Bant saw the death's head helmets on the Redcoats. He looked for an individual officer in command and finding none, focused on the other cavalry.

They were well out of musket range, perhaps just over three hundred yards away. Almost directly ahead, Bant noticed an officer in a green jacket wearing a high fur hat adorned with a dark grey plume. Bant was drawn to him as if it were written somewhere this was the target to drive away his demons. Kill him and his mind would be at peace. He sighted on the officer's head and waited. With a raised sword, the officer commanded the entire line to charge.

They came forward at a gallop. Even at that distance, the ground shook from their horses' hooves. Bant did not care if the militia around him fled and left him there all alone. He was as unruffled as if he were shooting at a patch of paper on a board. Details started to come into view. The officer's jacket with a broad collar, dark around the edges and open at the throat to form an inviting white V target. No. Bant would aim for the head. The horse's eyes, wild with excitement, foam flying back, the bit loose in his mouth. On they came, the troopers bunched together, as if they were aiming for Bant's corner of the line. He sighted down the barrel, knowing from experience the officer was a little more than two hundred yards away. His finger tightened on the trigger. A little closer he thought. Vaguely, he heard the order – "Ready! Aim!" It occurred to him the militia's officers were too hasty. Muskets at that range would do no damage. He fired a split second after the shouted command for the militia to fire. At that very moment the officer went down.

Bant knew immediately his ball had not struck home. Engrossed by the scene of tangled horses and his target now on foot Bant forgot to reload. By the time he remembered, the officer had been given another horse, his men had formed a protective ring around him, regrouped and the entire line of cavalry withdrew out of range.[1]

Scowling, Bant hoped they would charge again. He reloaded and thought about what had happened. The premature order for the militia to fire had spoiled his chance. These officers were unused to the role of riflemen in the line. Let them take down the officers at long range. Then, have the demoralized men charge into a solid wall of musket fire. Instead, some lucky musket ball had wounded a horse that in turn tripped the mount of the officer he was aiming at.

"I shot one of those green jackets," McNeil said matter of factly. He waited for Bant to give his account. "Not me," Bant replied. McNeil knew not to ask the question. Bant let it hang in the air and shrugged. "I would have had him if his horse did not go down. Next time, I will fire just within the three hundred yard mark." He waited in vain for another charge. The cavalry had disappeared from the field. Several French Hussars made a show of jumping the fence and riding out as a scouting party.

The next morning, the entire American and French force took down their tents, dismantled their camp, marched through the tiny town of Gloucester and relocated to within a thousand yards of the British fortifications. From here, there was ample opportunity to go out on patrols and snipe at those soldiers foolish enough to reveal themselves above the parapets. Bant took it as a challenge. The Redcoats presumed they were safe at what they deemed was too great a distance for any Continental rifleman.

He volunteered only for the daytime patrols. Sometimes, McNeil joined him and on the day he brought down a British officer on one of the redoubts, McNeil was there to witness it. They were in one of the few woods left standing by the British who had stripped the country bare of trees for firewood and fortifications. Bant rested his unloaded rifle where a low-lying branch joined the trunk. A few of the militia curiously watched him and squinted at the earthen wall in the distance. If Bant was aware of the chatter around him and the bets that were being placed by the militiamen, he gave no sign. He estimated the distance to be maybe three hundred and twenty yards. Lacking any knowledge of mathematics, he simply knew from experience how much extra powder he would need and the decline of the trajectory of the ball over that distance. He unpacked a cartridge and poured more powder down the paper cylinder. Next he loaded the ball, examining it first to make sure there were no defects that might alter its flight. He rammed it down hard and once again for good measure, primed the pan and waited. A sentry appeared on the wall. A little while later he was joined by another. The second Redcoat wore some insignia in his hat. Together they looked out over the gently sloping field and toward the rows of white tents and the smoke from the fires of the French and Continentals in the distance.

Bant decided he would aim for the one with the insignia. Morgan's riflemen called it "killing off the king birds." He could see it was more of a metal badge than a feathered cockade but he took it to signify the man was an officer. He nestled the long rifle in the crook of the tree and crouched a little, staring down the length of the barrel. His head was slightly to the left of the flashpan, his right eye seeing nothing but the officer's temple. Slowly, he squeezed the trigger, feeling the familiar point beyond which the pressure would bring the hammer down and ignite the spark from the flint. The smoke from the pan and muzzle momentarily obscured his vision. He heard the cheers of the militia and saw the back of the sentry as he scuttled down from the parapet for the protection of the wall.

McNeil patted him on the back. "You got him. I would say at three hundred and twenty maybe three hundred and thirty yards." For some reason, Bant was uncomfortable. He knew the militia would carry the news of his feat back to camp. The last time he had been with militia and they had bragged about his prowess, it had resulted in twelve men being hanged by British cavalry and Bant proving himself a coward. It was the beginning of his demons.

Sweating, although it was cool, he grabbed his rifle and walked back into the woods, away from the soldiers babbling as they exchanged money, the losers almost as happy as the winners, for both had seen Bant's remarkable exploit. He began to run quickly and slowed to a trot only when the sounds of words were indistinguishable. The woods ended at the edge of a flat tidal marsh. Across the York River, he could hear the British cannonade of the American and French lines. To his left, he could see the sandy beach and pier of Yorktown, with red brick houses lining streets now devoid of trees. Two ships lay at anchor in the river, both flying British flags. He wished his rifle was a cannon and he could blow their arrogant hulls out of the water.

Why was he so angry? It was not anger, he admitted to himself but fear. He was afraid bad things would follow the boasting of his shooting of the officer. He tried to imagine what could happen and became more terrified with the image of another cavalry sally, with McNeil, his only friend cut down because of Bant. This time, if that happened, he would not run. He would not climb a tree and hide. He would stand and fight to save McNeil. He must get back to his friend. The British could be sending out cavalry at this very moment to take revenge. He stood up and raced back through the low brush to where the patrol had been resting. Finding no one there, he ran all the way to camp. He arrived sweaty, his hair matted underneath his battered round hat, his eyes wild and searching. To his great relief, he found McNeil sitting on a rock with some of their mess mates, sewing his sole back onto his worn boot. Trying to appear unconcerned, Bant found a place a little away from the group and stretched out on the grass. He vowed he would never leave McNeil alone, nor go out on patrols without him. His lips moved silently as he made this promise to himself.

—⁂—

With the platforms in position, they began to bring the guns forward from the artillery park. In the darkness, the British trained their cannons on the newly constructed redoubts they had fired on during the daylight hours. Their balls did little damage other than to harass the work parties. However, the noise and the occasional errant cannon ball made even the most experienced artillery horse skittish. Big Red was teamed with another and with Will astride him, the horses pulled one of the three eighteen-pounders toward the siege line. Will was still weak. His fever had broken two days ago. He remembered nothing of his delirious dreams and could only recall the concerned faces of Hadley and more often Chandler hovering over him.

At the staging area, crews quickly detached the carriage and Will reluctantly returned with Big Red and the large sorrel mare to the artillery park. He wished to be in the trenches, lining up the cannons and commanding a battery when dawn came. Finally, the American artillery would give their answer to the incessant British bombardment of the past week. Instead, his orders were to bring the cannons up, then the wagons loaded with balls, side boxes and crates of charges. Men would move the guns and supplies down the trenches.

Beyond the staging area, the guns bogged down in the soft sandy soil. The loamy earth had been easy to dig for throwing up the fortifications but now hampered their efforts to get the guns into position. Soldiers pulled on drag chains in front and others behind put their shoulders to the carriages, pushing the muzzle or grappling with the spokes of the studded wheels. But once they reached the trenches, widened now to ten feet, the wheels rolled more easily on the earth more packed down by the toiling soldiers.

The main American battery was almost forty yards ahead of the siege line. The position had been laid out by direction of the French Engineers to best pound the British gun emplacements. Captains Holmes and Hadley, each in charge of positioning an eighteen-pounder, entered the connecting trench from the siege line to the battery.

As Hadley and the men under his command pulled one cannon further down the trench that ran the length of the battery, Holmes and Sergeant Cooper grabbed shovels and helped the squad of soldiers dig slots in the earth, perpendicular to the parapet. Adam lifted one end of a fifteen foot long log and with the aid of two others lowered it into the newly dug niches. Once another log had been placed on the other side, they laid planks across to create a ramp between the trench floor and the gun platform. It was difficult work in the dark. Adam was thankful there was no full moon and the British had not yet discovered the feverish work going on nine hundred yards away.

"All right, men," Holmes said in a hushed tone. "Now we must move the cannon into position." He pointed to the gun platform at the top of the steep makeshift ramp. At the rear of the trench, Nat found the commanding officer and directed him to have his men cease digging bomb shelters in the rear retaining wall and help push the two thousand pound cannon on to the platform. Together, the soldiers joined the artillerymen pulling hard on the drag chains over their shoulders and inched the eighteen-pounder slowly up the ramp. At one point, when it seemed the men could not hold it from rolling back, Adam jammed a thick log under one of the wheels. The cannon slid sideways as the other wheel slipped. Grabbing a hand spike, Adam stuck it between the spokes and struggled to hold it in place, hoping that the spoke itself would not crack and tumble the cannon off the ramp. Once another log was thrown behind the wheel, they were able to realign the gun and inch it up the ramp.

"Come on men," Adam said. "Put your shoulder to the wheel and carriage and push." The men grunted and the gun moved upward slightly and then faster as the soldiers pulling on the chains in front tugged in unison. The tail of the carriage was over the platform when the wheels caught on the edge of the first plank of the platform that was a few inches higher. Soldiers rushed forward to join the others in fighting to lift the wheels and barrel over the protruding edge.

Together now," Adam urged and with one final heave, the eighteen- pounder rolled on to the platform. A flare burst overhead, illuminating the battery's parapet before it was again enveloped in darkness. Adam hoped the British would not detect the activity and shift their fire to this sector.

But minutes later, the British gunners opened up on their position. Several balls lodged in the earthen works with a muffled thump. The Redcoats elevated their guns so that cannon balls whistled through the air overhead and fell - forty yards between the battery and the main trench or struck soldiers unfortunate enough to be in the open flat terrain beyond.

Adam clambered down the ramp and joined the soldiers digging concave shelters in the rear wall and filling barrels with sand to form blinds if mortar shells landed in the trench. Knowing generally there was activity in the trenches, the British now intensified their mortar bombardment. Eight and twelve-pound bombs whistled through the night sky, tracing a line of fire with their fuses. They exploded in the air over the trenches or landed within them. When they blew up, hot jagged iron fragments flew everywhere. Adam felt safer at the back of the trench making blinds than huddled against the earthen wall on the parapet next to the eighteen-pounder.

A runner came down the trench and trotted up the ramp, conferred with Captain Holmes and then disappeared into the brown-black darkness down the trench to the left. Nat waved for Adam to join him.

"Sergeant Cooper," Holmes said. "Assemble a squad with bill hooks, axes, and shovels. The guns are in position. We are ready to cut the embrasure in the parapet. Note my marks for the parameters." Nat placed several white pine strips upright against the seven-foot high wall. Adam wanted this accomplished as quickly as possible. It was dangerous work with some of the British cannons and howitzers firing directly at the parapet wall. Once the men cut through the parapet, a lucky shot could destroy the cannon and wipe out the entire crew. ²

"Hurry men. Careful with those axes. Look before you swing," Adam said as the soldiers attacked the parapet wall like a team of beavers anxious to destroy the dam they had constructed.

"Shell" someone from the parapet shouted, having seen the muzzle flash. They flattened themselves on the rough hewn planks of the gun platform. The sounds of shovel and axe blades striking the stones in the gabions rang out with such clarity, Adam feared they would draw down upon themselves the artillery from all the British positions within range. Fortunately, the American battery was at the very end of the British line of fortifications and beyond their guns in the middle of their line.

"Shot," someone shouted and the men ducked, waiting for the impact. No ball whistled overhead or struck the parapet.

"They do that sometimes," one of the soldiers said. "The bastards light a little powder in the muzzle, one of us sees the flash and calls out a warning. Keeps us alert, it does."

Adam tapped one of the soldiers hacking away ineffectively at the embrasure and motioned for him to step back. Rhythmically, swinging a pickaxe, he tore away at the packed earth and stone, ripping the branches and twigs that formed the gabion framework. He could not tell where one gabion began and the other ended, so seamlessly were they stacked together. Finally, his blade pushed through the five-foot thick wall. Loose stones clattered down the outer slope to the bottom of the parapet. Adam stepped back and let others with their broad bladed shovels widen the gap he had created and open the wall to the level of the gun platform.

"Shell" someone warned. Adam flattened himself against the solid earth of the thick parapet away from the opening. The mortar bomb descended slowly in a tumbling arc, the sputtering fuse marking its trajectory. It exploded overhead before fragments rained down on the trench. Adam silently thanked the British gunner for cutting the fuse too short and miscalculating the timing.

"Who ordered this embrasure," a man with a thick English accent shouted out from the darkness above. He was on the parapet coming toward the gun platform. Adam recognized the voice. It was Major Murnan. Adam held his pickaxe, his hands toward the lower end of the smooth hickory handle, the pointed part of the blade facing forward. He would embed that point in Murnan's side and tear his insides out.

"Which imbecile ordered this opening," Murnan shouted again, ignoring the danger of speaking loudly from his exposed position. "I did," Holmes replied. "On orders of Colonel Bonnay."

"Colonel Bonnay, you say. He did not tell me." Murnan said loudly. The Major was still on the parapet nimbly jumping over the rough surface and coming toward them. He was a few yards away. Adam tightened his grip on the pickaxe and waited in the dark against the earthen wall, certain that Murnan had no idea he was there.

"Shot," came the cry. This time Adam did not duck, so intent was he on watching Murnan. The sound of the whoosh of the ball through the air was followed by a soft sigh. The French Major toppled off the parapet and into the trench. His leg, sheared off from thigh to booted foot, splatted down onto the platform next to the eighteen-pounder.

"Stupid Frenchie," a soldier muttered, putting his shovel under the severed leg and tossing it down into the trench. Adam could see Murnan slumped against the back wall, as a few shadowy figures loaded him into a wheelbarrow and hurriedly carted him back up the trench. He loosened his grip on the pickaxe and turned toward the half opened embrasure. "Come on men," he said quietly. "Square up the opening."

A little before dawn, there were three eighteen-pounders, three twenty-four pounders and four ten and a half inch mortars in position, the latter squatting on their low, four wheeled gun carriages on their own smaller platforms. Their ugly squat barrels, instead of elevated to throw shot over the British fortifications, were leveled to pound them instead. [3] The balls and bombs were stacked on the platforms and the powder safely stored behind earthen walls and sandbags a distance away.

As the men trudged wearily down the trench and back to the entrance ravine, they shivered in the cold wind accompanied by the early morning mist. Adam put his worn blue jacket on over his damp sweaty shirt.

"Today will be the day our guns will finally respond to the British and begin hammering their positions." Hadley said. He, Holmes and Adam were walking behind one of the wagons sent to carry the men back to the artillery park. "I hope to be assigned as one of the gun captains."

"I doubt whether we will be sent to the parallel this morning," Nat said. "Our work is finished."

"I, for one, do not overestimate our ability from this range to force the British to surrender." Hadley looped in his arm over Nat's shoulder. "We will need another siege line, closer than this one and the guns will have to be moved and positioned again." He looked over Nat at Sergeant Cooper. "What say you Sergeant. Are you as eager as Captain Holmes here to return to the lines?"

"That I am, Sir, hopefully attached to Lieutenant Stoner's gun crew as I was at Monmouth. It will be all the more pleasurable for me knowing the ill-tempered French Major will not be in the trenches. Only a British cannonball prevented me from dealing with him myself and restoring my honor."

That cannonball, Nat thought, saved you from a court-martial and a firing squad, but he kept his thoughts to himself.

—⚔︎—

For the men of the New Jersey Regiment, their day began as usual with the drum-beat signaling Reveille. They rose in the chilly October morning under a grey sky and at the familiar drum signal lined up for roll-call. The men stood in ranks listening to the sound of the drums move from the left to the right from company to company and regiment to regiment.

"Sounds like the entire brigade is being called up," Private Vose said loudly to the others nearby. Wade merely grunted. The soldiers stood patiently awaiting orders. Usually, they were inspected by Lieutenant Phelps or one of the Captains. This morning, none of their officers appeared. Corporal Traynor, standing at the end of the first file, one in from Sergeant Henderson, noticed a group of mounted officers slowly making their way down the assembled ranks. They stopped in front of each Regiment and departed to three shouted huzzahs. He recognized their own Colonel Dayton, newly appointed as 2nd Brigade Commander of their Division. It was the General next to him who drew his attention. Two woven stars gleamed from his yellow epaulets. The blue cutaway coat with its wide buff lining was pristine clean and he sat in the saddle with the poise an experienced horseman. This must be General Lafayette, Traynor thought, staring curiously at the red-cheeked young face and the prominent thin nose. As they approached the Regiment, Colonel Dayton spurred his horse forward and stopped facing the ranks.

"Soldiers of my own New Jersey Regiment. Today, we have the honor to take part in the formal opening of the trenches. General Lafayette will lead the entire Division. Our color bearers will implant our flags upon the parapets in accordance with ancient customs of war." He paused and stood up in his stirrups and surveyed the soldiers arrayed before him. "However, we do not fight for the reasons of wars gone by. We fight for our independence and freedom. We fight as free men. We fight to overthrow the rule of a tyrannical king." He waited for the spontaneous cheers to end. "We are joined in our struggle by our French allies whose troops this very moment are preparing to open their section of the trench on the far left of our siege line. We are led by the best France has to offer, our own General Marquis de Lafayette. Three cheers for General Lafayette." The men erupted in loud full-throated huzzahs. The young aristocrat acknowledged by raising his tri-corn in salute, exposing a powdered wig. The officers' entourage moved on to the next Regiment and the New Jersey Continentals were left standing in ranks and talking amongst themselves as to what it meant to "open the trenches." [4]

"The trenches are already open. We dug them ourselves," Vose said a bit too loudly, earning a scowl from Sergeant Henderson. "All this means is we get to march in, man the parapets and watch our cannon balls blast the British to hell. I am all for that, especially if it means an extra gill of rum beforehand."

They stood in place, listening to the soldiers' cheers for Lafayette and the officers diminish to their left. "If they keep up at this pace," Vose said, "by the time they complete the review they will march us straight to the trenches without our rum."

"I would prefer they issue us enough cartridges," Wade said quietly. "If the Redcoats make a sortie, we will be in the thick of it. This may turn out to be more than a ceremony."

After they had been dismissed and struck their tents, they lined up and the regimental quartermaster issued every man thirty cartridges. The sutler's wagon arrived, when all had received their ammunition, to dispense the rum. Many of the soldiers eagerly held out their mugs for their gill and drank it on the spot.[5] Traynor and Wade took only half a gill each in their canteens adding it to the hard cider, already within.

A little before eleven a.m. when the morning mist had burned off and the sun warmed their shoulders, the drums beat to assemble. Led by the color bearers and drummers, General Lafayette and the Brigade Commanders, the entire Division, muskets at carry with bayonets fixed, marched past the grist mill, over the mill dam and through the ravines of Wormley Creek, out of sight of the British and into the shade of the trenches. Lieutenant Phelps led his company to a section of the trench where they mounted the earthen shelf, enabling them to fire if the British attacked, while protected from the waist down by the parapet.

Traynor stared out across the sandy field at the British fortifications less than one thousand yards away. A line of flashes followed instantaneously by the whistle of cannon balls was all he glimpsed before ducking down behind the parapet. When he next looked, the British ramparts were wreathed in white smoke that drifted slowly to his left in the light breeze.

"Where the hell is our artillery," Vose said angrily. "They

should be blasting those bastards to hell and back."

There was another enemy cannonade and the men sought the protection of the freshly dug earthen battlement. There was a ripple of shouts of disbelief coming from their right. Traynor still crouched down behind the earthen wall, gazed up. There, on the parapets in full view of the British gunners, a Regiment was brazenly executing the manual of arms. Traynor winced and braced himself for a cannonade that would blow the Continentals off the epaulment but there was only sporadic musket fire. At that range it was ineffective. The demonstration of the manual and the gesture of bravado completed, the men jumped off the parapet and were once again protected by the earthen works. [6]

"If any officer gave me a command to commit such a crazy act, I would refuse and he could go to hell with his order," Vose said. Others agreed as well. "Better to be court martialed than to have one's head blown off, " a soldier offered.

At the mention of court martial, Wade blanched. He said nothing, uttered a sigh and hunched back against the trench wall, making himself as small as he could. Traynor did not think Colonel Dayton nor any of the officers under him would risk the men's lives for such a senseless gesture but one never knew with officers. They had different ideas when it came to honor and bravado than the ordinary soldier. It is we, Traynor thought who do all the senseless marching, it seems mostly at night in the rain, only to be ordered to march back the way we came. We sleep outside exposed to the elements and our only constant companion is hunger. He had to admit that since arriving in Yorktown their rations had been regular and the addition of fresh beef and pork most welcome. It was the British who were suffering. Bottled up in Yorktown they must be on short rations. Their only course of action would be to break out of the siege. That would mean a frontal attack on the American and French lines.

As if his thought had simultaneously occurred to the officers, Lieutenant Tew appeared and moved down the parapet, passing on orders from Brigade Headquarters. When the British attacked the line, they were to give them one volley, leap over the parapet and drive them back with their bayonets. Wade smiled grimly at this order. He was skilled with the bayonet and his size and strength gave him an advantage. Traynor, for his part, relied on his quickness. He hoped it would not come to the bayonet. The image of the dead British soldier he had killed on night patrol came back to him. He removed the wooden stopper from his canteen. The warmth of the diluted rum going down his throat was helpful. Not to bolster his courage but to chase away the sightless eyes of the dead Redcoat and the feeling of the softness of the body he had stumbled over.[7]

Chapter 11- On the Siege Line

Immediately after Reveille, Colonel Lamb informed Will that he would command one of the eighteen-pounders. Together with Captain Hadley and the other eight gun commanders, he walked somewhat nervously to the Colonel's tent. It was the day after the American and French batteries had opened up on the British lines and begun bombarding their gun emplacements and Yorktown beyond.

"I have never commanded a gun in a siege before," he whispered to Hadley.

"Neither have I. Nor have any of the others," Hadley replied smiling. Seeing the consternation on Will's face, he nudged him with his shoulder. "Since you can fire a field piece rapidly in battle with the enemy charging at you, surely you are able to deliberately and coolly discharge your piece effectively."

"This requires more precise aiming and use of our gunner's quadrants and wedges," Will said. The thought of having to make precise mathematical calculations frightened him. His brain would seize up like a wheel jammed with a handspike. He would embarrass himself and betray the confidence General Knox had in him.

They stood around a map table showing the entire siege line and the British positions. Will focused on the main American battery and the location of the two British redoubts closest to it.

"Gentlemen. You may remove your hats if you desire. I keep mine on to warm my bald pate," the Colonel said with a smile. "Today 'tis my turn in command of the trenches. Captain Ferguson here is commander of the main American battery." Ferguson asked each of the gun commanders to introduce themselves. As a Lieutenant, Will was the lowest ranking officer in attendance. Ferguson openly looked him up and down. Will thought the Captain's face revealed his doubts about Will's selection.

"We relieve those manning the batteries at precisely noon," Colonel Lamb continued. "You and your crews will serve for twenty-four hours. General Knox, in accordance with the orders of His Excellency, requires that the bombardment continue through the night so as to give the enemy no respite. We have learned from our first day of the siege some useful lessons," he concluded and took a step back.

Ferguson stood with his tri-corn tucked under his arm, his back as straight as the shaft of an artillery rammer. "Our twenty-fours are most effective against the buildings in Yorktown. Our eighteens and mortars at first will target these two redoubts," Ferguson said placing a finger on the two wedge shapes facing the American battery." He spread his index finger and thumb between the two positions. "Tis no more than five hundred yards. We will pound them, weakening their outer wall, destroying any embrasures that remain, splinter their platforms and make life hell for the troops holding them." He paused to let the gun commanders absorb this. "Richochet firing at the redoubts has proven most destructive. You will need to remove some of the powder from the charge so that the ball rolls more slowly and does more damage. Yesterday's gun commanders report reduction by no more than a third of the powder accomplishes this end." Ferguson held up his index finger and repeated no more than one third.

"When you are directed to fire mark the position of your gun's wheels with chalk on the platforms before firing. That way, if the ball has been well directed, you will place the carriage in the exact same position again. Cannons will fire at no less than ten-minute intervals and no more than five times per hour. Every three hours, you will cease firing and clean out the barrels. Mortars to fire at will and also clean the tubes every three hours. I will schedule the rotation." [1]

Will felt slightly relieved. The ten-minute intervals would give him ample time to make the necessary calculations. The chalk would save him the necessity of recalculating the elevation and distance with the quadrant.

"You will receive a spyglass from the gun commander you relieve," Ferguson continued. "You are to personally aim and observe every shot. You are to ensure that your gun has ample supply of balls and powder at all times, including several canister charges in the event the enemy sorties and assaults our positions."

They left the Colonel's tent, gathered their gun crews and assembled on the Artillery Park's parade ground. Of the old crew that had fought together at the Battle of Brooklyn, only Sergeant Isaiah Chandler and Corporal Levi Tyler remained. Both displayed a single white V on their sleeves, signifying they had been in the army for at least three years. Will added Adam to the crew. He possessed the strength and endurance to carry cannon balls and charges over the twenty-four hour period they would be on the line. He wished for the guidance of Sergeant Merriam, a master at calculating range and elevation. But Merriam was back in Boston, having ended his service in bad health. At Trenton, when Will had first commanded a field piece, Merriam had told him firing grape shot was like shooting at birds with pellets. Now loading only balls, he feared, Captain Ferguson and the other gun commanders would see how accurate his fire was or, worse he thought, how far off the mark.

The men were lined up by order of the guns in the battery. Will's cannon was the fifth. Hadley's was the fourth. They marched off the parade grounds, down the ravine and into the trench. The battery was fifteen hundred yards down the eight foot wide newly dug corridor. They passed rows of soldiers standing on the shelf below the parapets, muskets at the ready. To Will, it seemed as if there were men every five feet. Inside the trench, those on fatigue duty were still at work improving the blinds and shelters or storing water and cartridges.

When they reached their emplacement, Will scampered up the ramp. He looked out of the embrasure for his first glimpse of the enemy camp and fortifications. The redoubts were within easy range. Beyond them, wisps of grey, dirty, smoke rose from the smoldering brick buildings in Yorktown and the fires from the now blackened canvas tents of the garrison within the town.

"We gave them several rounds of hot shot in the middle of the night," the gun captain said, handing Will the spyglass. "Their soldiers have gone to ground, probably in caves along the beach. More seem to be manning their defensive lines. Good. You will have the opportunity to make it warmer for them."

Through the glass he could see the roof of a large three-story building, holed in many places but with some of its windows still intact. The Captain followed his gaze. "Cornwallis' headquarters. No doubt he is somewhere else now. Maybe a lucky shot will get him." Will scanned the other brick buildings. Most had been damaged by cannon balls but were still obstinately standing, balls embedded in the brick. The outer earthen defensive works showed signs of being battered in a few places but the British artillery, mostly field guns, remained in action. He focused on the two redoubts about five hundred yards away.

"We only commenced firing at five p.m. There was much ceremony at the beginning what with General Knox and His Excellency here to begin the festivities. It was General Washington himself who fired the first gun." [2]

The roar of cannon fire from the French sector to their left was answered by lighter responses from the British artillery. Will saw splashes as the French balls fell short of two ships in the York River. Too far away for him to try with his eighteen-pounder.

A mortar bomb, fired from within the main British line, arced slowly into the air. The descending trail of dissipating white smoke pointed like a blurry arrow to the muzzle that had sent it skyward. The bomb exploded over one of the American's palisaded redoubts.

Will looked through the glass and marked the approximate location of the mortar. He would target it later in the day, he thought.

After the relieved gun crew left, Will inspected their battery. Embers glowed in the fire pit for heating hot shot. He hoped he would not be ordered to restart it. He was apprehensive about having flames close to the magazines. Never having fired hot shot before he was unsure if placing wadding or a sod plug in the barrel would completely protect the charge from the hot cannon ball inserted on top of it. If it did not, the heated ball could ignite the powder, the cannon would explode and kill the crew.

An aide to Captain Ferguson informed Will he was to target the closest redoubt and commence firing when the blue pennant was raised on the parapet at Hadley's battery, about twenty feet away. Will peered through the spyglass at the embrasures of the closest British redoubt. There were at least four cannon, eight and twelve pounders. Behind them, through the embrasure opening, he counted at least two mortars. There were probably more, visible from either Hadley's emplacement or the one another twenty feet further to Hadley's right. He would aim for the embrasure and hope the ball would destroy the field piece, continue on through and damage the mortars as well.

Will sighted down the cannon and directed the crew to turn the gun slightly until he was satisfied it was in line with the embrasure. He removed the gunner's quadrant from its canvas bag and placed the long end of the L into the bore of the brass cannon and let the plumb bob swing free. He noted the line on the quadrant. The eighteen-pounder would have to be depressed. He knew it would decrease the range but at five hundred yards, perhaps a little more, the cannon's range had many feet to spare. He waited while Chandler supervised the placing of the wedge between the breech and the carriage before measuring again. The elevation was at eight degrees, perhaps a little on the low side but Will intended richochet firing. Having no experience in weighing the powder charge, he simply reduced the charge by a little less than one third, as Captain Ferguson had instructed. He entrusted Adam, as a former Marblehead Mariner, to re-sew the canvas powder bag and make sure no powder leaked out.

Satisfied that the eighteen-pounder was properly aimed, Will called out the familiar orders, slowing his cadence from the battlefield when his gunners had been able to fire a ball every minute. The seven-man crew stood three on each side, with one behind. "Worm and sponge barrel." Corporal Tyler approached the muzzle with his long wood handled two headed tool, one end the soft wad of cloth, the other an iron headed double corkscrew. He thrust the wormer down the barrel, twisted it vigorously and withdrew it clean. He reversed the staff, plunged the sponge into a bucket of water and stuck it down the cannon. "Load cartridge." Tyler took the lighter canvas bag from one of the crew dropped it in and rammed it home, leaning on the pole for good measure. Chandler stood by the vent with his leather-encased thumb over the opening to keep out any residue.

"Load shot! Ram shot!" Will commanded. Adam dropped the ball down the barrel and stepped aside for Tyler to ram it home. "Lintstock! Make Ready!" Will had never used a lintstock in battle. The long handled staff with its Y shaped iron head curving back toward the shaft and rope twisted around it, was to light the priming tube from a distance. In battle, Will used a match inserted in a quill filled with powder. "Vent and Prime!" Chandler reached into the pouch at his hip, removed an eighteen-inch iron pin with a ring at the top for a better grip and jabbed it down the vent hole, piercing the canvas charge. Next he inserted the priming tube. One of the gun crew stood by with the frayed end of the rope on the lintstock glowing and waited.

Will glanced toward his right and saw the blue pennant flying from Hadley's battery. In preparing for firing he had neglected to see where Hadley's shot had fallen. Now it was his turn. He stepped up to the parapet and peered at the first gun embrasure of the redoubt. "Make Ready!" he yelled, elongating the last word. He steadied the spyglass with his elbow on his raised knee. "Fire!" Through the glass he saw the ball bounce about forty feet from the redoubt, bound forward, smash into the edge of the embrasure, shatter the gun carriage wheel, and richochet beyond into the interior of the redoubt. It was a shot worth repeating. To his chagrin he realized he had forgotten to mark the cannon wheels' position with the chalk.

With Chandler timing the intervals between shots, the gun crew continued to pound the redoubt, knocking chunks of earth, stone and wood from around the embrasure. After one hour, they had blasted a wide gap in the fortifications and silenced all but one of the British pieces.

Captain Ferguson ordered Will to redirect his fire at the second redoubt. This one was around six hundred yards away, still within easy range of the eighteen-pounder. Will took his time re-sighting the cannon and checked the reading on the quadrant twice before determining to increase the elevation to ten degrees. Adam drove the thicker wedge under the breech with a wooden mallet and stood back. Before loading, Will studied the redoubt through his glass. It had been directly pounded by ten-inch mortars, firing on a flat rather than an arced trajectory. Some of the bombs had exploded in front of the earthen wall, creating large craters and seemingly doing no real damage to it. Will thought that richochet firing would result in the ball being trapped in the craters, without further destroying a part of the redoubt. He decided to directly fire at the parapet.

Once the eighteen-pounder was loaded, before giving the order to fire, Will marked the wheel positions on the rough hewn wooden gun platform with a piece of chalk. "Make Ready!" he commanded. "Fire!" Through the glass he watched the ball sail a bit high over the embrasure and bounce across the field behind the redoubt. A wasted shot.

"Shell!" Someone shouted. A mortar bomb rose over the second redoubt, leaving an ugly black trail of smoke, arced high in the sky and landed in the trench no more than twenty feet from Will's gun. It did not explode but lay there, a hollow iron sphere filled with powder, its fuse sputtering menacingly.

Soldiers moving along the trench for a moment were immobilized by fear. Then, some dropped to the ground. Others hid behind the barrels that formed a blind. Adam was the first of the gun crew to react. Seizing the bucket of water used to sponge the cannon, he raced down the ramp to douse the fuse. He slipped on a loose board at the bottom and the water sloshed uselessly on to the ground.

"Sandbags, now!" Will yelled, grabbing a bag that lined the embrasure and tossing it down toward the smoldering bomb. The rest of the crew frantically began hurling the bags down. Several fell near the unexploded bomb but not close enough. We must get enough bags to cover it, Will thought frantically.[3]

"Adam. Get away! Get away." Will shouted desperately. Ignoring Will's call, Adam turned and gestured for those on the parapet to toss the sandbags to him. Catching one, he pivoted and threw it on top of the shell. He did this with three more bags and was turning to toss one more, the bag clutched to his chest, when the bomb exploded. Hot jagged pieces of iron flew in every direction. Adam blown backwards, crumpled against the earthen wall and lay motionless, his head sagging on his chest.

Will bounded down the ramp. Sharp smoldering fragments of the bomb stuck out from the sandbag that covered Adam. Sand poured from the rips in the fabric. One of Adam's hands was cut badly and blood oozed out of both of his ears. Will pulled the sandbag off of him and was relieved to see there were no visible wounds on his friend's chest or stomach. Chandler handed him a linen strip of cloth and Will bound it around Adam's hand. Gently, Will lifted Adam's head and examined it for injuries. The old scar from Major Murnan's slashing cut stood out against Adam's dark curly hair but outside of a few abrasions, he found no other wounds.

Adam moaned, opened his eyes and tried to sit up. Will put his hand on Adam's chest to restrain him. "You saved our lives," he said. Adam smiled at Will's familiar face.

"What? What did you say?" he repeated loudly. "I cannot hear you."

Will pointed to Adam's ears. "You are bleeding from the ears. We will get you to camp and the hospital," he said speaking louder and gesturing to the wheelbarrow a soldier had brought. Gently, he and Chandler helped Adam to his feet and lowered him into the barrow. They cushioned his head with Adam's Mariner's jacket, worn and tattered almost beyond recognition after five years of war.

"I will come to you when we are relieved," Will shouted after him. Whether Adam heard him or not, he seemed to understand. Adam lifted a hand feebly and waved goodbye.

Back on the gun platform, Will delegated Adam's role to another of the crew. They would operate with one less man. With Chandler and Tyler as experienced as they were, he did not think it would harm their efficiency. He stared through the glass at the second redoubt. He thought the mortar shell came from there.

"All right men. This ball is for Sergeant Cooper. We will aim to bounce it through the embrasure and to the mortars beyond." After making the proper sightings, and lowering the barrel slightly, Will supervised the removal of some of the powder from the charge, checked the stitching himself since Adam was not here and his friend was the only one he trusted to sew it up properly. "Make ready," he shouted. The men were now used to his stretching out the last word of the command. "Fire!" he shouted holding the spyglass with both hands. The ball struck just below the lip of the embrasure, ricocheted through the opening and veered to the right and bounced on out of sight. In its careening path, it must have struck a magazine because there was a loud explosion followed by a tall thin grey plume of smoke rising from well behind the redoubt walls. Will snapped the spyglass closed with satisfaction.

A runner from Captain Ferguson scrambled up the ramp. "Captain Ferguson's orders. You are to cease firing, cool and clean your piece. You are to resume once the blue pennant flies again on the battery to your right." Will only heard some of the words. Most of what the soldier had said was a blur of sounds indistinguishable of their meaning. He stepped closer to the man and made him repeat the orders directly into his ear.

His hearing must have been affected by the noise of the constant bombardment. It did not seem they had been firing for three hours. After fifteen rounds there was a distinct danger the heat of the explosions would soften the metal and the barrel would bend. Even worse for accuracy, the touchhole could expand, diminishing the force propelling the ball. Captain Ferguson had been alternating the fire of the three eighteen and twenty-four pounders so that some guns were rested and cleaned while others continued to fire. He heard the reassuring boom of one of the twenty-four pounders down the battery to his right, followed after several minutes by another shot fired from a cannon to his left.

Will waited for the men to bring the buckets of water and vinegar from the trench up to the platform. He left it to Sergeant Chandler to supervise the cleaning of the barrel and vent. After the gun had been cleaned, Chandler waited an appropriate time and then, as a precaution although the gun would not be fired for another hour, repeated the entire procedure. [4]

Some of the gun crew mingled with the soldiers manning the earthen wall while others slumped with fatigue, their backs against the sturdy parapet. A few descended the ramp and trotted back along the trench to the latrines in the field beyond the rear wall. Sergeant Chandler joined him on the parapet. Will studied the two enemy redoubts to assess the damage the American battery had done. The one closest to the York River had been erected on a cliff above the water. It was protected first by an abatis of sharpened sticks chest high, then a deep ditch in front of a palisade of thick pointed logs six or seven feet tall. The larger five-sided redoubt to the west of the first one had thicker earthen walls and the same defensive structures as the closer one. Most of the cannon fire had been directed at the gun emplacements. Their accurate fire had blown the embrasures apart, widening the gaps in the walls but the defenses against an infantry attack still stood mostly intact. Well, the goal had been to destroy the enemy's artillery first, Will thought and we have accomplished that. He assumed once they resumed fire, they would concentrate on shattering and setting fire to the abatis and palisades and crumbling the earthen protective wall. Will handed the glass to Chandler.

Looking up Will saw the sky crisscrossed from right to left with white smoking tracers of shells from both sides. The sound of bombardment and return fire was incessant. Occasionally, the lighter crack of musket fire filled the intervals between roar of cannons and the explosions of bombs. He wanted to return to the hospital to see how Adam was faring. It would have to wait until they were relieved. He guessed by the low position of the sun, obscured somewhat by the smoke from the siege guns, it was somewhere around four p.m. With his naked eye he could make out the brick buildings of Yorktown. After being battered for a second day, they were still standing but their roofs were shattered exposing the wooden beams in many places. The windows were gaping irregular holes and the tall chimneys had crumbled into piles of brick. Whatever wooden buildings remained in the town, having survived dismantling by the British to strengthen their fortifications, were now ablaze from the American cannon fire.

"There must be one hundred of them," Chandler said. As an artillery veteran he knew the loss of hearing all of them suffered from. He moved closer to Will and spoke more loudly.

"One hundred of what?"

Chandler pointed and Will took the glass back and scanned the river. Large brown, black and grey mounds dotted the beach and a few floated in the river riding the tide back from the bay to Yorktown. Flocks of gulls and other large birds stalked the sand and perched on the humps as if they were rocks. At first he could not identify them, even with the magnification. Then, he realized they were bloated horses, their bellies swollen with the gases of death, keeping them afloat until they were washed ashore.

"The British must have killed them as they ran low on forage and feed, and dumped their carcasses in the river," Will said with disgust. [5]

"Being soldiers rather than sailors, they did not allow for the tide," Chandler replied. "Now they will suffer the stench of their mistake. Let us hope the wind does not change during the night," he added waving his hand in front of his nose to push away an imaginary stink.

They resumed firing shortly after four p.m. aiming for the redoubts' walls. Will marked the position of the cannon wheels for shots that struck the fortifications straight on and lower down. He drew a different chalk line for those that struck the parapets. To aid the crew in setting the gun for the two targets at night, he drove a small wooden peg between the slats of the gun platform for each. In the darkness, if they were unable to see the chalk line in the light of the lintstock, they could feel for the two pegs and adjust the piece accordingly.

By seven, when the eighteen-pounder had been firing for another three hours, they again ceased fire for cleaning and cooling the gun. The night sky was lit with the arcing flames of mortar bombs and howitzer shells from the American and French lines. The British responded with cannons and mortars as well. Will watched the American troops move out into the grassy flat area between the lines. They were followed by fatigue parties of maybe five or six hundred men, armed with their usual shovels and pickaxes and carrying either fascines or gabions on their shoulders.

"We are digging a second parallel," Chandler guessed. "Once that is accomplished, our guns will be moved closer to the British lines of defense."

Will thought a moment. The two redoubts were obstacles to any such parallel since the enemy would flank the American lines and rain grapeshot and canister down onto the soldiers in the trenches. The enemy redoubts would have to be taken. He kept his thoughts to himself. Others of greater rank and experience would make the decision. The night was cooling. Will shivered and wrapped his worn coat closer to his body, thankful that he still had the neckstock Elizabeth had made for him.

They had been firing in the total darkness for close to two hours, five shots an hour, when there was the sound of voices and footsteps behind the battery. A body of men came down the trench. Even in the gloom, Will recognized General Knox by his large physique. He was accompanied by Colonel Lamb and other artillery officers.

Knox lumbered up the ramp, paused slightly out of breath and then clapped Will on the shoulders. "How goes it Will?" he asked, in his loud booming voice that fortunately was drowned out by several rounds of fire from the British fortifications to the left of the second redoubt. Knox perked his head up. "They are firing howitzers at our work crews and patrols. It sounds like balls instead of canister."

The General peered over the parapet into the darkness and the British lines beyond. "Note the gun flashes and aim for them. They move their howitzers around but perhaps you will catch them before they do so." He stood to the side with the other officers as Will's crew, using handspikes, re-aimed the eighteen-pounder. Will, keenly aware that Knox was observing him, decided to leave the elevation at ten degrees, although if asked he could not have given a reason. He barked the orders for the gun to be loaded and primed. When it was ready, he turned to General Knox.

"Sir. Would you like to bring the lintstock to the touchhole?"

"Nothing would please me more," Knox chortled. He took the long handled shaft in his hand, waited like the experienced artillery man he was for Will to shout "Make Ready," and "Fire," and lowered the burning rope to the hole. The cannon roared and the ball sped off across the darkness of no man's land, elevated enough to clear the American work parties and patrols. The cannon was aimed to strike high enough on the British parapet to crumble part of it before rampaging onward toward any guns sheltered behind. There was no way of knowing but any shot that landed behind the British lines fulfilled the purpose of maintaining a constant bombardment. [6]

"Well done, Will," Knox said. "I offered the same honor to His Excellency who indeed fired the first shot from this battery when we opened the trench."

As the officers departed, Knox paused at the bottom of the ramp and beckoned to Will, letting the others proceed up the trench toward the next guns without him.

"Will. Tomorrow, after you are relieved, I have a special task for you." He lowered his voice and bent down closer to Will's ear. "We are assaulting the two Redcoat redoubts tomorrow night. I intend to support the infantry with six field cannon. You will be in command of the battery." [7]

"I will do my utmost, Sir."

"If the assault goes as planned, we will take their redoubts in a matter of minutes and your cannons will not have fired a shot. I need your cool judgment as to when to fire in support and when to withhold fire." The General straightened up and wrapped his cloak more tightly around his shoulders.

"To be honest, Sir, firing siege cannons is too calm for my tastes."

Knox smiled at the comment. "Well, when we take the redoubts and open the second parallel, I am afraid you will once again be assigned to battering the British from a parapet. We will bring them to their knees, Will. I am certain of that.

The General gave Will a goodbye wave and lumbered down the trench. An aide discreetly waited for him a few yards ahead.

We are to be relieved at noon, Will thought. In about another twelve hours. First, I will find Adam and see to his welfare, then sleep for a few hours and be ready by sundown. It is true that he had battlefield experience supporting infantry but never at night. And he would be commanding gun crews not his own. He would need to meet the gun commanders and crews before leaving the artillery park. Best to know their capabilities in advance, he thought.

Chapter 12 - The Assault on the Rock Redoubt

Sergeant Henry Gillet, Private Gideon Hazzard and two platoons of sappers and miners crowded against each other in the trenches immediately behind the large American battery. A light mist lay low over the field between the battery and the two British redoubts. It was shortly before sunset and already there was a chill in the air. Henry watched the smoke from the firing of a twenty-four pounder waft slowly over the edge of the parapet. He imagined it drifting toward the two redoubts, less than a quarter of a mile beyond, creeping silently over the deep craters made by previous cannon balls, up over the abatis, down into the ditch, over the tall palisades, and then, enveloping the British soldiers manning the walls. He hoped the continuous American bombardment would disable any field guns the Redcoats had and demolish their defensive structures, or at least create gaps in the abatis and palisade. Gaps they would quickly widen.

The sappers and miners were armed only with axes and picks. Their rifles were racked in triangles before their tents in camp. Behind them, companies of soldiers stood silently in tight ranks in the dank corridor created by the trench leading past the battery. Gillet was the first to recognize the colors of their former Rhode Island Regiment with Captain Olney in the lead. The Captain was wearing a sword and carrying a long shafted spontoon with a blade affixed at the end. Gillet nudged Hazzard with his elbow. "We are to clear the way for our old Rhode Island Regiment." Hazzard followed his gaze. Private Mingo Power, a mulatto and brother from their old all black regiment was immediately behind the Captain.

Gillet looked down the trench. There were four hundred or so men - companies from different regiments - who comprised the assault force. He could not see any of the other colors among the soldiers for the flags hung limply against the staffs. Two men from each company, the bravest of the brave, would volunteer to be at the front of the assault. They would comprise The Forlorn Hope and gather directly behind Captain Olney before he led the attack. When they stepped forward, it would be an indication the command to advance was imminent.

They may be the "forlorn hope," Gillet thought but 'tis we sappers and miners who will advance first. Their orders were to hack away the sharp pointed stakes of the abatis and then chop gaps in the palisades for the troops to clamber through. How strange, Gillet thought. Because he had been afraid of heights and wanted no more of that, he was now about to lead an assault on a strongly fortified British redoubt, armed only with an axe. If he survived this evening, perhaps he should rejoin his regiment. At least with his musket and bayonet he had a fighting chance. He reached for his cartridge box to finger the worn piece of blue ribbon from the dress Judith had made for their daughter, his talisman of reassurance. But the ribbon was in the box and the box was back in his tent, deemed by the officers as unnecessary equipment and an encumbrance when the men were not carrying muskets. He fought off the premonition that without the piece of ribbon with him, he would die this night.

The ranks of soldiers bent and swayed as, pursuant to whispered orders, they unfixed and then re-fixed their bayonets. The sharp clicks of metal on metal moved down the trench toward the end of the line. After what seemed to Gillet an interminable time standing in place, he left the base of the ramp to the gun and approached Captain Olney. With his back to the twenty-four pounder, he did not see them fire and instinctively hunched his shoulders surprised by the roar of the cannon.

"Captain Olney, sir. Sergeant Henry Gillet, formerly of the 2nd Rhode Islanders. Me and Private Hazzard here are among the sappers and miners."

Olney studied his features in the darkness and recognized him. He nodded to Hazzard who had followed Henry.

"Ah yes, Sergeant. It will be a comfort to me to know that there are brave Rhode Island men in front as well as along side me in the attack." He smiled, Gillet thought a bit nervously. "I cannot claim I had the foresight to recommend you at West Point so you would be here tonight. It must be by the will of Providence." Gillet heard the tenseness in the Captain's voice. He felt the same. Better to get on with it instead of remaining stationary in this trench while balls whistled overhead. One of his knees began shaking but he kept his voice firm.

"We will clear the path for you, Captain. Private Hazzard swings his axe like a man possessed and with great strength."

Several pairs of soldiers approached Captain Olney at his forward position in the line of troops. Gillet listened as the men identified their rank and regiment. Gillet did not wait for the other volunteers for the "forlorn hope" to identify themselves. The time for leaving the trenches was near.

Private Hazzard squeezed past the Captain and the men of the "forlorn hope," and moved among the ranks of the Rhode Islanders. Many were the blacks of the old 1st Rhode Island Regiment, veterans of the retreat from Newport. They pressed around Gideon, speaking in low voices, grasping his hand and leaning forward to whisper in his ear.[1]

Gillet motioned to Hazzard and the two made their way back to the two platoons of sappers and miners assembled before the ladders leaning against the trench's outer wall.

"They are worried if they are killed their families will not know of it," Hazzard said matter-of-factly. "They have asked me to write letters home for them, in case Mungo is killed." Gillet looked puzzled. "Mungo, Warmsley and me are the only literate ones." He did not add among the black troops. It went without saying the blacks did not trust the whites of their Regiment to write their letters for them.

"And you?" Henry asked with a slight smile. "You do not intend to get killed?"

"Hell no," Hazzard grinned. "I intend to live to see these bloody Redcoats either blasted to bits or surrender." Gillet smiled at Gideon's bravado and wondered whether he felt as weak-kneed as he did. The order was given in a whisper to move out.

They climbed the ladders, stood on the parapets for a moment and then descended into the darkness of the fields of soft grass and sand. The roar of the American and French cannons firing along the line masked the gentle swishing sound as four hundred soldiers silently advanced on the cliff redoubt ahead. Thirty yards from the redoubt, they were ordered to lie down. Gillet could see the massive dark wall of the redoubt, blacker against the night sky. He felt the dampness seeping through his waistcoat, having left his jacket unbuttoned so as to swing his axe more freely. The American battery behind him had fallen silent. He lay with his face turned toward the west and the French occupied trenches. The signal to attack was to be three shells, fired by a French battery in quick succession. The watchword was Rochambeau, the name of the French General. The Americans had converted it to "Rush on Boys." It was easier on the tongue.

It was a clear night and Gillet fixed his gaze on Venus, the evening star, grateful to see a familiar object in the sky yet wishing for a more cloudy and darker night.

Then, there they were. Three bright fiery spheres arcing into the sky. "Up! Up! Up!" the orders were whispered. Gillet, Hazzard and the other sappers and miners rushed forward to the sharp pointed stakes of the abatis.

"Halt! Who goes there?" When there was no response, the wall erupted in flashes of musket fire. In the pitch blackness, the British had fired high. Gillet found several stakes broken by cannon fire and chopped at the adjacent ones to make a wider gap. Hazzard's powerful swings cut through the tangle of wood to enlarge it. They were jostled aside by soldiers screaming like Indians. He thought he recognized Captain Olney's voice slightly from behind – "Rush on boys. Rush on. The fort's our own." [2] Gillet and Hazzard were swept through the abatis and into the ditch before the palisade. Another flash of musket fire from above illuminated, for an instant, the deep craters formed by the American bombardment. Gillet skirted the rim of one and began furiously hacking away at the log palisade. Soldiers pushed through the gaps created by cannon balls and enlarged by the sappers and miners.

Gillet looked up at the parapet and heard the shouted cry – "Captain Olney's company form here." Without thinking he grabbed his axe, swung it hard into the earthen wall, struck something solid and hauled himself up. Hazzard was close behind, leaving the other sappers below. They were the first to reach the Captain and found themselves, armed only with axes, fighting off several Redcoats thrusting at them with their long, evil eighteen inch bayonets. Olney parried with his spontoon. Gillet stepped slightly ahead of him to one side and hacked down hard on the bayonet reaching up toward him. He felt the tremor in his forearms as the axe blade struck metal. His blow was hard enough to make the soldier drop his weapon. Hazzard was wielding his axe in vicious circles in front of him, blocking and battering away muzzles and bayonets alike. More Americans joined them on the parapet, having climbed up on the shoulders of others. Several of the Rhode Islanders, contrary to orders, had fortunately reloaded their muskets. An erratic volley, fired down on the British, drove them off their infantry platform. With a loud shout of "Huzzah!" the troops jumped down from the parapet and along with a surge of soldiers, pursued the routed British with a bayonet charge into the flat open ground of the redoubt.

From the vantage point of the parapet, Gillet looked around. Americans were swarming over every wall of the redoubt, chasing the Redcoats within the walled confines. There were shouts of "Remember New London," as some of the enemy threw down their muskets and tried to surrender. Gillet winced as he saw an unarmed soldier on his knees, bayoneted by a Continental. He turned to ask Captain Olney to stop this slaughter. The Captain was lying on the earth of the parapet where he had fallen. He was bleeding from the hand, and thigh, and worse there was an ominous patch of dark blood oozing from his waistcoat above his hip.[3]

Gillet ran to him. "It is my arm," he groaned, oblivious to the other wounds. "I have taken a ball in my arm and it causes me great pain." As gently as possible, Gillet and Hazzard lowered their Captain from the parapet and laid him on the shelf where, minutes before British infantry had been firing down on the attacking Americans. Below them, there were loud shouted "huzzahs." The redoubt was theirs. The twenty or more British prisoners stood somewhat apprehensively in the center of the redoubt, staring at the victorious Americans guarding them with bayonets at the ready. He was amazed only ten minutes had passed from the time they had charged the abatis till the Redcoats surrendered.

Gillet and Hazzard hurriedly left Captain Olney in the care of men from the Rhode Island Regiment and assembled at the open end of the redoubt facing the British lines. Frenetically, they began constructing a wall, filling the gabions that were brought up with reinforcements to guard against a British counter-attack. Gillet established a familiar rhythm – stick a gabion upright in the soil, dig like a madman, fill it with dirt and move down the line to the next gabion. He was intent on erecting some protection between the redoubt and the British line before the enemy either counter-attacked or directed their cannon fire at their former stronghold.

Less then three hundred yards to his left, the assault on the other redoubt, this one led by French troops was still going on. Gillet ignored the crackle of musket volleys and shouts and screams in French, German and English as he dug furiously through the soft sand, his shovel blade in constant motion. There was a lull in the musket fire and then shouts of "Vive le Roi! Vive le Roi!" reached the American captured redoubt. They answered with "Huzzahs!" of their own before returning to the urgent task of fortifying the unprotected opening in the redoubt facing to the British lines.[4]

The night sky erupted in a fusillade of howitzer shells and mortar bombs, accompanied by the deeper roar of field artillery. It seemed to Gillet that every British gun was concentrated on this redoubt although he knew that the barrage must be aimed at the newly captured French redoubt as well. The noise and fear of a counter-attack prompted the sappers and miners to a greater burst of energy. Their efforts were aided by the arrival of soldiers who had been sent to reinforce the redoubt but now were given shovels and were digging like fiends possessed.

As the night wore on, despite the ferocious concentration of enemy fire, more and more fascines and gabions were brought up. By the time dawn broke, the sappers, miners and soldiers had constructed a rear wall as high as the British built defenses they had overcome in the early evening. There was an infantry platform, now manned by some of the exhausted troops who had helped build the wall upon which they now stood. They stared across a distance of no more than three hundred yards at the battered British fortifications and the pulverized buildings of Yorktown beyond.

The sappers and miners, upon being relieved, marched from the redoubt through a newly dug trench to the American battery in the first parallel. It would not be long, Gillet thought before these cannons will be moved to the newly captured redoubts to pound the British defenses at almost point blank range. It would be over soon, he thought, as he reached for his cartridge box before remembering it was back in their tent. Maybe it was the thought of his talisman ribbon that enabled him to survive this night. Only one more attack on the main British inner lines before he would be furloughed and return home. One more time of sheer terror to survive. For that assault, he would carry Judith's ribbon with him.

—☙—

"You are drunk," Private Caleb Wade said, more as a statement of fact than an accusation.

"I have had my ration and more," Vose replied angrily. " Ballocks. What God damn business is it of yours, you oafish crock of shit. Leave me alone unless you want my bayonet sticking up your ass someday." Wade shook his head at his former friend's blasphemy but said nothing.

It was close to 4 a.m. Wade, Vose and two companies of the 3rd New Jersey Regiment were on guard duty at the American battery on the far left of the line, at the seam where it joined the French trenches. There was a brisk wind blowing the smoke from the British lines toward them. The cannonade had ceased in their sector, while further to the west, the lighter bark of field cannon and the deeper boom of mortars indicated the French trenches were bearing the brunt of the continuous bombardment. British mortar shells arced high and fell to earth like bright shooting stars, followed by the ominous dull boom of a deadly explosion.

Wade stood behind the low earthen works and peered across the field at the British fortifications. They were partially hidden by a thick copse of trees about four hundred yards away. Vose belched and settled his head against the top of the earthen wall as if sighting down his musket. It did not fool Wade who saw he was dozing. He gestured with his head to Corporal Traynor walking behind them down the line. Traynor shrugged and moved on. The men had been on the line since midday yesterday, relieving the soldiers who had held these positions in anticipation of a British counterattack following the fall of the two redoubts. None had occurred and with the opening of the second parallel, almost on top of the British defenses, the end was obvious. They would pound the Redcoats into submission.

Traynor hoped there would be no need for a final assault. The artillery would do the work for them. It should be all over by the time they were rotated back into the trenches twenty-four hours after this coming noon. At least that was the rumor among the soldiers, who eagerly placed bets on when the British would show the white flag and surrender. A lot of money was being wagered. Although he never gambled at dice or cards, he himself had contributed one half a dollar in coin, picking October 17th, one day from today. It was the date General Burgoyne had surrendered the British army at Saratoga. It seemed to Traynor an especially propitious date.

The wind rustled in the leaves on the trees behind him. He reached the end of his platoon and met Sergeant Henderson coming toward him.

"Lieutenant 'Nuthatch' is making his rounds," Henderson said. "Make sure your men are alert. No sense anyone drawing

The Assault on the Rock Redoubt

extra duty or the lash for mistakes this late in the war."

Traynor nodded in appreciation. Henderson was a good sort in his own gruff way. They were both from the same county. He wondered if they would be furloughed at the same time and could travel to New Jersey together. He saw Wade's tall silhouette ahead and was moving a little faster to make sure Vose would pass muster with the Lieutenant when one of the pickets shouted a challenge into the darkness ahead.

"What troops?"

"French" came the husky response.

It was followed by a shouted command – "Push on boys and skin the bastards." Redcoats surged over the wall and jumped into the trench, stabbing and plunging ahead in a ferocious bayonet attack. The surprised Americans fell back toward the three eighteen-pounders. In the screaming and shouting and discharge of muskets, Traynor heard Henderson's shouted command – "Rally round the cannons, men. Rally to me."

There were too many of the Redcoats. Light infantry swarmed over the low wall behind them and fought their way up the line instead of encircling them. Henderson called for the men to retreat and they abandoned the gun emplacement and pursued by the British ran into the field behind their battery and toward their main lines. The Redcoats broke off the pursuit and soon, the metallic sound of spikes being hammered into the cannons' touchholes echoed in the early dawn.

Lieutenant Tew ordered them to regroup and reload their muskets. "Fire one volley on my command and then 'tis bayonets boys. Recapture our guns." They advanced on the run, shouting to be heard and to drive away any fear of the coming hand-to-hand fighting that would ensue. Traynor saw white uniformed infantry to his left. The French were sending reinforcements as well. The Redcoats discharged one volley at the attackers to hold them off while others tried to complete the spiking of the cannons. They lingered too long. Traynor caught one of them with his arm raised, a hammer ready to drive a bayonet further into the touchhole. He pierced the Redcoat through the ribs. The man collapsed on the cannon, spewing a torrent of blood from his mouth.

"After them, boys!" Lieutenant Tew shouted. They jumped the low wall and ran out into the field. On command, they knelt and fired a volley at the retreating Redcoats. There was a light boom from the British lines and a cannon ball from a six-pounder skipped across the field, taking down a few men before lodging in the earthen wall with a thud.

"Back to our positions," Tew ordered and the men of his company marched in good order into their lines to man the fortifications once again. It was daylight by now. There were several dead and wounded Redcoats lying around the cannons, all three of which had been spiked. How permanently, Traynor did not know. They had hammered bayonets in the touchholes instead of the thicker steel spikes which were harder to remove. [5]

"God. I am dying. Please do not let me die. I do not want to die!" The piteous scream of Private Vose continued as Wade and Traynor attempted to staunch the flow of blood. He had been bayoneted several times, in the legs and arms as he had tried to ward off the vicious attack. They pulled back his jacket, checking for any stomach or chest wounds.

"Be quiet," Wade said firmly. "You have no fatal wounds." Traynor wrapped a linen tourniquet tightly around Vose's left thigh and stuffed linen into the slash below the hip bone. It was bleeding profusely. Poor Vose might lose enough blood to kill him unless the surgeons were able to sew him up in time.

"Caleb, my old drinking friend," Vose gasped, motioning for Wade to bend closer. "Pray for me. If you believe God is with us, pray for your besotted drinking companion. I meant no harm. I just like my rum. Is that a sin?"

Caleb put his hand on Vose's forehead, as if in benediction. "It will be all right, Mathias. Be calm and place your faith in God and your trust in our surgeons."

Vose reached out and took Caleb's large hand in his. "Visit me. Please. I beg of you. Come to the hospital. Do not leave me to die alone," he pleaded like a frightened child.

"You are not dying and I promise to visit you," Caleb replied, removing his friend's hand and folding his arms across his abdomen. Vose screamed when they lifted him into the wheelbarrow and carted him back toward the encampment.

Traynor stood up, his dirty white breeches now stained with Vose's blood or was it that of the dead Redcoat he had bayoneted at the eighteen-pounder. It did not matter. Although it was not his, he felt drained as if he had been bled by the doctors.

"All able bodied men to the line," Tew commanded. It was after dawn. Six more hours before they would be relieved. Already, the line had been reinforced by some Virginia militia. A company of Continentals, flags flying were quick marching across the field toward them. If the British renewed their attack, Traynor thought, there would be fresh troops on the line to greet them. He would like to still be on the line when the cannons were fixed. It would do the men good to hear them firing again.

—⚜—

In the darkness before midnight the guns were silent. The lack of booming and the menacing lighted descent of mortar bombs and howitzer shells was disconcerting. Will guessed they fired their last ball from the eighteen-pounder about an hour ago. Accompanied by strong winds blowing up the Bay to Yorktown, the rains lashed at them in driving sheets, soaking them in minutes. All the artillery men could do was plug the vents securely, cover the muzzles with leather caps and place canvas over the powder magazines and hope they remained dry.

Will huddled, together with the gun crew, under a makeshift lean-to opposite the new battery established in the redoubt the Americans had captured the day before. The field cannons he commanded in support of the infantry attack had not been necessary. The troops had carried the redoubt by their determined charge and at dawn they had brought the six-pounders back to the artillery park. Exhausted as he was, he visited Adam to find him unwinding the bandage around his head and wiping the liquid oozing from his ears onto a linen cloth. He did it awkwardly, hampered by the thick wrapping around his hand, binding his wound from the bomb's shrapnel. "Dr. Thaxter said my hearing may come back,"Adam said too loudly, startling the wounded soldiers in adjacent cots. Will assured his friend that his hearing also improved with time away from manning the guns. He left him for some much-needed sleep.

When he awoke, he slogged through the mud to rejoin the battery. The canvas cloth, pegged to the trench wall sloped downward to the top of the sand filled barrels that served as blinds against bombs. Water gushed over the edges in torrents, forming muddy puddles on either side of their meager shelter. Will shivered from the cold and hoped his fever was not returning. He was angry and frustrated. Now they were within easy range of pulverizing the British into submission, the weather was conspiring against them. By orders of Colonel Lamb, the Trench Commander for this day, it was the specially mounted mortars and howitzers that had done most of the firing. The guns had not been ready until dark when they commenced a sporadic bombardment around five p.m. Will's cannon had shot only ten rounds before the storm began. He hoped daylight would give him the opportunity to blast the British positions unless the rain continued into the morning.

He shifted his position, feeling the cold wetness on his rear and the water on the floor of the trench seeping through his worn boots and freezing his toes. Sergeant Chandler pulled his tri-corn tightly on his head and frog-marched out of their shelter. Grunting, he stood up and sloshed through the mud toward the inner wall of the redoubt. He returned shortly, water coursing off his hat and long tufts of grey hair matted to his temples, clutching a length of folded canvas under his jacket. He squatted down in the mud and motioned for everyone to stand.

"No sense soaking from the bottom up as well as the top down," he said, causing the others in the crew to chuckle. They spread the canvas on the ground and sat down appreciating the relative dryness.

"Old bookbinders are always able to scrounge up whatever is needed," Levi Tyler said appreciatively of his long time crewmember. The rain continued to drum on the canvas above their heads as the men talked softly among themselves.

Will found himself thinking of Elisabeth and little Henry. The last letter from his wife came from Philadelphia. She was enjoying the hospitality of Mrs. Knox and her friends and continuing as nanny to little Lucy. It was dated more than a month before, after the ladies arduous trip from West Point. He drifted off to sleep, thinking how pleasant it would be to hold her once again and to carry their son on his shoulders.

He woke to Chandler shaking him gently. "Lieutenant. The rain has stopped." The wind had abated and a few stars were visible through the rapidly clearing clouds.

Will emerged from the canvas lean to and stretched. He was alert but stiff, chilled and hungry. On the parapets around the battery, soldiers moved about, brushing the mud from their jackets and reloading their muskets.

"Have the men wipe down the cannon as best they can. Keep the vent blocked but uncover the muzzle. Sponge the barrel with a dry cloth. I will check the magazine."

Occasionally slipping in the mud, Will sloshed through the puddles to the powder magazine in the far northwest corner of the redoubt. The kegs of powder and the side boxes of charges were raised off the ground on thick logs under a slanting wooden roofed shelter. A canvas sheet, double folded covered the kegs but not the side boxes. Two tired but dry sentries stood aside as he pried boxes open. He felt the top layer. It was dry. He smiled. They would be able to resume firing when Colonel Lamb gave the orders. He waited impatiently as other guns along the American line began to fire. From the sounds, he knew that only the howitzers and mortars were in action.

Just before dawn, a runner from Captain Ferguson's adjacent battery on the second parallel, ordered Will's cannon to commence firing. There were two pentagonal shaped fortifications protruding from the British line. These were his targets. He decided the ground was too muddy for a richochet and instead aimed directly at the angled wall closest to the battery. Satisfied that the gun was aimed properly, he put his gunner's quadrant away and crisply gave the orders to load.

"Make ready," he shouted, hearing his own voice echo in his ears. "Give Fire!"

The eighteen-pounder roared, a sheet of flame blasted from the muzzle and the ball struck the wall a bit high, sheering off an irregular chunk of earth and wood before careening beyond into the streets of Yorktown.

Chandler tapped Will's shoulder and pointed toward the river. Through the glass, Will saw several large high gunwaled boats, crammed with Redcoats emerging from the mist opposite Gloucester Point. The helmsman struggled to keep the boat on course, as the sailors rowed frantically to bring the craft to Yorktown, fighting against the strong current and tide that would take them into the American lines.

Without waiting for orders, Will directed the crew to wrestle the eighteen- pounder around. The men slipped and slid on the muddy, wet gun platform until they had the muzzle pointing at the York River. The British boats were difficult targets as they bobbed and drifted in the waves. They were less than a half a mile away, approaching slowly in an irregular, weaving manner, caused more by current than deliberate evasive maneuvers. Will checked the lines on his gunner's quadrant and ordered a wedge to be inserted until he was satisfied the breech was at the proper angle. No need to mark the position of the wheels because each shot would have to be recalculated.

"Make Ready," he shouted as he stepped to the right of the gun and trained his spyglass on the first boat. "Give Fire." A large spout appeared just to the left of the prow of the crowded craft, almost upending it. As the crew sponged the gun and reloaded, Will kept his glass on the boats and their desperate struggle to reach shore. Geysers of brown water spewed skyward as American mortars and howitzers concentrated their fire on the helpless Redcoats.

"Poor bastards," Will said. The lead boat was almost to the Yorktown beach. Will decided to target it as they landed. The crew used their pry bars to re-aim the cannon and a mallet to remove the wedge and depress the muzzle. The Redcoats, spurred on by the fear of being sitting ducks in a beached boat, frantically jumped over the gunwales into the shallow waters and ran up the sandy strip of land, seeking the shelter of the low, grassy dunes.

"Make Ready!" Will yelled followed by "Give Fire." Through the glass he saw the last two Redcoats wade into the water as the ball smashed the middle of the boat, splintering it and sending lethal sharp shards of wood flying everywhere. One of the soldiers lay face down in the water. The other was nowhere to be seen. He may have escaped. Good for him, Will thought.

The soldiers in the other boats, following the example of those in the first one, leaped into the water as they approached the shore and raced up the beach. There were no direct hits despite the concentrated fire directed at them while on the river, The bombs and shells cut down some of them on the sandy beach leading up to Yorktown. [6]

All along the entire line, from the main French batteries on the extreme left in the closer second parallel to the American guns in the newly recaptured redoubts on the far right, the combined firing of more than one hundred pieces of artillery, shook the earth. The roar was continuous, with the wind blowing the smoke north of the British lines and Yorktown, giving the allies' gunners a clear view of the besieged Redcoats. Only a few British cannons fired in response.

The sun rose higher in the morning sky. Will standing along side the eighteen-pounder with his back facing east, welcomed the warmth it provided. His damp shirt clung to his body, chilling his skin. His wet jacket hung heavily on his shoulders. The crew had reloaded the cannon and Will was about to shout "Make Ready!" when the cry of "Hold Your Fire," came from the adjacent battery.

There was no need for the spyglass. A red-coated officer stood on the parapet less than one hundred yards to Will's left, waving a white handkerchief. Will cupped his hands to his mouth and shouted down to the next battery, "Hold Your Fire." As the cannons fell silent, he heard the beat of the drum in the customary "chamade" signaling a desire to cease hostilities and confer. [7] The officer, accompanied by a drummer boy, clambered down the battered parapet and walked slowly onto the field separating the two armies.

Will watched as an American Captain met him halfway, blindfolded him with the handkerchief, and escorted him within the lines.

After the British messenger returned carrying the Americans' response, and for the remainder of the morning, Will and the other gunners continued to bombard the British positions, blasting away at the earthen fortifications that had crumbled in places. When they were relieved at noon they marched out of the redoubt and down the communications trench to the main second parallel and back to camp. Will was so exhausted, he pulled off his boots, covered himself with a blanket and collapsed on his cot. He slept until morning.

When he awoke, he was chilled and aching in every joint. It was his fever coming back. He wondered whether he had lost his hearing entirely. There was no constant roar of the Allied cannonade, not even a single shot. Hurriedly, he left the relative warmth of his tent and walked quickly in the cool dawn air to General Knox's tent. He took a moment to stand as close to the orange flames and hissing wood of the fire burning outside as possible while the General's orderly ducked inside the tent. The two sentries on either side of the flap looked at him curiously but said nothing.

"Ah, Will, my lad," Knox called as he entered. The General was seated in a canvas chair, his hefty bulk causing it to sag significantly. A sheaf of papers lay on his camp desk. A large trunk was off to the side with a book splayed open perched on top of it, as if its owner had hastily but reluctantly put it down mid-page. Knox ceased writing in his copy book and returned the quill to its stand. The light from two lamps shone on his ruddy cheeks and illuminated a table with a map of the new Allied line and the British defenses. Could it have only been six days Will thought since he had stood in Colonel Lamb's tent listening to Captain Ferguson describe the firing procedures for targeting the two redoubts?

"Do you hear this significant silence," Knox said throwing his arms out. "It is this lack of sound that portends surrender is imminent," Knox chortled. "I have been with His Excellency most of the night. The British have agreed to negotiate terms. A cease fire has been in effect since 5 am," Knox said. "Our two commissioners and the British representatives will meet at nine o'clock this morning to agree on the Articles of Capitulation. By God how I am eager to write my dearest Lucy to tell her of this glorious moment for America."

Will felt dizzy and reached for the corner of the table to steady himself. Knox saw him stumble, stood up and held Will by the shoulders. "My dear boy. You look unwell," Knox said looking down and moving to guide him to his cot.

"No. I am simply tired, Sir. No need for any concern on your part." Will sat in one of the chairs opposite Knox who had returned to his camp desk.

"Sir. We are on camp duty today but it would please my men, two of whom were with us at Dorchester Heights in '76, to be on the lines, to observe the events of this truly remarkable day."

The tent flap opened and a cook from the officer's mess tent came in with a bowl of hot porridge mixed with molasses. Knox insisted Will eat first and sent the cook back to bring another bowl and some tea laced with rum.

"Of course you and your crew may observe from the lines. I myself may join you if His Excellency does not need my advice to confer on the Redcoats' counter proposals." Knox leaned forward and stared at Will's eyes. "You look feverish," he observed. "Before returning to the parapets, let Dr. Thaxter examine you. You must return healthy to your beloved Elisabeth and your baby boy."

"Yes sir." Will tucked his head down to avoid the General's stare, and eagerly spooned the hot porridge into his mouth. He could not lie outright while meeting his eyes. He had no intention of going anywhere near a doctor. He would not be bedridden and bled, confined to some field hospital when the British surrendered.

Chapter 13- Confrontation on Surrender Field

Camp before York, eight o'clock A.M.19th October (1781)

My dearest Lucy,

I have detained my brother until this moment that I might be the first to communicate good news to the Charmer of my soul. A glorious moment for America! This day Lord Cornwallis & his army marches out and piles their Arms in the face of our victorious Army. The day before Yesterday he desir'd commissioners might be named to treat of the surrender of his troops, their ships, and everything they possess. He at first requested that the Britons might be sent to Britain, and the Germans to Germany; but this the General refused, and they have now agreed to surrender prisoners of War, to be kept in America until exchanged or released. They will have the same honors as the garrison of Charlestown; that is, they will not be permitted to unfurl their colors, or play Yankee Doodle. We know not yet how many they are. The General has just requested me to be at head quarters instantly. Therefore I cannot be more particular. . .

Excuse this hasty scrawl. My brother will be able to inform you how little time I have had even for sleep.

Adieu the best beloved of my heart, and believe me to be your ever affectionate

    Love
        HKnox

"Why are the church bells tolling a death knell?" Adam asked in a loud voice. He was seated on a borrowed horse, holding the reins awkwardly in his bandaged hand, a part of a contingent of General Knox's Artillery Regiment, awaiting the arrival of the surrendering British.

The Americans lined the east side of the Hampton Road together with the other Continental Regiments in the first and second ranks, the soldiers standing at attention in their shabby and battle worn blue uniforms. Those who were fortunate enough to have boots, had polished them as best they could, as well as any leather straps they wore. Almost every company was a mixture of tall and short men of all ages, with a few blacks and mulattos interspersed throughout. Quite a few had dull grey linen bandages wrapped around their wounds and limbs.

In the third rank, mostly hidden from the road were the militiamen in their hunting shirts, floppy hats, breeches with deerskin leggings and their individual assortment of weapons – muskets, rifles, hatchets, hunting knives and tomahawks. Behind them were crowds of civilians who had come from the surrounding area - plantation owners with their wives in carriages, attended by Negro slaves on foot, and townspeople, merchants and shopkeepers, some with their families. A few intrepid barefoot boys had climbed nearby trees. Greatly excited, they pointed here and there at the array of troops beneath them – far more than they had ever seen in their young lifetimes.

General Washington, accompanied by Generals Lincoln, Lafayette, Knox and others, as well as his headquarters staff, were mounted waiting at the beginning of the American lines. They were positioned, on the east side of the road, at the point where Lord Cornwallis would first emerge at the head of his army to surrender. Opposite them were General Rochambeau, his senior officers and staff.

The French troops, all of about the same height and age, were arrayed beyond their generals on the west side. They presented a precise military appearance, immaculate in their uniforms of white, sparkling with silver, each regiment with different colored lapels and collars.

Will shivered in the noonday sun. Regimental flags fluttered in the mild breeze that chilled him. He leaned forward and patted Big Red's neck. The horse's flesh was brushed to a bright smooth sheen. He heard no church bells, only the music played by the French military band that seemed muffled and dull. He turned to Captain Hadley. "Samuel. Are you hearing church bells?" he asked anxiously.

Hadley gave him a puzzled frown. "The only nearby church is in Yorktown and we blasted the steeple four days ago. How could there be bells?"

Adam heard the Captain's response and shrugged. "I am either going daft or the bells ring inside my ears from that explosion."

There was an almost imperceptible ripple of activity among the troops, a stiffening of their posture, a straightening of the muskets held at shoulder arms, a moving of the feet closer together. The British and Hessians were coming to surrender.

Captain Hadley sat up taller and turned his eyes toward where a British General was presenting his sword to General Lincoln. There was a brief discussion and then the British came on, their drums and fifes playing a melancholy tune, the troops led by their flag bearers with the colors cased in glistening leather tubes. [2] Their jackets were clean and of such bright red they appeared to be new, their silver colored buttons highly polished.

Some of the officers wore sashes, others had cockades in their black tri-corns. They sat erect in the saddle, the perfect picture of gentlemen accustomed to horses. Yet their faces were sullen and pouting, as if to indicate they thought they had been bested by their inferiors in some unfair and underhanded way.

The regular troops were equally ill-tempered, intoxicated or both. Barely a single platoon was in step and many of the marching soldiers were bent and hunched, as if they were too encumbered by their equipment. Their marching was sloppy and from the side, Hadley could see their ranks were as curved and crooked as those of new recruits. All of the officers and their troops, as they proceeded down the road between the lines of the victorious allied troops, had their heads turned to the right, facing the French. Hadley was incensed at this insult to the Americans and almost shattered the silence by crying out in anger to force them to notice.

Suddenly, the American drummers and fifers, interspersed between the regiments, burst into Yankee Doodle. The British troops, compelled as if by some uniform command, turned their heads to their left and morosely took notice of the Continentals who had beaten and defeated them. While the Americans maintained their silence, many of the Continentals could no longer keep a stoic countenance. Still standing at attention, they smiled and grinned at the spectacle of the passing Redcoats.

Will swayed in the saddle and gripped the pommel with one hand. The British soldiers marching past were a red blur and across the road, the French troops seemed to be moving first toward and then away from him. He lifted his tri-corn, feeling the cool air on his damp hair. The fever was returning. He rubbed his temples with his thumb and fingers in a vain attempt to relieve the intense, dull throbbing that deprived him of the joy of the moment.

The last of the British infantry were passing by. Now it was the cavalry's turn. They trotted by, the troopers immaculate in their red uniforms, wearing hard black caps with the death's head insignia adorned with a crest of dyed red horse hair, sabers held at the shoulder. Their horses had suffered from the deprivations of the siege. Nothing could disguise they were poorly fed boney images of their former selves, now only fit for ceremonial use, incapable of charging into battle.[3]

As he turned his gaze to the blue unformed Hessians marching behind, something among the cavalry caught his eye. Some irregularity caused him to examine them again. There, in the middle of five riders abreast, in the next to last row, was a trooper wearing a tri-corn instead of the dragoons' black cap and carrying a sword rather than a saber. He was heavier than the others around him, with a paunch stretching his waistcoat. Will concentrated on his face, partially shaded by the tri-corn. It was his brother.

Confrontation on Surrender Field

Involuntarily, Will broke the silence of the surrender march. "John! John Stoner!" His voice sounded gravelly and rough. His brother jerked up in the saddle, cast a fearful look at Will on Big Red and quickly turned away, hunching his shoulders down as if he expected to be shot in the back. The troopers trotted further down the road and now the Hessian regiments were opposite Will.

Hadley guided his horse between the first and second ranks and stopped next to Big Red.

"That was my brother," Will said excitedly. "He answered to his name. I will kill him for what he did to Elisabeth. I swore I would."

Samuel reached out and squeezed Will's arm. "If indeed it was your brother, you will do what is allowed by the Terms of Surrender and no more," Hadley said firmly. "Right now, you belong in the Regimental Hospital. Your eyes betray the fever wracking you. They burn brightly and you shiver as it consumes you."

The blue sky, the grass, the brown ribbon of road all swirled around in dizzying circles. Will slumped forward in the saddle, trying to escape from the painful throbbing in his head. His chin nestled against the long coarse strands of Big Red's mane. Hadley handed the reins to Adam. The two left the line and headed toward the Warwick Road and the field hospital beyond the Artillery Park.

—⁂—

Private Caleb Wade stood proud and tall. His New Jersey Regiment, by luck or design of Colonel Dayton, was the last of the American troops lining the road before the British soldiers turned from the road into a field to give up their arms and surrender their standards. He was convinced, watching the ranks of what was the best Army in Europe march by, all spit and polish in their bright red uniforms, that Providence had indeed been and was with the American cause. How else to explain the fall of this invincible foe to the Continentals, who a few years ago were untrained and poorly equipped. Even now, rations were short, soldiers lacked shoes and jackets, their tents were full of holes and their blankets threadbare. And yet they had triumphed.

Over three hundred French Hussars sat motionless on their horses, their buttons and braid sparkling in the mid-afternoon sun, their freshly oiled high leather boots gleaming and their wicked looking lances upright. Saluting the Almighty, Wade thought.

The French cavalry formed a long oval perimeter in a grassy meadow, surrounding the defeated British soldiers who entered to complete the last gesture of surrender. The Hussars' white uniforms stood out against the background of the cathedral of tall trees of the forest behind them.

The first company reached the center of the field. "Present Arms! Lay Down Arms!" Wade smiled at the orders given by a grizzled British Master Sergeant. There was an audible clatter as muskets were tossed to the ground.

"Put off swords and cartridge boxes." More clatter before an American officer rode forward and directed the Redcoats to put their muskets in one pile, swords in another and cartridge boxes in a third. The soldiers grumbled and their officers, who had been sulking, now appeared more angry at what they took as an additional indignity.[4]

As the afternoon wore on, Wade marveled at the growing pile of captured muskets and equipment. It truly was an offering to Providence. He looked forward to the Regimental Chaplain's sermon which he was certain would praise God for their victory.

The stoic, blue-jacketed Hessians were the last of the defeated army to march up the Hampton Road and lay down their arms. As they began the long march back to their tents in Yorktown, Lieutenant Tew on horseback and his company fell in behind them. The New Jersey soldiers had been assigned guard duty that night. Some of the men grumbled at their bad luck, having anticipated a night of gambling and celebrating with drink and song. For Wade, it was simply another task to be performed willingly as part of the great victory the Army had achieved.

The stench of rotting corpses hit them as they passed through the now unblocked entrances to the British fortifications and on into the town itself. Huge craters from cannon balls were everywhere, some filled with fetid, scummy water. Corporal Traynor covered his nose with a linen cloth and others in his platoon followed his example but it was not enough to keep the sickening smell out of their nostrils. The scenes of the dead were even more appalling. The bloated red-coated torso of a soldier or officer, his rank no longer identifiable, lay on the top step of a brick building, in front of a gaping door frame. A leg belonging to that corpse or perhaps another, lay in the mud of a crater nearby.

They quick-marched through the desolate streets and took up guard at a low stone building, that had been shielded from much of the Allied bombardment by a four-foot high brick wall. A Georgian style mansion to the rear had also offered some protection, first by drawing fire and then as a barrier before it was pounded into rubble by constant cannon fire.

"This is one of the British Regiment's commissaries," Lieutenant Tew said, pulling his mount up before the arched wooden double doors. "Inside, are food stuffs, clothing, bedding and barrels of rum." He paused studying the men standing before him.

"Sergeant Henderson! You are under orders to protect this commissary until relieved. You may avail yourselves of blankets to keep warm. Under no circumstances are you to break open the barrels." He waited for Henderson to acknowledge he understood, and then led the rest of the company down a darkened street to take up another position.

"Corporal Traynor!" Henderson barked. "Take two men and bring out blankets for all." The Sergeant directed the other members of the platoon to gather together whatever they thought would burn and start a fire. They removed their bayonets and used them to hack at the wood from broken wagons, crates and splintered barrels. In short order, they had fires going about twenty feet in front of the two corners of the commissary. The orange flames cast enlarged shadows of the armed Americans against the stones, making it seem as if giants were on guard.

"Corporal?" one of the soldiers asked Traynor as he stood warming his hands near the fire, a blanket draped over his shoulders. "Are there boots and shoes within? I could use a pair to replace these scraps of leather and cover my bloody toes."

"That is enough of that," Traynor replied brusquely. "The clothing and shoes in all of the commissaries will be distributed fairly and equally to our soldiers in need. There will be no independent purloining in Lieutenant Tew's company."

"It makes sense to me," another soldier said in the darkness. "It seems though everyone has access to rum, except us. It would warm our insides and help us through this cold night." As if to support his claim, they heard drunken shouts of British soldiers singing and cursing in the streets nearby.

"You heard the Lieutenant," Caleb said. "We are not a drunken rabble of defeated soldiers. We are proud, God-fearing New Jersey men. Today, we saw that Providence is with us. Tomorrow. . ." He was interrupted by cries of "On to the Commissary! Come on boys."

A large mass of drunken, unarmed British soldiers surged out of the darkness toward their fires. "There it is! The rum is inside for the taking, my lads." They stopped in front of the line of Americans, surprised to see them barring the way.

"What is this?" a heavy-set man in the lead cried out. "'Tis our rum and we have come to get it and no scummy rebels are going to stop us." He tilted his canteen back and took a long continuous swallow. He tipped it upside down to show it was empty. "We are running out now and need more. It is our due! Now, out of the way you traitorous bastards." Behind him the mass of soldiers, unarmed and drunk, shouted their agreement.

Sergeant Henderson stepped in front of the fire. "You men will disperse." He raised his hand and Traynor shouted, "Front rank! Make ready!" The men threw off their blankets. The sound of twelve muskets being cocked had a sobering effect on the drunken Redcoats. Their leader retreated a step while those behind him, safe in the dark shouted more curses at the Americans.

Seeing that the Continentals were not backing down and a hostile attitude toward the Americans had not persuaded them to step aside, the heavy set man approached them again. "Why do you confront us so," he said, in a cajoling manner. "The siege is over. You have won. We have surrendered. Why cannot we have a drink, together – as comrades in arms?"

"State your Regiment! Where are your officers?" Henderson asked. The drunken Redcoats erupted in laughter. "Our officers? Why they were invited and are dining with yours, stuffing themselves with fine foods and wines, sitting down with those fancy Frenchies and the like."

"Yeah," a voice yelled from the crowd. "Nice and warm they are before some fire, finishing off their dinner with port and brandy."

"And what do we have for our portion," voice cried out angrily. "Nothing but our rum and the ruins of this shithole to shelter us."

As they continued pleading for access to the barrels of rum, the Redcoats spread out, until some outflanked the line of Americans on either side of the commissary. One soldier edged forward and seized a bayonet that had been carelessly left lying on a splintered crate. Stumbling drunkenly and seething with all the shame and anger at being confronted by rebel soldiers, he rushed at Traynor and stabbed him in the chest. Wade, standing next to Traynor, turned and plunged his bayonet into the Redcoat's stomach so forcefully it pierced the man's back. He withdrew the blade, cast his musket to the side and sat astride the dying soldier, smashing his head against the hard ground, oblivious to the drunken mob that had hastily retreated down the street. Fearful of being killed by a volley from the shocked and outraged Americans, they disappeared around a corner.

Caleb cradled Traynor's shoulders in his arms, as blood oozed from the corner of the Corporal's mouth. He tried to speak as his mouth filled with blood. A horrible gurgle came from his throat and his head fell to one side. Caleb remained holding Traynor, questioning over and over in his mind, why this senseless death now O Lord? After all he has been through. Why now?[5]

—⁂—

John Stoner had almost soiled his breeches when Will called his name. He was fearful of being shot in the back and then of being cut down by Will as he returned on this same road. If he got past him, his brother would hunt him down in Yorktown and kill him with impunity. When the 17th Light Dragoons had added their fuzees to the pile of muskets and looped back to pass once more between the lines of French and American troops, John had slouched so low in the saddle that Lieutenant Chatsworth had reprimanded him for not sitting up straight as trooper. John altered his posture only after he was sure they had ridden past the place where his brother had been.

Late in the afternoon, when the British officers received invitations to dine with their counterparts amongst the victorious Americans and French forces, John feigned illness. If he went into the American camp, Will would find him easily. He imagined Will would seize him by the throat and strangle him. Or challenge him to a duel that very evening and shoot him through the heart, or worse, intentionally fire to maim him for life. His imagination ran rampant as he stalked through the Yorktown ruins, covering his nose with a handkerchief to block out the stench of human corpses, dead horses and rotting amputated limbs.

Where to hide when Will came looking for him? At first, he thought of the Nelson House, Lord Cornwallis's headquarters, abandoned at the height of the siege as shot and shell rained down, and then reclaimed during the cease fire. There would be orderlies and some of the General's staff and even his black servants about. But what protection could they offer? Will would arrive with an armed patrol and simply take him away. That the terms of surrender allowed British officers to give their word and remain free of imprisonment would carry little weight with his brother.

Quickly, he rejected remaining in the ruined barracks with the troopers. He had always been an outsider and they had treated him as such. "Ramrod John" they called him to his face and knew him to be a coward. Worse, they recognized he was not a gentleman born but the son of an upstate New York farmer. Their condescending manner was evident in all manner of dealing with him. With their idiotic sense of honor they would suggest Will challenge his brother to a duel and gleefully provide the seconds and witnesses.

No, he would have to find a safe place to hide and wait until the morning when there would be more senior officers around.

They would demand that the surrender terms be honored.

Having resolved this, John scurried along the cratered streets, keeping to the shadows and avoiding the noisy clusters of drunken soldiers cursing and carousing their way through town. Damn, he thought. Why had not someone thought to keep some officers in camp to maintain some discipline. He headed toward the Grace Church. It was one of the few buildings to survive the intense bombardment with its thick marl walls and low steeple. He was familiar with its interior. The troopers had sacked the church of its pews for firewood and even stabled their horses inside to protect them from the cannonades.

The moon had not yet risen and the church was dark as he approached. The arched door was ajar and a collective low moaning came from the interior. The only distinguishable words he heard repeatedly were "water" and "help me." He stood on the porch undecided what to do. John yelped in terror as a hand grabbed at his ankle and slid off the leather of his boot. He bent down and stared at the face of a young Negro laborer, shivering with the ague. He pushed open the broken door to the church. The sharp metallic sound of the broken hinges stirred those inside. The calls for help and water increased in volume. In the dim light, John saw a mass of black bodies on the floor, some lying so still they must be dead, others feebly rising up on their elbows to beg for help. He turned and fled back into the night.[6]

He ran awkwardly toward the beach, the boots chaffing his feet, one hand on his sword, the other one pumping up and down. Panting heavily from the exertion, he recognized he was near the Customs House, or that was what it had been before the British had arrived. The clapboard structure with multiple dormers had been stripped of its wood by the Negro laborers to reinforce the fortifications. What was left had been destroyed during the siege. He recalled there were stone outbuildings, one covering a well, the other, lower than the first, perhaps a storage or smokehouse. Once, when the troopers had exercised their horses riding up and down the beach, which it was possible to do before the rebel scum with their French allies had shown up, he had seen sentries guarding one of the stone buildings.

John thought it safer to move closer to the bluffs and away from the openness of the beach. No telling if there would be American patrols ready to assert their authority and harass a lone British officer. He crossed an exposed area between two bluffs with trepidation and hid in the shadow of the first stone house. The moon had just risen and the sounds of drunken revelry continued unabated from the streets beyond the beach. This was the well house. The thick door had been shattered by axes. Judging by the whiteness of the splinters this had been done recently. John looked furtively around and ducked inside. It was empty except for the well, rope and bucket on the floor and a large wooden trough with iron handles. This will do as a place to spend the night, John concluded, settling himself in a corner and wrapping his cloak around his shoulders. He unsheathed his sword and laid it across his knees, feeling all the better to see the glint of the blade in the sliver of light coming from the small, square window.

In the security of his hideaway, John began to reason a way out of his dilemma. British officers were required to sign an affidavit of parole. Once that was done, they were free to proceed to either New York or Charleston, or some other port held by the British and not take up arms against the Colonists until an official exchange for a Continental Officer.[7]

John had no intention of ever going into battle again. He would be among the first to sign this affidavit and wheedle his way on to the earliest ship for New York. He preferred the sea. If he traveled overland, he would not be safe from Will's pursuit until he reached Paulus Hook opposite Staten Island. John would gladly give up his horse and his liaison role with the Light Dragoons for a berth on any ship taking him away from Yorktown.

The more he thought of it, the more confident he became he could pull it off. But then, in a moment of panic, he saw a flaw. If the Americans required the British officers to sign the parole affidavit in front of them, Will would be there waiting for him. On the other hand, if the British merely had to submit signed affidavits, he was as good as safe. With this uncertainty gnawing at him, he permitted himself to doze off, with the hope that all would be resolved in his favor in the morning.

Chapter 14 - The Aftermath of Triumph

The soldiers of Colonel Dayton's 2nd Brigade, including the 3rd New Jersey and Rhode Island Regiments, stood on the parade ground, their hands loosely at their sides. It was Sunday. The Brigade Chaplain, Enoch Hunter climbed onto the flat bed of a wagon, ready to preach. At any other time, Private Caleb Wade would have been eager to hear the sermon from this good Presbyterian, a man who knew his bible well.

Yet, his mind was in turmoil, his faith shaken. How could it be that with the end in sight, Traynor was stabbed to death by one drunk Redcoat after they had beaten the entire British army? And after all Lieutenant Tew's Company had been through, starving and sick at Jockey Hollow in '79, the British cannons blasting away at them and the vicious hand to hand fighting with Skinner's hated Jersey Volunteers at Connecticut Farms. It was so senseless and meaningless a death. If God was with them, why had He forsaken Traynor at this moment when it was all but over?

Wade had gone through his friend's haversack and found the letter from the dead man's sister. Perhaps the Corporal had nothing more to live for. Yet his newborn daughter, named for his wife who had died bearing her, could be alive. He owed it to Traynor to find out, to meet the sister and tell her how her brother had died. To tell her how he had fought courageously at Yorktown. No! To tell her that Traynor had saved him after he had shot two of the ringleaders of the mutiny at a range so close he saw their skulls disintegrate and their brains splatter the snow - when he was so tormented by his actions, he thought of taking his own life.

Wade claimed Traynor's winnings from the wagering on when the British would surrender. Twelve dollars worth in pieces of eight. No one doubted him when he said he would deliver the hard currency to Traynor's new born daughter.

The Chaplain had chosen the one hundred and fifteenth psalm for his text. With a loud voice, turning first to his right and then his left, he boomed out a paean of praise for the Lord:

"Not unto us, O Lord, not unto us, but unto thy name give glory for thy mercy and for thy truth's sake." As the Chaplain called on them to recall how God had raised a mighty fog enabling them to escape across the East River in '76, there was a restless shifting in the ranks as the men realized he intended to detail five more years of retreats, bitter winters and bloody battles while they stood there in the chill fall air.

Wade was captivated by Reverend Hunter's cadence and tone more than the words. He perked up at the reference to the glorious victory at Yorktown.

"Not unto our commanders and armies, though they have behaved themselves so valiantly – yet give glory not unto them but unto the name of God, for He it was who girded our soldiers with courage and strength. It is the Lord our God who has fought for us in every successful battle, and has supported our righteous cause against those who hate us without any just reason. O Sing unto the Lord a new song, for His right hand and His holy arm hath gotten him this victory."

The Chaplain paused and looked toward the distant rows of neat white tents of the French camp.

"We thank God for the stalwart aid of our French Allies, who with the sacrifice of their blood on this battlefield, have become our brothers before the Lord." Caleb knew the Frenchies were Catholic and was not sure who or how they worshipped. Their chaplains wore enough gold braid to pass for generals but it did not seem to matter to Hunter. So Wade was inclined to give thanks to the

Frenchies as well. The Reverend was pacing back on forth on the wagon platform and coming to the climax of his sermon.

"Oh, give thanks to the Lord our God for our brave General, the Commander-in-Chief, of all our armies. A virtuous and humane General possessed of such unparalleled fortitude and patience, I venture to say of that true patriot and most excellent hero, that if you search for faults in his conduct, you will find none. . ." Here Hunter paused for dramatic effect.

"unless you call it a fault to exercise compassion and lenity toward those negligent and guilty offenders, who by their sloth or disobedience to the best orders, counteract the wisest plans and frustrate the best schemes of military discipline.

"I see the illustrious Washington, with but two or three thousand men retreating indeed before ten or twelve thousand of the enemy, but checking their progress through the countryside. Oh America, give glory to God for such a faithful hero! Then your countrymen saw him, greatly resolved to be the bulwark of liberty or fall in its defense, surrounded by you his courageous followers, until on this now sacred field, you achieved a glorious victory over your enemies and ensured liberty for all our people. The end of the war is nigh. Soon you will return to your hearth and home. Do not be startled by unanticipated sufferings that may follow. Bear them like all men, and refrain from profane swearing and all ungodly acts. Live the lives of true Christians and recall you were courageous soldiers who served the Lord under the wise, compassionate and virtuous General Washington." [1]

In a pent up release of energy, previously constrained by military discipline, the soldiers erupted spontaneously into huzzah's for General Washington, exuberantly throwing their tri-corns in the air, catching them and tossing them up again. Now, they could publicly cheer their victory, anticipate the end of the war and the return to their farms and towns.

Caleb joined in the tumultuous shouting. He took to heart the message that when the war ended there might be tribulations of a different sort. The grief he felt over the death of Traynor was one such tribulation. If he continued to live his life as a good Christian, then God would be with him, no matter what. When they marched through Williamsburg, he would ask the Lieutenant for leave to visit Vose at the hospital. To tell him first of Traynor's death and then of the Chaplain's sermon and perhaps wean Vose away from his rum and ungodly ways.

Two days after the surrender, five gallows were erected on the west side on the field where the defeated Redcoats and Hessians had cast down their arms. According to camp rumor, the location was supposed to have been chosen by General Washington himself to associate desertion with the shame of surrender, to afford a large enough space for every division and brigade to muster and see the punishment that awaited deserters.

Major General Benjamin Lincoln's entire division was assembled on this chill morning as the mist lifted off the meadow grass. The men stomped their feet to keep warm, still buoyed by the exhilaration of victory and the hope that the war was over. The men of the 2nd Rhode Islanders, flanked by their regimental officers and the Lieutenants of each company, waited in straight lines for Colonel Israel Angell, to address them. Their Colonel sat patiently on his mare, until he determined the men were properly settled. He trotted his mount forward, stood up in the stirrups and in his broad, unmistakable, familiar Rhode Island accent praised them for their courage before the British guns of Yorktown and announced the good news - Captain Olney was recovering at the military hospital in Williamsburg. The men gave a hearty cheer, startling the nearby regiments. Lieutenant Tew, rode forward as the Colonel backed his horse up a few lengths. He removed a paper from underneath his jacket and held it up in one hand.

"By order of the American Commissary of Prisoners, approved by Major Generals Lincoln, Lafayette and Von Steuben and Brigadier Generals Knox, Wayne and Gist, this twenty first day of October, the following men, having been surrendered within the garrison of the enemy and been examined and proven to have previously been enlisted in the Continental Army of the United

States, are deemed deserters and shall be hanged by the neck until dead."

Tew read the list. Private Mingo Power counted seventeen names. The ranks stiffened as five men, their hands tied behind their backs, their heads bare, led by a drummer boy and escorted by two squads of armed soldiers were paraded in front of the ranks. Two of the men were sobbing and one cried out in loud and piteous wails – "Oh God. I am so sorry. Please forgive me. Let me live. Oh God, please help me."

As the condemned men reached the end of the ranks of soldiers and saw, for the first time the empty gallows awaiting them, two of them dropped to their knees screaming and had to be lifted and dragged forward. Mingo heard one begging the chaplain who followed them to intercede on their behalf, whether it was with God or the military authority that had condemned them, he did not know.[2] At the command, "Eyes Right," they turned their heads and watched as one after another of the five mounted the scaffold, were blindfolded, some still pleading for their lives until the trap doors opened and they hung lifeless with their necks broken.

"With the war over, what would be the harm in sparing their lives and giving them the lash," Mingo muttered to Jeremiah Warmsley who stood next to him.

"You would not have thought that way if there was the certainty of more battles to be fought," he replied. They trudged back to camp in loose order, keeping to the east side of the Hampton Road as company after company led by their regimental colors, drums beating and fifes playing marched past heading in the opposite direction.

"Another morning of drills?" a passing soldier called out. "No," came the reply. "'Tis the hanging of the deserters, poor bastards." That comment started a fierce shouted debate as to whether the punishment was too harsh, or just, with soldiers loudly arguing amongst themselves.

Bant paid no attention to the rowdiness of the passing troops until he heard the word hanging. "What hanging they talking about?" he asked McNeil who was beside him.

"As near as I can tell, it seems we are all marching to witness the hanging of deserters on Surrender Field. Something about the General making an example of them. To encourage us not to desert," he said. "Although if the war is over with, there is no reason to desert, that is even if I was inclined to do so."

The closer they came to the field, the more agitated Bant became. I cannot watch men be hanged and see them swinging afterwards, he thought. No. It is too much to bear. I have caused enough deaths by hanging through my own cowardice. He slowed half a pace and darted out between the ranks, holding his rifle loosely at his side and dashed off into the woods. No officer saw him and he knew McNeil would not betray him. He was Bant's only friend. The others thought he was possessed. Some of them called him a "lunatick." No matter. After it was all over, he would come out of the woods and return to camp.

The fall leaves crunched under his moccasins as he hurried to get as far away from the hanging field as he could. He glanced apprehensively over his shoulder and stopped only when he could no longer see the meadow and the mass of assembled troops. He eased himself down with his back against a tree trunk, his long rifle resting on his knees. Four Continentals appeared at the edge of a clearing to his left, two armed with muskets and the others carrying axes with three foot long hardwood handles. They noticed Bant as they scanned the clearing and the trees bordering it, waved to him and skirted the edge of the sunlit meadow.

The leader introduced himself at Sergeant Henry Gillet. "This is Private Gideon Hazzard," he said nodding at the Negro. "We are both with the Sappers and Miners Corps. These other two are our former brothers in arms with the 2nd Rhode Islanders. What regiment are you with?" he asked in a friendly manner.

"Virginia Riflemen," Bant answered vaguely, noting the white V on Gillet's left arm, indicating he had been serving in the Continental Army for at least three years. The solid stocky Negro, the other one carrying a musket, appraised Bant carefully.

"We are hunting pigs. They run loose in these woods. For farm animals they are devilishly skittish," he added ruefully. "We cannot get in range before they scent us and take off." The Negro soldier scratched his head and pointed to Bant's long rifle. "You any good with that?"

When Bant stood up, the four men could see his rifle was a shade taller than he was.

"Better than some, worse than others," he said, repressing a desire to boast about his prowess.

Gillet grinned at his modesty.

"If we get a pig, you will get you a share of the meat," Gillet offered. Bant thought it over. He was not quick and did not want to be outsmarted by these fast talking Yankees. Yet it would be nice to bring back fresh meat for his messmates.

"A hind quarter will do," he replied and then quickly added, "whether it is my shot that kills it or not."

"That seems fair enough," Gillet said and the five entered the woods, heading west away from the camp and the river. The trees thinned and soon they were moving through brambles and low lying shrubs. As they crouched behind the remains of a weathered rail fence, Hazzard who was acting as the scout, spotted two large sows, rooting at the edge of a burned corn field. He put his arm out in warning and then pointed.

Bant estimated the distance to be under two hundred yards, an easy shot. The light midday breeze was blowing toward them. The pigs' keen sense of smell was of no avail. He aimed for the eye of the larger of the two sows, thinking he should also have asked for the pigs' jowls. A blue jay screeched a warning too late as he fired. The sow went down. With a squeal of fright, the other pig dashed into the bushes beyond.

The men eagerly raced through the stubs of cornstalks and quickly set to work butchering the pig.

"That other pig may not be far away," Gillet said as he watched Bant ram in the powder cartridge and test the ball in his hand for roundness before dropping it down the barrel.

"Another haunch and the jowls as well," Bant replied. "Done," and the two of them set off after the second sow. With the breeze still blowing toward them, they spotted her grubbing in a pile of corn stalks at the edge of the next field. Bant brought her down with another well-aimed killing shot.

Using the thick ropes they carried, they hoisted the two pigs up so they hung from stout tree limbs a few feet from the ground. Bant sat several yards away from the pools of blood that had immediately attracted swarms of flies, as the four soldiers, stripped to their breeches, bled and gutted the pigs. Even after field dressing, each pig weighed close to two hundred pounds. They cut down saplings, tied the carcasses on the poles, slung them over their shoulders and headed back to camp.

"No need for you to carry," Gillet said to Bant, with the other men readily agreeing. "You did all the shooting." Bant nodded his acceptance and said nothing. He was more concerned about whether they would approach the camp from the woods beyond Surrender Field and pass the gallows. Maybe the deserters' bodies were still hanging there, with their necks broken and their breeches stained with their shit. He shuddered at the thought, trudging with his head down, bringing up the rear of the hunting party, although, since he was unencumbered, he was capable of walking much faster.

Despite the clouds of flies and mosquitos that followed them in the late afternoon, the soldiers were in a jovial mood, anticipating the fresh pork they would enjoy not only for dinner but for several more meals as well. Ahead, a line of soldiers, perhaps twenty in number, were spaced out across a field, ropes looped over their shoulders, searching for someone or something. Two of them noticed the hunters and the pigs they were carrying and veered off from their brethren methodically moving toward the woods.

"You seen any of the Negroes the British turned loose from Yorktown?" one shouted, in a broad New England accent. "Their owners are offering one guinea a piece for each one brought in," the other said, gleeful at the thought of easily earned money.[3]

The four soldiers laid the gutted pigs on the ground and flexed their tired shoulder muscles. Hazzard stood rigidly to the side, his musket held firmly across his chest, his expression fixed and tense.

"What is your Regiment?" one asked Gillet. "When we get

paid, I want to come by and purchase some of that tasty fresh pork you have there."

"No need," Henry said sullenly. "This meat is for our messmates and 'tis not for sale." He gestured toward Hazzard to make sure the two Yankees understood. "Him and me are with the Sappers and Miners. There are a lot of our messmates to feed."

They entered the camp by way of the Williamsburg road, their happiness of the hunt and the anticipation of a fine pork roast, dampened by their encounter with the slave catching soldiers. Their mood improved as they passed others relieved of duty, idling by the road, who greeted them with shouts of appreciation. Some asked for the bristles and bones. Others offered to have their regimental baker put the hogs in their oven, asking only for a shank or prime cut in payment. All but Hazzard responded good-naturedly to the congratulations and comments. As they paraded triumphantly down the road, a tall man standing on a wagon to the side hailed them.

"Those had better not be my pigs you killed." He was wearing a long maroon colored topcoat over a waistcoat, embroidered with silver thread to match the buttons. A clean tan planter's hat covered his head to keep the sun off his pale skin.

"And who might you be," Gillet asked slowing his pace as they approached the rear of the wagon. Three emaciated, sad faced Negroes in rags sat in the back of the wagon, slumped against the rough boards.

"I am John Bannister come to reclaim my Negrahs taken by the British when they plundered my plantation south of Petersburg." He had the broad slow accent of the Tidewater Virginians. "They took my horses, cattle and pigs off as well as eighty-two of my best slaves." He waved casually toward the poor wretches in the back. "And now look at them. It will take a month before they are fit for any decent work. All I have left are some old wooly haired men, bent and toothless women and a few children too young to cut tobacco leaves."

"These sows were running loose in the woods," Gillet replied.

"Besides, the starving besieged Redcoats would have eaten your pigs long ago."

"I say they are mine and belong up on this wagon."

"I care not a whit for what you say," Gillet said angrily. "These pigs are ours."

"Who is your commanding officer? I will report your theft and insolence to him," the planter shouted turning red in the face.

Other soldiers on the road, drawn to the argument began taunting the planter with cries of derision and showering him with insults and curses.

"Take it up with General Washington, you loud-mouthed assbag," one yelled.

"Where were you when they recruited in Virginia? Hiding in your tobacco barn while we were fighting Cornwallis for you, I wager."

"Look at this dandy all dressed up for a fancy ball with his silver buttons and embroidered waistcoat," one soldier said, grabbing the side of the wagon and rocking it hard. "You are lucky we do not tar and feather you as a Loyalist sympathizer. Tell us what you are," he demanded. "A coward or a bloody Tory."

Other soldiers joined the first one, taking hold of one side of the wagon. They would have tipped it over and handled the planter roughly, if two mounted officers had not come up the road and intervened. While the soldiers shouted their complaints and accusations against the man, demanding the officers dispense justice, Gillet signaled they should take up the slings and move on.

Hazzard slung the pole on to his right shoulder and glared at Gillet. "Our own brother soldiers, out hunting these poor escaped slaves for a guinea. I would rather be left in the woods to starve and die then to be enslaved again," he hissed.

"You are a free man," Gillet said emphatically.

"If I were given the choice," Hazzard said, "I would never return to being a slave. Never."

They stopped first at the camp of the Rhode Islanders and cut off two hind quarters and one head off a sow. It was obvious that it was too much for Bant to carry by himself. Hazzard went with him, the two haunches in a sack over his shoulder, dripping a bloody trail on the well-worn path to the Virginia Militia's tents. The black Private could sense the hostility of some of the men. Even though he was a Continental, they saw him as a Negro, and if he stayed there, would treat him as such. Still, he could not resist reaching out and hugging Bant around the shoulders, thanking him loudly for his two killing shots.

Returning to the encampment of the 2nd Rhode Islanders, Gideon thought over Gillet's proposal. They would resign from the Sappers and Miners Corps and return to their old Regiment. There would be no promotion for him either way. It would be good to be around his old messmates, Mingo and Warmsley and the other blacks of the disbanded 1st. He had been treated decently in the Sappers and Miners, but he was the only Negro in the ranks. He would wait to see what their orders were. If they stayed down south, he would ask for a transfer. It would be unbearable to remain in Virginia. He needed the comfort of being with his own kind, back north.

—⚜—

The road from Yorktown to Williamsburg was clogged with Continental soldiers, marching with a spring to their step, confident that at the end of an easy thirteen-mile march, they would sleep in a camp away from the stench of death that hung over the siege lines. The smiles and laughter were those of men who had defeated the hated British and were now looking forward to furloughs and even receiving some of their back pay. Many talked of the war being over and being able to return to their farms and towns for good.[4] Others had been able to scrounge around the ruins of Yorktown before leaving and carried in their haversacks, odd pieces of silverware, sconces and the like. Items to barter for rum, food and soap, with the townspeople of Williamsburg.

Captains Hadley and Holmes, together with newly promoted Master Sergeant Adam Cooper, rode into town ahead of their artillery regiment. Adam who was more comfortable on water than mounted, managed the broad-backed plow horse reasonably well for a former Mariner.

Rows of neat white tents, many of them captured from the British and Hessians, lined the fields on the outskirts of Williamsburg. Their orderliness and the clear blue late October sky contrasted with the grim picture of bodies piled outside church yards, as pairs of soldiers dug fresh graves for those who had died at the hospital.

All of the structures of the College of William and Mary - from the elegant main brick building with its white trimmed windows and portico to the plain wooden framed structures, previously used as storage, housing, maintenance, and stables - now served as a hospital for the wounded and diseased soldiers, evacuated from Yorktown during the siege.

Adam dismounted awkwardly and went inside the large brick building to make inquiries. He emerged with an exasperated look on his face.

"They say they have not yet compiled lists of either those being treated or," he paused and swallowed hard, "those who have died. The orderly suggested we either find our Regimental Surgeon or inquire at the former Governor's Palace in the middle of town. He heard there they were writing down the names."

Adam waved off Hadley's offer to help him remount and walked the remaining quarter of a mile, leading his docile horse behind him. Occasionally, he shook his head from side to side trying to rid himself of the ringing within. The noise was not as loud as before. It was more like chimes from a hand bell one used to summon a servant, but constant.

By a stroke of luck, they encountered Dr. Timothy Thaxter in the vast great hall, instructing some women who had newly volunteered as nurses.

He shook his head in frustration as the women hurriedly left. "There are more than one thousand sick, most with ague, fevers and the blood flux and a few wounded. We lack everything," the Regimental Surgeon said gloomily – "food, vinegar and wine, chamber pots, blankets, straw for bedding and the like. The women of the town help with the nursing. There is only so much they can do. Far too often I am afraid, it is only to hold the hand of a dying soldier and give him comfort in his last moments."

"We are looking for Will Stoner," Hadley said. His voice was tense, waiting to hear the worst.

"Ah, Lieutenant Stoner," Thaxter said with a smile, as Hadley, Holmes and Adam breathed an audible sigh of relief. "He is upstairs on the west side, close to the end of the inner row. If I had been allowed to bleed him more, perhaps the fever would not have returned," he added, recalling how Hadley had challenged his medical knowledge.

They found Will lying in a crowded ward of feverish men, the windows wide open to provide relief from the stink of accumulated human waste, vomit, and blood. His face was skeletal, the weathered skin drawn tight over his flushed cheeks. Even under the blanket, lying on a thin pallet of linen filled with straw, his wasted frame shook with the chills that accompanied the fever.

The diseased soldiers lay feet to feet, with a narrow corridor between them for the doctors and nurses. Adam, who had seen enough dead men during the war, nevertheless quivered as he noticed that the young soldier lying two over from Will was definitely gone. His unshaven jaw hung open and his eyes stared sightlessly at the ornate, yellow and white painted ceiling. Why do they cramp all of those with fever in large rooms? The very air was unhealthy. Soldiers in the camps talked frequently about how the sick recovered better when housed in small sheds or homes.

"This recurrence is not good," Hadley said softly, removing his tri-corn and running his fingers through his thick shock of dark brown hair. "He was weak to begin with from the rain and cold." He stepped aside to make room for a matronly woman making her way toward their end of the ward. She wore a stained bib and apron over her normal dress and her grey hair was covered by a puffy white cap with a large white cockade.

"Would one of you hold up his head while I feed him?" she asked kneeling next to Will and dipping a wooden ladle into a round iron pot.

Adam placed both of his hands under Will's head, feeling his clammy skin and hair damp with sweat. As he propped Will up, his friend opened his eyes, recognized him and smiled faintly.

"Adam. It is you. You have come for me yet again." Adam nodded.

"Yes, Will. I am here."

"What is it you feed him?" Nat asked the nurse, pointing at the pot.

"It is a posset of wine, water, vinegar and crackers," she replied. "We give it twice a day, four ladles per serving.[5] As Adam held Will's head steady she carefully spooned his ration into his open mouth.

"'Tis good that you are eating," Adam said softly. "Soon you will regain your strength," hoping that it would be true.

The nurse motioned for Hadley and Holmes to accompany her. "Your friend rages and calls out for John, that he is coming after him and will kill him. Other times, he sobs for Elisabeth and begs her forgiveness."

Hadley bit his lip and lowered his eyes, not wanting the kindly woman to see he was overcome. "Elisabeth is his wife," he said by way of explanation, clearing his throat. "Do not get the wrong impression. He has done nothing for her to forgive, other than being bed-ridden with this fever and unable to return to her as soon as possible."

"Who is this John he wants to kill?"

"John is his brother, a Loyalist and a trooper in the Light Dragoons."

The matron gasped and immediately grabbed Hadley's arm. "I was widowed by British cavalry when they rampaged through our farm outside Petersburg, not more than six months ago. They murdered my husband as he tried to protect me and our daughter." Her eyes opened wide in horror as she relived the moment. "One trooper cut him down in our yard, splitting his skull open with a saber."

Hadley and Nat let her regain her composure before asking the question they wanted answered.

"Will our friend recover?"

She shrugged. "I am no doctor and our apothecary's shelves are empty. Still, I have familiarity with these fevers and agues. Those who burn with the fever and rage in anger have a force to live that those who lie meekly and accept their fate do not." She wiped her hands on her apron. "I suggest you pray for his recovery. I will also, for the reason I wish him to ride away from here and seek out his brother. To avenge my dearly deceased husband, even though his brother's sword may not have been the one to strike him down."

The next morning, when they visited Will, he seemed slightly stronger. Adam said it was their hopes that made it seem so. He insisted there had been no change, but Hadley and Holmes disagreed. They stayed with Will that afternoon and at night, agreed that Adam would remain in Williamsburg with Will. He did not know where his wife Sarah was, whether at West Point or somewhere south of there. Hadley and Holmes would ride on, Samuel home to Morristown to be with his wife and greet his newborn son for the first time. Nat would seek out a schooner or other vessel in Baltimore and return to Salem by sea.

"I hope to find my sweet Anna and my two sons, John and Benjamin, the little one, in good health."

"It is dangerous to travel up the New England coast what with British frigates prowling the seas," Adam observed. "It will be safer to travel overland with the army. It took us a mere three weeks from Dobbs Ferry to Yorktown."

"In September, the British Navy was beaten by the French men of war and have learned their lesson," Nat replied confidently. "They will keep to their safe harbor of New York. And three days at sea is far better than three weeks by land," he said merrily, anticipating the feel of a deck beneath his feet and the smell of the ocean's salt air.

The following morning before departing, Hadley and Holmes, accompanied by Adam, went to the hospital to say goodbye to Will. General Knox was conferring with Dr. Thaxter, towering over the smaller man like a tall, wide oak over a squat shrub.

Knox greeted them with his usual infectious optimism. "The

lad is getting better. I am certain of it. Why this morning, he asked me if Big Red was being taken care of. A man does not think of his horse, unless he intends to ride again and soon."

"It will be a few days before he is strong enough to ride in a wagon, let alone mount a horse," Dr. Thaxter said. "I warn you if he leaves before he is ready, the fever will come back while he is on the road."

The General put his arm around the surgeon's shoulder and squeezed him hard. "But you do agree he is improving, do you not?" Thaxter nodded, although to Adam it seemed he did so reluctantly.

"Will made me an unusual request," the General went on. "At first, I thought it was a product of the fever effecting his mind. He demanded to know how to find the destination of a paroled British officer captured at Yorktown."

"Tis his brother" Hadley explained. "He assaulted Elisabeth in Philadelphia and Will has vowed to kill him."

Knox for once was speechless. "Well," he finally said, gathering his thoughts. "When he reaches Philadelphia to be reunited with his wife and son, the chief of the Commissary of Prisoners of War will be able to provide him with that information. His Elisabeth is nanny to my daughter Lucy, while my dearest wife enjoys the hospitality of His Excellency and his wife at Mt. Vernon. There she shall deliver to us another babe within the fortnight." [6]

"Sir? Does Will know Elisabeth is in Philadelphia?" Hadley asked.

Knox nodded. "Of course," he boomed out too loudly. "I told him myself when I received a letter from Lucy. That was before the siege began. All the lad needs now is rest and nourishment." Knox laughed. "Yesterday evening I brought the lad a mutton pie when I visited after having dined with Rector Blair. However, I am certain 'tis the desire to be reunited with Elisabeth that improves his condition."

"We too, wish to be reunited with our wives," Hadley said, explaining that he and Holmes would be leaving by mid-day on furlough and Adam would accompany Will to Philadelphia.

"Well Master Sergeant Cooper," Knox said, putting his thick

hand on Adam's shoulder. "Affix the proper white cockade to your tri-corn to distinguish your rank and bring Will safely to the bosom of his family." He turned to Dr. Thaxter. "I trust you will look in on the lad, assess his improving condition and release him, when appropriate."

"I will rely upon my best medical knowledge to determine when that moment shall be," Thaxter said, preserving some modicum of dignity by asserting it was his decision to make.

Adam and Will left Williamsburg on the third of November, delayed one day by a cold rainstorm and Dr. Thaxter's absolute refusal to let him depart in such bone-chilling weather. Will for his part, rejected the Doctor's suggestion to travel by wagon. He mounted Big Red unaided, wincing from the pain of the effort, and settled himself in the saddle, unaccustomed to being on a horse since the surrender two weeks ago.

The first one hundred miles or so to the Maryland border were the roughest for both of them. During the day, they passed militias from Maryland and Delaware marching eagerly north, making good progress to achieve the reward of lengthy furloughs. Toward nightfall, after covering about thirty miles, Will and Adam stopped and inquired about lodging in a house near the road. The woman who answered the door explained while she had no objection to their staying, an elderly lady close to death was within and she did not want to disturb perhaps her last moments on earth.

Adam did not wait to hear any further explanations. They remounted and rode on.

"Just a pretense to avoid giving hospitality to a uniformed black man," he said bitterly.

Will, who had not thought that was the reason at all responded, "'Twas my impression there were no men of the house about. The ladies simply did not want to admit either of us."

They proceeded in silence as darkness fell. Ahead, a broad turnoff led to a substantial brick house, well lit on the first floor by candles visible through the un-shuttered windows. Will left Big Red standing in the yard and knocked on the door. A mostly bald elderly man, in his shirt-sleeves opened it. He appraised Will and then Adam who had tied the horses reins to a rail post and come up the front steps.

"Good evening sir. I am Lieutenant Will Stoner of General Knox's artillery regiment," he said loudly, still unable to correctly assess the volume of his own voice. The man smiled, assuming Will was simply announcing their arrival. "We are on our way from Yorktown to Philadelphia and desire lodging for the night and feed and shelter for our horses."

"The heroes of Yorktown are most welcome in my house," he said opening the door wider. "I can provide a hot meal and ale, and a hearty fire, in return for your regaling our small family with an account of the glorious victory."

As Will took a step forward, the man gestured to Adam. "Your servant can sleep in the barn. I will see to it some food is brought to him as well."

Will stopped one step short of the threshold. "This is Master Sergeant Adam Cooper of my regiment, a true hero of Yorktown. We will both partake of your hospitality within your home or within the barn."

The man stood hesitantly in his own doorway, sputtering at his natural order of things being challenged by a stranger. "I cannot have him . . ."

Will firmly cut him off. "Very well, sir. I appreciate your offer of the shelter of your barn, and any food you can provide." He turned and took Big Red's reins in his hand and led the horse toward the nearby barn. Adam followed him. They unsaddled their mounts, rubbed them down and after feeding and watering them, collected some clean straw for their own bedding in an empty stall away from the cold and wind of the entrance. They hauled some bales into the stall to lessen the drafts.

"We have slept in cold damp trenches during the siege. This is cozy by comparison," Will said. He coughed up some phlegm and Adam looked alarmed. Will shook his head and smiled indicating it was nothing.

"You should sleep in the house and I will stay here. 'Tis but one night."

"Absolutely not. I refuse. Say no more about it," Will replied, waving his hand in dismissal.

They remained silent until Adam asked, "Do you still believe the matron turned us away to avoid having men in the house?" his tone implying he thought it was otherwise.

Before Will could respond, two boys, one about fourteen, the other by the similarity of looks his younger brother, halloed from the yard outside. In the lantern light held by one, Will and Adam saw a tray laden with cheese, cured ham and bread, and two tankards of ale.

"Mother asks your pardon for not preparing a warm meal," the older one said.

"Were you really at Yorktown?" the younger one asked. He had blond spiky hair and a gap toothed grin. His voice was still high-pitched, almost squeaky in tone.

"We were," Will replied. "Master Sergeant Cooper here was the bravest amongst us, saving us from the blast of a British mortar shell that landed in our battery trench. Do you know what a battery is?" Both boys shook their heads.

"Well. Adam. Why not explain that to these young lads and how we fired shot after shot at the British and how you saved our lives." He winked at Adam, ripped a piece of bread off the loaf, cut a slice of the ham and leaned back against a bale. As Adam regaled the two boys with stories of fiery shot and shell arcing through the night sky and the glorious surrender ceremony, Will thought, he would tell his son Henry of their wartime adventures. But he would begin with his coming to the Marblehead Mariners' barracks in the winter of '76 and the beginning of his friendship with Adam.

Each day, Will found his strength returning. His cough had subsided and his joints ached less. His headaches were almost gone. Despite Adam's protestations, Will increased the pace, feeling Big Red's muscles effortlessly flow beneath him. They reached Baltimore in two more days and Adam insisted they remain there for one entire day. He disappeared, leaving Will alone to wander the city, crowded with troops passing through to the north. That night, in the one small loft they rented for the privilege of not having to share their bed with anyone else, they lay next to each other under the thin coverlet, their worn soldier's blankets on top for additional warmth.

"I was down at the port all day," Adam said. Will waited for his friend to continue. "The smell of the salt air did me some good. It cleared my mind that has been troubled of late."

"Surely you have not let that bald man refusing both of us lodging continue to gnaw at you."

"Tis more than that Will. Something you are not able to understand. I felt more dignity fighting for Colonel Tye to liberate slaves from their Whig owners in New Jersey than I did with our army at Yorktown."

Will looked over at Adam, surprised by both the vehemence of his words as well as the thought.

In the darkness, Will could not see his friend's face but he imagined his brow furrowed with deep concern and the scar from Major Murnan's cut emerging from the tight, curly hair line down part of his forehead.

"Surely you cannot mean that. You were attacking the farms and homes of men who, like us, seek to be free from the tyranny of the crown," he said indignantly. "Did you not feel proud of thwarting a plot to kidnap General Washington?"

"I acted as I did because it was the only way to buy Sarah's freedom. I did it for her. Not General Washington."

Adam was silent for a long time, letting Will absorb what he had said, something that could be deemed treasonous if repeated elsewhere.

"The cause I am fighting and risking my life for is one that permits my brother soldiers to hunt down freed slaves for a guinea. I serve under commanders who welcome slave owners to our camp and return their blacks, freed by the British, to a life of slavery. These Negroes are deemed the same as the stolen wagons and horses plundered by the Redcoats. They are only property to be reclaimed."

"General Knox did no such thing," Will said indignantly. "He is not a slave owner himself."

"I grant you that, Will. It is General Washington, as Commander-in-Chief, at whom I direct my anger.[7]

Adam exhaled loudly. "Remember when we left Morristown for the hospital at Princeton and I told you I was consumed by rage? I am once again. Even more so after seeing those poor sick wretches returned to their slave masters."

"The difference this time," Will said softly, "is Sarah is free and now your wife. Soon, you will be reunited with her and the rage you speak of will be soothed by her presence.

Adam's words were hushed and wistful. "I do miss Sarah most terribly."

He sensed Adam turn back toward him.

"I do not even know where she is or whether she is safe," he cried out in anguish. "All I desire now is to live free, as a man, with my wife, in peace and dignity. To raise a family and see my children grow. I am entitled to that after my years of service. They owe me no less than that," he concluded vehemently.

Will twisted on to his side and stared out the small window at the night sky. It was beyond his power to resolve what tore at Adam. He could not make others see him as a man and not a Negro.

Chapter 15 - Reunion in Philadelphia

Sarah hoisted herself from the chair in the kitchen. It was better to stand. The baby seemed to kick more when she was sitting, objecting to being confined and curled up in such a small space. She rolled the flour on the board, wincing at the sudden sharp pain in her ribcage. It must be a boy. He is so active. He was kicking higher up her body. That meant his head was now down. That was good. She remembered her mother telling her that as she approached the end of her own numerous pregnancies. Sarah wished her mother could be with her, although she was not afraid.

The news of the surrender of an entire British army at Yorktown had reached Philadelphia within days of the victory. Bells rang out all over the city. Sarah had joined grateful throngs at the free black Bethel church, as had congregants at churches throughout the city, thanking God for this triumph.

Sarah also prayed fervently for the safe return of her husband. The army would be marching back from Virginia. Maybe Adam would arrive in Philadelphia before she gave birth. It would be a great comfort to her to have him there. She had not written him since early May when the army went south toward New York City. Paper cost money and she was saving all her earnings for their unborn child. Adam may not even know she was pregnant. She had suspected she was before he decamped but had not told him.

Will's wife, Elisabeth, had promised she would write her husband and ask him to tell Adam of Sarah's pregnancy. Maybe

Elisabeth had not written, or the letter had not reached Will. She suppressed the thought that both Will and Adam were dead, killed at Yorktown or felled by the vile fevers she knew were prevalent in the Tidewater regions. She dreaded that when the army passed through Philadelphia, neither of their husbands would appear. That could explain why there had been no word from them. No, she reassured herself, rubbing her distended belly and feeling the baby stir within. Elisabeth's letter simply must not have reached them.

Months ago, she had traveled from near West Point by wagon, a free black woman, denied decent lodgings at modest homes and farmhouses on the roads south through New Jersey toward Philadelphia. Normally, she stayed in the servants' quarters. On a few occasions she was compelled to sleep in the stables. Somewhere, in New Jersey, the white master of the house they stopped at for the night had questioned her status and proposed she share his bed. He had slaves of his own, both house servants and field hands. She had defiantly stood up to him, recounting how General Henry Knox himself had arranged for her freedom and if he dared to lay a hand on her, he would have the men of General Knox's Artillery Regiment to contend with. He bothered her no more that night.

Upon her arrival, she was welcomed into the home of Mr. and Mrs. Absalom Jones, one of Philadelphia's many free black families.[1] Initially, she took in laundry and paid for her lodging and board with her meager earnings. Then, she began making pepper pot soups and savory meat pies and peddling them, first down at the wharves to rough workmen and sailors and then on the fringes of Market Street. The stalls of free blacks were not as well situated, nor as sturdy as those in the central market. However, people knew where to come for her pies. Her humble-meat pie, made with sheep innards, spiced with savory, sage and rosemary and simmered in crab apple juice was a favorite.

Then, one clear September market day, Elisabeth fortuitously appeared at her stall. Mutually surprised, the two women hugged, prompting many curious and in some cases, disapproving looks. They reminisced about their time at West Point and shared the anxieties they felt for their husbands who had passed through

Philadelphia in July and were now somewhere with the army in Virginia. Elisabeth confided that she had had no word from Will and this daily silence filled her with dread.

She was staying with the Lewis's, just north of Market. When Sarah visited she met twenty-month old Henry, a sweet little boy with Will's eyes who had just learned the word Papa. When he uttered that word over and over, Elisabeth's eyes filled with tears and Sarah prayed that Providence would watch over both their husbands and return them safely.

Elisabeth spread the word among her friends, the wealthy white women who entertained in their elegant salons and at their afternoon teas. Sarah Penrose, the renowned baker and cook to General Knox and the Marquis de Lafayette was living in Philadelphia. Soon, Sarah was inundated with so many orders for apple, cranberry, peach and pear pies, she had to rise well before dawn and begin baking to fulfill them. She hired three young black boys to deliver them and once they were on their way, usually shortly after noon, she would sit in a wooden arm chair in the Absalom's warm kitchen and doze, her hands crossed on her stomach, feeling the life grow within her, and dream of Adam.

—⁂—

They arrived in Philadelphia on a crisp, cold Sunday. Adam was saddle sore. They had been pushing their horses hard since dawn. Will was anxious to reach the city and took no notice of Adam's pleas for a more deliberate pace. Big Red, invigorated by the fall weather was more than willing to flex his muscles. Will held him in check as they threaded streets filled with fancy coaches, farmer's wagons and carts of every description. Although it was the Sabbath and the market was closed, many of the taverns seemed to be doing a lively business.

Somewhere a church bell rang and then another. Adam smiled to hear them. Because they were real, not just in his head. His hearing had improved to the point now where he no longer heard bells chiming. However, the ringing was still constant, a muted annoying noise, somewhat louder when he first awakened in the morning. He had learned to live with it ever since the shell had exploded in the trench.

They found a stable for their horses and walked rapidly, Will leading the way, to the Quaker area north of Market and the Lewis's home. Elisabeth would be staying there or Mary Lewis would know where she was.

"You have recovered from your bout with the fever, very well," Adam called out limping several steps behind, the muscles of his inner thighs still stretched from the ride and his lower back aching from the constant jarring.

"I am eager to find Elisabeth and Henry," Will called back over his shoulder. He sprinted up the three steps, grabbed the brass knocker in his hand and rapped it loudly. No one answered. He knocked again, if anything harder. No one came to the door.

"Perhaps they are at church," Adam suggested. "After all, 'tis Sunday and they are Quakers you say and thus religious folk."

Will debated with himself whether to walk to the Quaker Meeting House, remain here on the steps or return later. He could not disturb Mary at her worship. Never having been to a Quaker meeting, he had no idea how long it lasted. Waiting here could be interminable.

"Come," he said to Adam.

Adam groaned and rose stiffly to his feet. "Whereto?"

Will did not know himself. He felt a strong urge to keep moving to search, to roam about. The office of the Commissary of Prisoners would be closed. A visit there would have to wait until Monday. Without making a conscious decision, Will set out, away from the Quaker area of the city and the recently developed section of clapboard houses above the city boundary, toward the steeples and spires of the Philadelphia he knew. The cobblestoned streets were crowded with merchants, ladies, soldiers, workmen, wood carriers pushing wheelbarrows and even chimney sweeps with their distinctive long handled wire brushes, presumably on their way to clean the flues at homes where the Sabbath was not strictly observed. They passed tall, well-kept brick buildings that Will thought he recognized from his walks with Elisabeth. He stared at each entrance, as if willing her to emerge from the white-framed doors.

After wandering aimlessly for more than an hour, he led a tired and complaining Adam back toward the Quaker Meeting House and the Lewis's home. Ahead, in the throng of people, he noticed a tall thin man carrying a small boy on his shoulders. The little one's head turned this way and that, curious at all he could see from such a height. When he chanced to look behind him Will recognized the face of his son, no longer chubby cheeked but with the clear features of his wife. A sharp knife of fear stabbed at his heart and he gasped. If the man, whoever he was, was carrying Henry, then Elisabeth must be dead, of a fever, an accident, something to separate her from their precious child.

He roared out for the man to stop. Edward Lewis halted, a broad smile of recognition on his face. "Will. Is that you? Come relieve an elderly man of this delightful burden." He swung Henry off his shoulders and handed him to Will.

"Papa," Henry said, as Will grabbed him in his arms and threw him into the air. Will melted with joy. He pulled his son to his chest and smothered his smooth skin with kisses.

"Is Elisabeth here? Is she well? Where is she?" His questions tumbled out one after another.

"She is with Mary, calling on a friend before coming home from the meeting house."

"Adam," Will gestured. "Meet Edward Lewis, a man who has sheltered my Elisabeth for the long months she was in Philadelphia." Will put his arm around Adam's shoulder. "Master Sergeant Adam Cooper and I are old friends. He has saved my life on two occasions and protected me several times over." The two men acknowledged each other while Henry squirmed in Will's arms.

"You have a fine looking son," Adam said grinning at the little boy. "May I hold him?" Will passed Henry to his friend's outstretched arms.

Adam hugged the child to his chest. "Papa," Henry said. "Papa," he repeated, pleased with himself for saying the word.

Will looked at Edward and laughed. "He calls every man who holds him Papa, does he not?"

Edward nodded. "It has been one of my joys to have your son live with us. Now, he will have to learn who is his real father and entitled to that accolade."

They settled in the parlor of the Lewis home. Will and Adam took turns bouncing Henry on their knees to keep him occupied as they described the siege of Yorktown. Will related how Adam had smothered the mortar shell in the trench and saved their lives. Adam told of Will's near fatal bout of fever. Both men spoke in loud and animated voices, unaware of how the sounds filled the small room. Henry began to fuss and cry. Will was puzzled as what to do.

"It will take a woman's touch to persuade him to nap. He is much excited by your presence. We helpless men are saved. I hear Mary's voice at the door."

The two women continued chattering as they hung up their cloaks at the door. Will was on his feet with Adam at his side holding Henry, when Elisabeth came into the parlor. She paused in surprise and then rushed at Will, clinging to him, running her hands over his face and neck, smothering him with kisses, oblivious to the others.

"Oh my dear, dear Will. You are here, unharmed and well. You are here," she repeated, tears streaming down her cheeks.

"And Adam. You too. What do you think of our son? Soon you too will know the joys of fatherhood."

"What? What do you mean?" Adam said, shocked by her words.

"Did you not get my letter?" she turned looking at Will quizzically. "No? I wrote Will to tell you Sarah is here in Philadelphia and expecting your first child."

"Where is she? I must go to her," Adam shouted. Henry began to cry alarmed by his loud voice. Quickly, Elisabeth took the little boy from Adam's strong arms, rocked him gently and gave Adam directions to the free blacks' neighborhood of the city. With scarcely a nod, Adam grabbed his tri-corn from the coat rack and dashed out into the street, unthinkingly slamming the door behind him.

The room was quiet and peaceful.

"Now, my love, let me put our little one to sleep and then we have much to tell each other." She tenderly reached out and touched Will's cheek. "You look so thin and worn since we last were together. I pray that God who granted us the victory at Yorktown will see fit to bless us with an end to this war."

Will nodded in agreement. Whether the war ends quickly or not, he thought, there is the unfinished business with my brother. He will find out tomorrow where John had fled to and if possible, hunt him down and kill him.

―⚍―

For the next several days, Adam arose with his wife at three a.m. He could not bear to be apart from her. He watched Sarah as she assembled the ingredients for baking, rolled the flour and sorted the fruit and spices. He took on the tasks of bringing in the water and wood, building up the fire for the oven and cutting the apples, or pears for her. He hovered over her, making sure she wore her cloak when she went out, urging her to rest when she was tired and content to sit quietly and watch her while she napped in her big armchair in the kitchen. Most of all, he loved it when she would beckon to him, a pained yet joyful expression on her face and put his hand on her distended belly.

"Do you feel that Adam?" she would ask. "He knows you are here. He is kicking to say hello. He wants to meet you." Adam would nod as he felt the boy within and place his ear to her stomach. Through her clothing he imagined he could hear a heart beat although he knew it could not be true. His hearing was not back to normal. Many times, especially when others were in the kitchen talking, Sarah would have to repeat what she said to him.

At night when they lay together, Sarah propped up by pillows because it was more comfortable for her, he would tell her about Yorktown. Somehow, his recollections of the slave owners coming to the Army camp and paying soldiers to capture "their property," or the indignities he had suffered traveling with Will to Philadelphia, did not consume him with rage as before. They were injustices, an affront to his dignity as a man, but with Sarah and their as yet unborn son, he could see his way to having a life worth living in Marblehead, as a fisherman, a life back on the eternal sea. He squeezed Sarah's hand and uttered a silent prayer for the birth of a hearty, strong son, Sarah to remain healthy and a swift end to this war. In the dark Adam smiled to himself. It was possible, he thought.

End Notes

Part One – Treason of the Blackest Dye

Chapter 1 – The Raid on the Ford House

1) Most readers are familiar with the Continental Army starving and freezing to death at Valley Forge in the winter of 1777-1778. The winter of 1779-1780 was far worse. There were twenty-eight snowstorms, the last one occurring in April. The Hudson River around New York City and the waters of Newark Bay froze solid in the frigid winter. It was one of the coldest of the century. A 24-pounder hauled across the ice approaching Paulus Hook (now Jersey City) from Staten Island "made no impression . . . an event unknown in the memory of man." (McBurney, Christian, Abductions in the American Revolution – Attempts to Kidnap George Washington, Benedict Arnold and Other Military and Civilian Leaders, pp. 83, 90.)

2) The size of the force sent to kidnap George Washington is unclear. The cavalry may have been as many as 300 with 175 from the 17th Light Dragoons and 70 hussars from Simcoe's Queen's Rangers. Estimates for the infantry range from 350 to 3,000. (McBurney, p. 88.)

3) The initial mission to capture General Washington was scheduled for February 8th. However, it was postponed due to a snowstorm that began on February 7th and continued throughout the following day. The raid actually took place on February 11-12, 1780.

4) The mission failed. According to General Knyphausen, the cavalry proceeded about five or six miles from Hackensack toward Morristown and were forced to turn back due to the earlier snowstorm that made the roads impassable. Another source claimed it was due to "an uncommon fall of rain, which encrusted the top of the snow, cut the fetlocks of [the] horses, and rendered it absolutely impossible for [Captain Beckwith, the cavalry commander] to succeed." Loyalist Judge Thomas Jones placed the blame on other than the weather. "The guides got frightened, the party bewildered, they lost the road, and after a cold, tedious and fatiguing excursion of twenty-four hours, without ever seeing a Rebel, returned to New York, all frost-bitten." (McBurney, p. 93.)

5) During that winter at Morristown, when there had been false alarms of an enemy attack on Washington's quarters at the Ford Mansion, "the Life Guard would rush from their huts into the [Ford] house, barricade the doors, open the windows, and about five men would place themselves at each window, with their muskets brought to a charge, loaded and cocked ready for defense...These occasions were annoying to the ladies of the household, for both Mrs. Washington and Mrs. Ford were obliged to lie in bed, sometimes for hours, with their rooms full of soldiers, and the keen winter air from the open windows piercing through their drawn curtains... [Washington's] tender care for the comfort of Mrs. Ford was often evinced. On the occasions when the alarms . . . were given, he always went to her room, drew the curtains close, and soothed her by assurances of safety." (McBurney, pp. 85-86.)

6) William Livingston, the Whig Governor of New Jersey (the Loyalist Governor, was William Franklin, Ben Franklin's son), was a frequent target of kidnapping attempts by British raiding parties and

Loyalist militias. His home was in Elizabethtown, dangerously and temptingly close to British forces on Staten Island. He was staunchly anti-Tory, having written that "A Tory is an incorrigible animal and nothing but extinction of life will extinguish his malevolence against liberty." (McBurney, p. 72.)

Chapter 2 – Against Overwhelming Odds

1) According to British spies, the Rebel army was down to 3,500 "sullen, mutinous men." In fact on May 25,1780 , at the Jockey Hollow camp outside of Morristown, soldiers of the 4th and 8th Regiments of the 2nd Connecticut Brigade had mutinied primarily for lack of food. They threatened to raid the depleted commissary for food and march home to Connecticut. (Fleming, Thomas, The Forgotten Victory – The Battle for New Jersey – 1780, pp. 18, 51-59.)

Private Joseph Plumb Martin of one of the soldiers in the mutinous Connecticut Regiments described the causes of the mutiny as follows:

. . .[W]e got a little musty bread and a little beef, about every other day, but this lasted only a short time and then we got nothing at all. The men were now exasperated beyond endurance; they could not stand it any longer. They saw no other alternative but to starve to death, or break up the army, give all up and go home. . . They were truly patriotic, they loved their country, and they had already suffered everything short of death in its cause; and now, after such extreme hardships to give up all was too much, but to starve to death was too much also." (Martin, Joseph Plumb, Private Yankee Doodle – Being a Narrative of Some of the Adventures, Dangers and Sufferings of a Revolutionary Soldier, George Sheer, Editor, pp. 182-187.)

Washington sympathized with his soldiers, writing to Congress – "The men have borne their distress with a firmness and patience never exceeded. . . but there are certain bounds beyond which it is impossible for human nature to go." (Chernow, Ron, Washington – A Life, p. 370.)

To his brother, Washington wrote he was amazed "that an army reduced almost to nothing (by the expiration of short enlistments) should sometimes be five or six days together without bread, then as many without meat, and once or twice two or three without either; that the same army should have had numbers of men in it with scarcely clothes enough to cover their nakedness and a full fourth of it without even a shadow of a blanket, severe as the winter was, and that men under these circumstances were held together, is hardly within the bounds of credibility, but is nevertheless true."
(Chernow, p. 370.)

2) Black Sam Francis' tavern, or the Queen's Head Tavern, which later became Fraunce's Tavern, was a place where Loyalists in New York City came to drink and talk. William Franklin composed a song blaming the rebellion on the "New England breed," whose Ministers "taught them to 'snarl and bite and rail and fight for religion – without having any.' The song ended by commending the man:

Who dirt never flings
At Bishops and Kings
Nor treason will speak tho he's mellow
But takes a full glass
To his friend or his lass
This – This is an honest brave fellow."

(Fleming, p. 29.)

3) Soldiers from New England were generally called Yankees by those from other states. The army was well aware of the Connecticut Regiments' mutiny, and especially the failure of the officers to discipline any of the men. The Connecticut men complained they

were "as ignorant of making [Indian corn meal or Indian corn flour] into bread as a wild Indian would be of making pound cake." (Martin, p. 175.)

4) Washington had set the rations for soldiers by order dated January 18, 1776. Rarely, had the soldiers received their allotted amount, and in many cases, had not even been paid so as to be able to purchase their own food. (Fleming, p. 65.)

5) Skinner's Greens were named for their commander, Brigadier General Cortland Skinner. They wore green coats with white cross belts and most of them were from New Jersey. Loyalism was rampant in New Jersey with more than 2,450 men enrolled on the side of the British, while men from the same family often fought for the Americans. It is estimated that there were about 50,000 Loyalist adherents or sympathizers out of a total population of 140,000. (Fleming, pp. 81,114-115.)

6) Fleming describes this part of the battle with the air filled with a "howl of mutual contempt" with men darting from tree to tree and "shouting insults" while firing their muskets. (Fleming, pp. 250-251.)

7) The 2nd Rhode Islanders were integrated again in May 1780 with the addition of soldiers of color formerly of the 1st Rhode Island Regiment. (Popek, Daniel M., "They . . . fought bravely but were unfortunate" The True Story of Rhode Island's 'Black Regiment' and the Failure of Segregation in Rhode Island's Continental Line, 1777-1783, p. 318.)

8) The Rhode Islanders regarded themselves as suicide troops. Captain Olney wrote that "[i]n all the various situations I had been placed in, before an expected engagement, I never had so much difficulty to reconcile my mind with the fate contemplated. . . I expected soon to have an enemy in rear, as well as a powerful one in front." (Fleming, p. 254.)

Washington wrote to the Governor of Rhode Island on June 29, 1780:

"The gallant behavior of Coll. Angell's regiment on the 23rd inst, at Springfield, reflects the highest honor upon the officers and men. They disputed an important pass with so obstinate a bravery, that they lost upwards of forty in killed, wounded and missing, before they gave up their ground to a vast superiority of force." (Angell, Israel, Diary of Colonel Israel Angell, pp. 118-119).)

9) When the Rhode Islanders moved to higher ground they, and the other wing of the American army, were in a strong position to block a British advance if they attempted to assault Hobart Pass, the entranceway through the Wachung Mountains to Morristown. Apparently, General Knyphausen saw the situation the same way. The British began to retreat toward Elizabethtown. However, before they did, they set fire to Springfield, sparing only four houses, known to belong to British sympathizers. It is reasonable to assume the fires, including the torching of the Presbyterian Church, where the Americans had left some of their wounded, were set by New Jersey Loyalists. "Not even a pig sty was left standing." (Fleming, pp. 280-281.)

10) Captain Stephen Olney actually endured the suffering from his wound alone as he went from home to home seeking a place to rest and heal. The people whose property had been saved by the heroic stand of the Continentals immorally refused to help him. The wounded Captain, with his arm dressed by the Regimental Surgeon went from one house to another, "entreat[ing] quarters (for pay) for a few days," but was turned away from "houses where they appeared to be wealthy." Finally, he went to "a poor looking house" and was taken in by a weaver. Olney's conclusion was "Those people who feel adversity have the most sympathy for those in distress." (Fleming, pp. 287-288.)

Nor did much change for the surviving Continental officers and soldiers following the British defeat. Colonel Ebenezer Huntington wrote to his father in Connecticut:

"I despise my countrymen. I wish I could say I was not born in America. I once gloried in it but now am ashamed of it . . . The insults and neglects which the army have met with from the country beggars all description. . . I am in rags, have lain in the rain on the ground for forty hours past, and only a hunk of fresh beef and that without salt to dine on this day, received no pay since last December." (Fleming, p. 291.)

The Americans suffered 146 Continentals killed or wounded and the New Jersey Militia had ten killed, forty wounded and ten taken prisoner. The British incursion cost them 307 men dead and wounded. It is not clear whether this includes the one hundred or so Jaegers who fell in battle. (Fleming, pp. 286, 290.)

Chapter 3 – The Lovesick Hessian

1) The fictional Weiser family is roughly based on the German speaking Hartman family, Lutherans who arrived in Philadelphia in August 1750. They settled in the upper part of Chester County near the Schuykill River. One of their daughters, Abigail, married Zachariah Rice who built "a clover mill in the 1760s." (McCready, Blake, "Abigail Hartman Rice, Revolutionary War Nurse," Journal of the American Revolution, All Things Liberty, November 28, 2016.)

James Kierney's puzzlement about a clover mill is understandable. Clover does not lend itself to being cut between the bed stone and the rotating running stone of a typical grain or flour mill. In an exchange of emails with a friend who is a volunteer at the National Park Service's Peirce Mill in Rock Creek Park, Washington, D.C. and an acquaintance of his, the answer to what is a clover mill appears to be as follows:

A clover mill does not grind the seeds. After the clover is cut and dried in the field, it is taken to a barn where it is hulled and threshed by a machine. The seeds are separated from the flower by a shaker screen and used to plant next year's clover fields.

2) Abigail Hartman's father and older brother, Peter, fought in the French and Indian War as British soldiers. Their families were Whigs and supported the Revolution. Peter Hartman was a Major in the Chester County Militia. Abigail herself, became a nurse at the military hospital in Yellow Springs, about ten miles away from Valley Forge. She and other nurses, having not been paid for months, went on strike until the matter was resolved to their satisfaction. Abigail contracted typhoid fever while serving as a nurse at the hospital. She never fully recovered and died in 1789, "still suffering from the disease she contracted years prior." (McCready, Journal of the American Revolution, All Things Liberty, November 28, 2016.)

She is buried in St. Peter's Church in Pikeland, Pennsylvania. The original inscription on her gravestone read: "Some have children, some have none, here lies the mother of twenty-one." A new headstone, placed by the Abigail Hartman Rice Chapter of the Daughters of the American Revolution recognizes her service as a nurse at the Yellow Springs Hospital. There is also a plaque in the bell tower of the Washington Memorial Chapel at Valley Forge. (McCready, Journal of the American Revolution, All Things Liberty, November 28, 2016.)

Chapter 4 – The Hysterical Wife

1) Henry Jackson Knox, their first son, was born on May 24, 1780. He was named after Colonel Henry Jackson, a Continental Army Officer from Boston, a lifelong friend of General Henry Knox and a close business associate.

2) General Knox in a letter to his brother Billy, noted that Arnold had, in addition to escorting Lucy and their infant daughter to

Valley Forge, also "provided the horses for the trip – 'no small service.'" (Loane, Nancy K., Following the Drum – Women at the Valley Forge Encampment, p. 82.)

3) In the early months of 1777, Lucy Knox introduced General Arnold to Boston society and the many ladies from families of "divided loyalties" who attended the gatherings in her Cambridge drawing room. Among them, was a sixteen-year old debutante, Elizabeth DeBlois, daughter of a rich Tory merchant. Her mother was "a notorious snob who hoped the rebels would leave Boston at the point of British bayonets." (Randall, Willard S., Benedict Arnold – Patriot and Traitor, p. 326.)

Arnold penned a love letter to her and on March 4th, delivered it, together with a note to Mrs. Knox asking her assistance in his courtship. The transmittal note to Lucy Knox read in part:

"I have taken the liberty of enclosing a letter to the heavenly Miss DeBlois, which I beg the favour of your delivering with the trunk of gowns, etc., which Mrs. ____ promised me to send to you. I hope she will soon have the pleasure of receiving them. . . I shall remain under the most anxious suspense for the favor of a line from you who, if I may judge, will, from your own experience, consider the fond anxiety, the glowing hopes and the chilling fears that alternately possess the heart of, dear Madam,
      Your obedient and humble servant
        Benedict Arnold
(Randall, p. 327.)

4) West Point, as denoted on the charts of the time, was simply a rocky outcropping or point, jutting into the Hudson River opposite Constitution Island. Above it was Fort Arnold, later renamed Fort Clinton after Benedict Arnold's treason was discovered. (Randall, p. 563.) Arnold's headquarters were at Robinson House on the east side of the Hudson.

5) The story of Peggy Shippen Arnold's behavior when her husband was revealed to be a traitor reads like a Revolutionary War soap opera. General Arnold received by courier, a letter from a Continental Army Lieutenant reporting that Major John Andre had been captured with incriminating documents concerning the defenses at West Point. He hurriedly went to Peggy's bedroom, spoke briefly with her and then fled his headquarters. He rode downstream and took his barge to the Vulture, a British sloop waiting in the Hudson River. When General Washington arrived at Robinson House, he was told that Arnold had departed for the West Point fortifications. While Peggy remained upstairs, Washington and his staff had breakfast and then left to "meet" Arnold at West Point.

Then occurred what some historians have called the "Mad Scene." With Washington at West Point, Peggy emerged from her room shouting and screaming. Colonel Varick, one of Arnold's aides, came out of his room where he was lying sick and saw Mrs. Arnold "with her hair disheveled and flowing around her neck; her morning gown with few other clothes remained on her, too few to be seen even by a gentleman of the family, much less by many strangers." (Jacob, Mark and Case, Stephen H., Treacherous Beauty – Peggy Shippen, The Woman Behind Benedict Arnold's Plot to Betray America, pp. 160-161.)

In a letter to his sister Varick described the scene with Peggy Shippen asking him, "Colonel Varick, have you ordered my child to be killed? Then, she fell on her knees at my feet with prayers and entreaties to spare her innocent babe." (Stuart, Nancy Rubin, Defiant Brides – The Untold Story of Two Revolutionary-Era Women and the Radical Men They Married, p. 96.) Another of Arnold's aides came in with Dr. Eustis and together they carried her up to the bedroom, according to Varick "raving mad" and in an "utter frenzy." (Jacob and Case, p. 161.) Back in her room, Peggy told Colonel Varick that General Arnold was gone as she pointed to the ceiling, and that 'the spirits' "have put hot irons in his head," and "hot irons were bedeviling her too." (Jacob and Case, p.161.) She claimed that no one but General Washington could take the hot iron from her head. (Stuart, p. 97.)

When Washington returned to the Robinson House and read the letter and saw the documents about top-secret information pertaining to West Point's defenses, he knew Arnold had betrayed them. Washington was escorted to Peggy's room. She denied that he was General Washington. "That is the man who was a-going to assist Colonel Varick in killing my child." In Washington's presence she pointed to the ceiling insisting that Arnold was up there. (Jacob and Case, p. 161; Stuart, p. 97.)

This account of Peggy's hysteria, based on Colonel Varick's letter to his sister, is accepted by other historians. See Randall, p. 559; Chernow, Ron, Washington, p. 383.) Chernow describes the scene in Peggy's bedroom as follows:

"When Washington went upstairs to calm her, he found her hugging her baby to her breast, her abundant blond curls tumbling across her face and her dressing gown thrown open for easy viewing."

6) The meeting between Elisabeth and Peggy Shippen Arnold is of course fictitious. The letter from General Arnold to his wife is real. One historian reports that Washington, acting according to "chivalric behavior," forwarded Arnold's letter to his wife unopened. (Chernow, p. 384.) Whether he read it or not is unclear. The letter was in fact opened and read by Washington's staff. A copy of General Arnold's letter in the handwriting of Washington's Secretary, James McHenry resides in the Library of Congress. (Jacob and Case, pp. 163-164.)

7) The text of the letter in the novel is that as written by Arnold. The relevant part is: Thou loveliest and best of women. Words are wanting to express my feelings and distress on your account, who are incapable of doing any wrong yet are exposed to suffer

wrong. I have requested the Excellency General Washington to take you under his protection and permit you to go to your friends in Philadelphia – or to come to me. I am at present incapable of giving advice. Follow your own intentions. But do not forget that I shall be miserable until we meet. Adieu – kiss my dear boy for me. God almighty bless and protect you, sincerely prays Thy affectionate and devoted B. Arnold."

Arnold added a postscript – Write me one line if possible to ease my anxious heart.
(Jacob and Case, p. 164; Stuart, p. 98.)

8) Historians now agree that Peggy Shippen Arnold, if not an active participant in her husband's treasonous correspondence, at least knew of Arnold's plan to betray the Americans and turn West Point over to the British, in payment for 10,000 pounds. Her hysteria was a calculated mad act, "played to perfection," to better enable her husband to escape. ("played her mad scene to perfection," Chernow, p. 383; "a calculated piece of theater," Jacob and Case, p. 165; "her marathon display of insanity, the grandest theatrical performance of her life," Stuart, p. 100.)

Peggy Arnold's ability to deceive Washington, Hamilton, Lafayette, Knox, Arnold's two aides and Dr. Eustis, may all be attributed to men's understanding, at the time, of the nature of women. Females were thought prone to "hysteria" or "too flighty" to be involved in nefarious plots. In keeping with this concept of women's nature and perhaps also beguiled by her beauty, Lafayette along with all of the other general officers concluded that " the unhappy Mrs. Arnold did not know a word of this conspiracy, her husband told her before going away that he was flying never to come back and he left her lying unconscious. When she came to herself, she fell into frightful convulsions, and completely lost her reason. . . General Washington and everyone else here sympathizes warmly with this estimable woman, whose face and youthfulness make her so interesting."
(Jacob and Case, p. 165.)

End Notes

Washington was reported to have declared that he had "every reason to believe she is innocent, and requests all persons treat her with that humanity and tenderness due to her sex and virtues." (Jacob and Case, p.166.) The official story that emerged from the Robinson House, without a single officer questioning Peggy Arnold about what she knew of the plot, was that she "had been betrayed by the dastardly Arnold." (Jacob and Case, p. 166.) The other part of the argument that she was not involved was the "too flighty for treason" line, that is women lacked the intelligence and talents to engage in elaborate crimes. (Jacob and Case, p. 167.)

In late September 1780, on the way to Philadelphia she spent the night at The Hermitage, an estate near Paramus, New Jersey owned by Theodosia Prevost and her husband, a Swiss born Lieutenant Colonel serving as a British Army Officer in the Caribbean. Following the death of her husband, Theodosia married Aaron Burr. According to Burr's memoirs, published in 1836, "Mrs. Arnold . . . assured Mrs. Prevost that she was heartily sick of the theatrics she was exhibiting. . . . She stated that she had corresponded with the British Commander [General Clinton] – that she was disgusted with the American cause and those who had the management of public affairs – and that through great persuasion and unceasing perseverance, she had ultimately brought the general into an arrangement to surrender West Point to the British." (Jacob and Case, p. 170.)

Chapter 5 – The Aftermath of Treason

1) General Washington was returning from a secret journey to Hartford, Connecticut where he met and developed a joint strategy with the French high command. Thus, in Washington's absence, Major General Nathanael Greene was temporarily commander of the Continental Army. Greene's General Orders to the troops of September 26, 1780, issued from his headquarters at Tappan, New York stated:

"Treason of the blackest dye was yesterday discovered! General Arnold who commanded at Westpoint, lost to every sentiment of honor, of public and private obligation, was about to deliver up that important Post into the hands of the enemy. Such an event must have given the American cause a deadly wound if not a fatal stab. Happily the treason has been timely discovered to prevent the fatal misfortune. The providential train of circumstances which led to it affords the most convincing proof that the Liberties of America are the object of divine Protection." (Nathanael Greene, General Orders, Library of Congress; George Washington Papers Series 3, Varick Transcripts, 1775-1785, Subseries 3G, loc.gov)

Alexander Hamilton, in his correspondence to General Greene, advising him of what had transpired wrote "There has just unfolded at this place (West Point) a scene of the blackest treason." In a letter to his fiancée, Elizabeth Schulyer, Hamilton, in describing Arnold's actions, wrote about "the discovery of a treason of the deepest dye." One historian concludes, "Given the wording, which so closely follows Hamilton's distinctive choice of vocabulary, it's tempting to detect his hand [in General Greene's orders]. (Journal of the American Revolution, 2017, Brumwell, Stephen, "Alexander Hamilton, Benedict Arnold, and a 'Forgotten' Publius," pp. 380.)

Colonel Israel Angell in his diary entry for September 26th, 1780, gave this vivid, contemporaneous account of Arnold's betrayal in his own, inimitable and ungrammatical style:

"The most Extraordinary affair happened yesterday that Ever has taken place Since the war, General Benedict Arnold who Commanded at west point went to the enemy, His Excellency the Commander in Chief having ben to Hartford to meet the French Genl. and Admiral was on his way to the join the army . . . Genl. Arnold went down to the River Side with Six men with him got into a boat and went down the river to the English Friggat that Lay there and went on board of her, and She Imeadetly Set Sail for New York, and by the best information he had ben Carrying on a treacherous

Corrispondence with the Enemy. and had agreed to Sell them that post with all the men, but Heavens directed it otherways. on Receiving this intelligence, the whole Army was ordered to be ready to march as Soon as possible we all turned out went to Cooking and packing up their Baggage the Pennsylvania line marched of[f] and left their Baggage to follow it being Expected that the Enemy would attempt to take west point this night the News Come to us alittle after midnight, . . ." (Angell, pp. 123-125.)

Arnold's treason threatened the geographic unity of the rebelling colonies. If the British, utilizing their naval superiority, could sail up the Hudson, conquer and occupy the forts at West Point and control the river, it would split and isolate New England, which they deemed to be the seat of the rebellion, from the rest of the colonies. (Chernow, p. 380.)

Not only did Arnold plot to turn the forts, troops and munitions over to the British, he also alerted them to Washington's return route from Hartford. Washington, traveling with Generals Knox and Lafayette, and a troop of about forty men, was highly vulnerable to a British cavalry strike force. Fortunately, Arnold's letter informing General Clinton of Washington's whereabouts and the timing of his visit to West Point arrived too late for the British to act upon it. (Randall, pp.562-563.)

2) The chain, installed in April 1778, was forged at the Sterling Iron Works in Chester, New York. It consisted of seven hundred and fifty iron chain links, eight swivels and eighty clevises. The width of the Hudson, from West Point to Constitution Island, where the chain was installed was fifteen hundred feet wide. There were about fifty-three sets of nine links with swivels installed every one hundred feet supported by log rafts that were fifty feet long and twelve feet wide. The logs were waterproofed with tar and oakum and sharpened at each end "to give them less resistance to the flowing water." (Journal of the American Revolution, Harrington, Hugh, T., "The Great West Point Chain," All Things Liberty, September 25, 2014,)

As Harrington notes, "Surprisingly, during the Revolutionary War the United States was producing an astonishing 14 percent of the world's iron, 30,000 tons. . . . The colonies boasted 72 cold blast furnaces plus many smaller ones. Their production was greater than that of England and Wales combined. Each day an acre of forest was consumed while the furnaces were making the iron for the chain."

3) The colonists used elm for the hubs of wheels "because the tight, twisted grain resists splitting even when the spokes are driven in." (Boston 1775, "Wheels and What They're Worth," June 7, 2017.) I have assumed that the same would be true in the making of capstans.

4) Major Jean Louis Ambroise de Genton, the Chevalier de Villefranche, was appointed the Chief Engineer of West Point by General Washington in August 1780. His initial plans to improve and bolster the defenses were undermined by General Benedict Arnold, until his treason was discovered. Arnold sent troops sorely needed for the work of repairs and new construction away from West Point on meaningless missions. (Walker, Paul K., Engineers of Independence – A Documentary History of the Army of Engineers in the American Revolution, 1775-1783, p. 233.)

Major Jean Bernard-Bourg Gauthier de Murnan, of the corps of engineers, was "arguably, the most violently erratic officer to serve in the Continental Army." His first recorded incident involved his stabbing a quartermaster sergeant in a Connecticut Regiment. He faced a court-martial for "unofficer and ungentlemanlike" behavior in another incident involving a chaplain. When confronted by a sentry guarding a boat that Murnan wanted, he spit in the man's face. He attacked a Continental Captain who was protecting his men in a work party under Murnan's command, struck at him with his sword and was subsequently beaten by the captain with an espontoon. Murnan was court-martialed and was dismissed from the service. Washington ultimately reinstated the Frenchman. (Journal of the American Revolution, 2017, Shepherd, Joshua,

"Temper, Temper: Officers and Gentlemen Go Beserk, pp. 172-173.)

5) Private Martin describes a work detail on Constitution Island, in which their duty was "chiefly, wheeling dirt upon a stone building intended for a magazine . . . to the top of the wall, which was about twenty feet high, upon a way two planks wide, and in the passage we had to cross a chasm in the rocks thirty or forty feet wide . . . . [I]t often made my head swim when crossing it . . . . From the planks, which we wheeled upon, to the bottom . . . could not be less than sixty feet. . . ." (Martin, pp. 192-193)

6) In July 1780 General Washington ordered that one man be drawn from each regiment to comprise a special corps of Sappers and Miners. (Martin, p. 194.) Major General Louis Lebegue Duportail, as Chief Engineer to General Washington, had originally proposed the creation of such a corps in 1778. (Walker, p. 14.)

7) Major Andre was hung on October 2, 1780. He had hoped, as an officer to be shot by firing squad. He wrote Washington, "Sympathy toward a soldier will surely induce your Excellency and a military tribunal to adapt the mode of my death to the feelings of a man of honor." (Jacob and Case, p. 183.) Washington firmly ordered that he be hung as a spy for he was caught behind enemy lines, in civilian clothes with secret documents.

Andre's last words were: "I pray you to bear witness that I meet my fate like a brave man." He was buried in Tappan, New York. In 1821 his body was disinterred and reburied in Poet's Corner at Westminster Abbey, London. (Randall, pp. 568-569.)

8) In perhaps an apochraphyl story, during the Virginia campaign, Arnold, now a British General was interrogating an American prisoner who did not know his identity. When Arnold asked him "what local residents would do with Arnold if they somehow managed to capture him, the prisoner said they would cut off the leg that had been wounded at Saratoga and bury it with honors. The

rest of Arnold they would hang." (Jacob and Case, p. 192;) Another historian states that ". . .all over America, men swore that if they caught Arnold, they would cut off the leg wounded in the nation's service at Quebec and Saratoga, bury it with full honors, and then hang the rest of him on a gibbet." (Randall, p. 564.)

9) The British paid Arnold Six Thousand Pounds, which was the agreed price in the event of failure and Three Hundred and Fifteen Pounds in expenses. The total was the equivalent of about $200,000 in 1990 U.S. purchasing power. Arnold had originally asked for Twenty Thousand Pounds if he succeeded and Ten Thousand if he failed. Arnold also received an annual pension of Two Hundred and Twenty Five Pound for life that amounted to another $210,000 in 1990 terms. (Randall, p. 575.)

The three men who captured Major Andre and foiled General Arnold's treasonous plot were John Paulding, Isaac Van Wert, and Daniel Williams. They were militia men who were part of a gang, waylaying and robbing Loyalist travelers, although there is some question as to whether they were simply highway men robbing anyone who came their way. They were given gold medals by Congress and awarded lifetime pensions of $200 each in gold. In 1817, they petitioned Congress for an increase in their pensions. Their petition was denied. Congressman Benjamin Tallmadge described the three as "plundering Cowboys" who were "roving and lurking above the lines, sometimes plundering on one side and sometimes on the other." (Randall, p. 570.) Whether they were true patriots or opportunistic highwaymen, they were the ones who captured Major Andre and thus, averted a major disaster to the American cause.

10) In May 1780, nine hundred Continental paper dollars were worth one dollar in gold or silver. (Randall, p. 574.)

Chapter 6 – Of Balls, Teas and Dinner Parties

1) On October 27, 1780 the Pennsylvania Council, with Arnold's long time nemesis Joseph Reed as President, passed a resolution banishing Peggy Shippen Arnold from the State, determining that her "residence in the city has become dangerous to the public safety," and resolved that she "depart from this state within fourteen days. . .and that she do not return again during the continuance of the present war." She was escorted by her father through New Jersey as far as Paulus Hook and arrived in New York City November 14, 1780. (Randall, p. 577; Jacob and Case, p. 177.)

2) Besides the animosity among British officers engendered by Arnold's failure to offer himself in exchange for their friend Major Andre, he was also despised for his disloyalty and treachery to the American cause. "While senior officers were civil to Arnold if not all that friendly, lower-ranking officers shunned him. 'General Arnold is a very unpopular character in the British Army. . .'" (Randall, pp. 580-581.)

3) Arnold published a proclamation "To the Inhabitants of America," attempting to justify his treason and assure his former fellow soldiers that Great Britain would willingly give to the Americans "the rights and privileges of colonies unimpaired together with perpetual exemption from taxation," and there was no need to continue fighting to achieve less than the colonies could obtain by grant from the King. (Randall, pp. 574-575.) He also wrote an open letter to Americans with the long explanatory title, "Proclamation by Brigadier General Arnold to the officers and soldiers of the Continental Army who have the real interest of the country at heart, and who are determined to be no longer the tools and dupes of Congress and of France." The letter was virulently anti-Catholic, and was designed to separate the Americans from their newly arrived allies. (Jacob and Case, p. 178.)

Arnold also seriously misjudged the character of many of his former fellow officers. One can only assume he was completely delusional when he wrote Lord Germain, Britain's Secretary of State for the Colonies, about recruiting George Washington. "A title offered to General Washington, might not prove unacceptable." (Jacob and Case, pp. 178-179; Chernow, p. 387.)

4) General Arnold led a 1,600 man expeditionary force into Virginia consisting of his American Legion composed exclusively of deserters from the Continental Army, the Virginia born Queen's Rangers under the command of Colonel Simcoe, the Royal Edinburgh Volunteers and some Hessians. They left on December 11, 1780 from New York for the James River. (Randall, pp.581-582.)

5) There was a well-conceived plot to kidnap General Arnold from New York City that almost succeeded. Sergeant Major John Champe of Major Light Horse Harry Lee's Dragoons pretended to desert, successfully eluded his pursuers in a wild horse chase, was taken aboard a British armed galley off Paulus Hook, New Jersey and brought to New York. There, posing as a deserter, he contrived to meet with General Arnold who recruited him as a Sergeant Major in Arnold's American Legion. Champe planned to kidnap Arnold from the General's garden before he went to bed, and together with an accomplice, bring him through the alley to the Hudson and row him across to where Lee's cavalry were waiting to take Arnold into custody. (Chernow, p. 387.)

The plan was foiled because Arnold embarked for Virginia, with his American Legion, Champe included, December 11, 1780, the very night of the intended kidnapping. Champe subsequently deserted from Arnold's Legion in Petersburg, Virginia and rejoined Lee's dragoons. Washington forced him to retire from service for his own safety because, were he to be captured, he would be executed as a spy. (McBurney, pp. 97-103; Randall, p. 582.)

6) The Mischianza, to celebrate General Howe's achievements and mark his return to Britain was held in Philadelphia on May 18, 1778. The weight of evidence is that Peggy Shippen not only attended but was one of the ladies designated by Major Andre as worthy of bestowing their favors on the costumed knights. Andre wrote a detailed account of the festivities for London's Gentleman's Magazine. (Randall, pp. 394-397; see also End Note 2 to Chapter 7 in Spies and Deserters.)

7) Animosity to the traitor Arnold was virulent in Philadelphia. A two-faced life sized image of Arnold, dressed in a military uniform and riding in a cart with the Devil carrying a pitchfork and a purse of gold to tempt the traitor, was driven through the streets, escorted by drummers and fifers playing "The Rogue's March." The effigy of Arnold was then set on fire. His property, including a carriage and a "valuable negro man slave 22 years old" were confiscated and sold for one hundred pounds sterling each. (Jacob and Case, pp. 171-172.)

8) Even though Betsy Franks was an open Loyalist, she was invited to balls and social events held in liberated, American administrated Philadelphia. Her comment is quoted in Jacob and Case's book about Peggy Shippen. (Jacob and Case, p. 56.) Becky married Colonel Henry Johnson in 1782 and moved to Bath, England. As a reward for service in suppressing the Irish Rebellion of 1798, Johnson was promoted to General in the British Army. He subsequently became a Baronet. That entitled Becky to be called Lady Johnson. Not bad for a half Jewish girl from Philadelphia. (Jacob and Case, pp. 56-57.)

9) Francois Jean de Beauvoir, the Marquis of Chastellux, was a Major-General in the French Army. He spoke English fluently and served as liaison between French Lieutenant General Rochambeau and General Washington and his staff, and commanded the Army when Rochambeau was away. It is a historical fact that Chastellux visited General Knox at his headquarters near West Point in either late November or December 1780. Chastellux's own "Travels in

North America in the Years 1780, 1781 and 1782" suggests that the visit occurred in December 1780. (Journal of the American Revolution, Kelly, Jack, "Revolutionary Tourist: Chastellux in America," Journal of the American Revolution, All Things Liberty, March 4, 2016.") Drake quotes the Chevalier as finding a "real 'family,' formed besides the general and his wife of a little girl of three years and an infant of six months." (Drake, Francis S., Life and Correspondence of Henry Knox, p. 62.) Since Henry Jackson Knox was born on May 24, 1780, he would have been six months old in December 1780, assuming Chastellux's description of the infant's age is precise.

Besides being an esteemed military man, Chastellux was "a thinker and philosopher, one of the leading men of the French Enlightment." (Kelly, Journal of the American Revolution, All Things Liberty, March 4, 2016.)

The entire account of the dinner of Chastellux and his entourage with General and Mrs. Knox and Knox's headquarters staff is fictitious. For a description of the murderous Major Murnan's actual violent and despicable conduct, see End Note 4 to the previous chapter.

Chapter 7 – Mutiny

1) According to the editors of "In the Words of Women," women were "the first line of medical defense," in the household. They "diagnosed ailments, dispensed remedies, and 'watched' family members who were ill or abed. Some with more expertise, knew how to "bind wounds, dress burns and treat dysentery, sore throat, frostbite, whooping cough, and 'the itch,' as well as deliver babies. (North, Louise V., Wedge, Janet M., Freeman, Landa M., In the Words of Women – The Revolutionary War and the Birth of the Nation, 1765-1799, p. 163.) Those who served as nurses were familiar with "camp" or "putrid fever," (probably typhus,) "the bloody flux," (probably dysentery,) and "the itch," or scabies. (North, Wedge and Freeman, p. 167.)

Much of Mercy Ford Hadley's letter to her husband draws on letters from "In the Words of Women," pertaining to their treatment of medical problems, particularly Chapter 6 – This week . . . my Family are all sick." Mercy's mention of "throat distemper," is a reference to diphtheria and scarlet fever that were thought at the time to be one disease. (North, Wedge, and Freeman, p.170.)

2) Washington was faced with two mutinies of Continental troops in January 1781. He had sent the Army into winter quarters and pleaded with Congress to provide funds to support the Army. He wrote:

"We have neither money nor credit adequate for the purchase of a few boards for doors to our log huts. . . It would be well for the troops if, like chameleons, they could live upon air or like the bear, suck their paws for sustenance during the rigor of the approaching [winter.]" (Chernow, p. 388.)

The first mutiny, described in Mercy Hadley's fictitious letter to her husband, occurred on January 1, 1781 when the troops of the 11th Pennsylvania, under the command of Brigadier General Anthony Wayne, mutinied while in their winter quarters on Mt. Kemble outside Morristown. Inflamed by rum and legitimate grievances of insufficient food, clothing and pay, they soon were joined by soldiers of other Pennsylvania Regiments until a total of about 1,300 men were involved. This was about half of all of the Pennsylvania Line and the largest uprising in the Continental Army to date. (Chernow, p.389; Journal of the American Revolution, Schellhammer, Michael, "Mutiny of the Pennsylvania Line, All Things Liberty, January 14, 2014.) Some mutineers fired over the head of General Wayne when he attempted to stop them from leaving camp for Philadelphia.

Negotiations between a Board of Sergeants, representing the mutinous troops, and General Wayne, Colonels Butler and Stewart, joined by Joseph Reed of the Pennsylvania Council, took place in a small town south of Princeton. Mercy's reference to General W. and Colonel S. are to General Wayne and Colonel Stewart. The end result was that half were discharged and the other half furloughed until April. The soldiers were issued clothing and certificates for pay when money was available. (Chernow, pp. 389-390.)

According to Chernow, the ringleaders were rounded up by General Wayne, with Washington's approval, and executed by firing squad, composed of their fellow soldiers. "The distance that the platoons stood from [the condemned men] at the time they fired could not have been more than ten feet." (Chernow, p. 390.)

However, another account clearly states that following the conclusion of negotiations, the Pennsylvanians marched to Trenton where the terms of their original enlistments were reviewed. The soldiers received shirts, shoes, blankets, woolen overalls and fifty Pennsylvania shillings (about one month's pay). Those who claimed they were entitled to discharge by terms of their enlistment were discharged and the others furloughed. "None of the mutineers received punishment." (Schellhammer, Journal of the American Revolution, All Things Liberty, January 14, 2014.) The editor of a compilation of General Washington's Revolutionary War Letters also agrees with Schellhammer that none of the Pennyslvania mutineers were punished. (Lengel, Edward G., The Glorious Struggle – George Washington's Revolutionary War Letters, p. 222.)

3) Colonel Dayton's speech is fictitious. However, many of the phrases are taken from George Washington's General Orders of January 30,1781 thanking Major General Robert Howe for "the judicious measures he pursued" in quelling the mutiny of the New Jersey Continentals at Pompton, New Jersey. (Lengel, pp. 223-224.)

4) Colonel Dayton after polling the New Jersey 3rd, prudently furloughed most of the Regiment to their homes and sent the others out of the mutineers' path to Springfield. He did keep a few soldiers with him in Chatham. (Journal of the American Revolution,

Schellhammer, Michael "Mutiny of the New Jersey Line," All Things Liberty, March 19, 2014.)

5) Following the seemingly successful negotiations, the New Jersey mutineers left Chatham and marched back to Pompton. It was there the mutiny was put down by a force led by Major General Robert Howe and some five hundred armed troops from Massachusetts, Connecticut and New Hampshire. My description of how the mutineers were disarmed and the punishment that followed is a composite of Chernow's erroneous account applied to the Pennsylvania Mutiny earlier in the month and Schellhammer's version. Schellhammer describes the on-the-spot court martial of Sergeants David Gilmore, John Tuttle, and Sergeant Major Grant and the brutal execution of the first two. (Chernow, p.390; Schellhammer, Journal of the American Revolution, All Things Liberty, March 19, 2014.)

For purposes of the plot, I have kept the mutineers in Chatham where they are surprised, surrounded and punished by Major General Robert Howe's force.

Chapter 8 – Madness on the March

1) Washington's original plan for the 1781 campaign was to assault the British positions guarding New York City with the ultimate goal of retaking the city. In July, together with the newly arrived French forces under General Rochambeau, he mounted a major reconnaissance of the British defenses. The combined American-French forces of about 4,000 soldiers, cavalry and field artillery probed the outer British redoubts at the northern end of Manhattan Island that was about fifteen miles from the city itself at the lower tip. They noted that while there were some weaknesses, the forts on Manhattan Island itself were formidable. The ultimate conclusion was attacking northern Manhattan would be extremely difficult, and thoughts, at least on the French side, turned to trapping Cornwallis's army at Yorktown. (Journal of the American Revolution, Stoltz III,

Joseph F., "Le Plus Detaillee: The July 1781 Reconnaissance of New York, All Things Liberty, June 12, 2017);

Chernow is of the opinion that Washington was fixated on attacking New York, even after the reconnaissance. He urged Rochambeau to advise the French fleet, under Admiral de Grasse, to sail from the Caribbean to New York rather than Chesapeake Bay. Rochambeau "played a delicate game of deception," pretending that New York was the "top priority," while secretly communicating with de Grasse to think instead about Chesapeake Bay. (Chernow, pp. 401-402.) Washington went on to claim that he was the architect of the Yorktown campaign and the focus on New York was a deliberate deception to mislead, not only the British, but the Americans as well. (Chernow, p. 404.)

According to a French Engineer who attended the conference between Washington and Rochambeau, the French General after first refusing to order de Grasse to come to New York and then revealing that de Grasse was not under his command, stated that he would set out with the French troops for Virginia and invited Washington "to place himself at our head with as large a following of his army as he felt able to withdraw from New York. . . and he (Rochambeau) added that if it was necessary to share our army's money to set his (Washington's) in motion he was willing to do this. . ." (Fleming, Thomas, Beat the Last Drum – The Siege of Yorktown, 1781, p. 90.) Private Martin brings a soldier's eye view to the reconnaissance, depicting much skirmishing and exchanges of shouted insults, as well as long distance sniping. (Martin, pp. 214-218.) Bant and McNeil's patrols are based upon Martin's account.

2) Washington engaged in an extensive campaign to deceive General Clinton that the Americans were preparing an attack on New York City. To convince the British that the base in Chatham, New Jersey was a permanent one from where troops would be ferried across the waters to capture Staten Island, he ordered the construction of bakeries. Bricks were purchased and ovens were constructed for the French troops. By the time the French marched into Chatham

a sixty-five foot long shed was in place, "producing 3,000 loaves of aromatic, crusty French bread, per day." (Journal of the American Revolution, Shachtman, Tom, "The French Bread Connection," All Things Liberty, September 12, 2017.)

Chernow describes Washington as having to deceive his own troops and officers of his true intentions while the Army, divided into three columns, was strung out from Dobbs Ferry north of New York City to Trenton, New Jersey, and vulnerable to a major British attack with troops sallying forth from New York. (Chernow, pp. 407-408; see also, Clarke, Jeffrey J., Director, U.S. Army Center of Military History, "March to Victory, Washington, Rochambeau and the Yorktown Campaign of 1781, pp. 26-27.)

It appears that Washington also contrived for dispatches ordering the construction of the camp at Chatham to fall into British hands. In addition, thirty large flat boats, mounted on wheels, were part of the equipment heading south to Chatham. "Putting it all together, the British were convinced that Washington intended to attack New York via Staten Island." (Fleming, p.97.)

3) The character of Reverend Israel Avery is based, in part, on the Reverend Samuel Eakin, the pastor of a Presbyterian Church in Penn's Neck, New Jersey. He was a strong Whig and his addresses to soldiers passing by were so eloquent as "excite their emotions of patriotism to the highest Pitch." His words to the soldiers of the 3rd New Jersey are a composite of various sermons preached at the time and are taken from "The Chaplains and Clergy of the Revolution," J. T. Headley, printed in 1864.) Reverend Avery's line about a spirit of patriotism firing the soldiers' breath comes from a story in The New York Times about a 1776 sermon discovered at the First Presbyterian Church in Greenwich Village in 2003. (Wakin, Daniel J., "Sermons of 1776, With a Spirit of 2003; Newly Found Papers Reflect New York's Mood in Time of War," The New York Times, March 16, 2003.)

4) The distance from Dobbs Ferry above the northern tip of Manhattan Island to Yorktown was approximately 450 miles. The Quartermaster General, Colonel Timothy Pickering, was responsible for procuring and distributing supplies along the army's route through New Jersey and beyond, including the use of private contractors.

Depots were established along the route and supplies were paid for by pledges by Robert Morris, Superintendent of Finance, from his private finances, "interest bearing State or Continental loan certificates, promissory notes that were redeemable at some future date and the goodwill of providers to accept them." (Clarke, pp. 27-28.) The promises to pay backed by Morris's personal finances were known as "Morris Notes." Those that were redeemable immediately were known as "short Bobs," and "the ones with a longer length of time specified were called 'long Bobs'" . . . (Journal of the American Revolution, 2017, Smith, Jr., John L., "How Yorktown Almost Couldn't Afford to Happen," p. 399.)

5) There is an historical basis for this description of the distribution of the 26,000 pieces of eight, one half of Rochambeau's treasury. The Paymaster-General of the Continental Army, John Pierce, displayed the French barrels of coins to the disgruntled soldiers. Morris instructed Pierce to "make a spectacle showing of the specie coin when paying the sullen soldiers. So Pierce cracked open the top of one of the barrels and for grand effect, dumped the barrel on its side, letting the silver coins spill out." (Smith, Jr. p. 402.)

Private Martin wrote that while in Philadelphia, "we each received a MONTH'S PAY, in specie, borrowed, as I was informed, by our French Officers from the officers in the French Army. This was the first that could be called money, which we had received as wages since the year '76, or that we ever did receive till the close of the war, or indeed, ever after, as wages. (Martin, pp. 222-223.)

However, Clarke states the coins were paid to the troops at Head of Elk, Maryland when they arrived from Philadelphia at the top of the Chesapeake Bay. He cites the recollection of Private John Hudson of the 1st New York Regiment (who had turned thirteen in July 1781) "that it was at Elkton [Head of Elk] that 'I received the only pay that I ever drew for my services during the war, being six French crowns which were a part of what Robert Morris borrowed on his own credit from the French commander to supply the most urgent necessities of the soldiers. My comrades received the same amount." (Clarke, pp. 39-40.)

6) In planning for the Yorktown campaign, General Knox requested two hundred and five horses for the artillery alone and another forty to pull the ammunition wagons. When the horses that had been disbursed during the winter encampment returned in early July, there were fewer than expected. The Quartermaster General, with Washington's approval, authorized the seizure of draft horses from those with "known or suspected Loyalist sympathies" in Bergen County, New Jersey. (Clarke, pp. 29-30.)

Chapter 9 – Small Pox, Fever and Dangerous Night Duty

1) Washington, with the help of General von Steuben, issued "Regulations for the Service of the Siege." In this detailed and lengthy document, the Commander specified "The Faschines [fascines] to be 6 Feet long . . . this to be made of Branchery, the twigs of which are to be crossed, to be bound with [widths] at each end & the middle of each Faschine, 3 Pickets of three feet long, & 2 or three Inches diameter."

Gabions "are to be 3 Feet high including the end of the Pickets, which are to enter the Ground, they are to have 2 Feet & a half Diameter, and be formed of nine pickets each of two & a half Inches in Circumference interlaced with Branchery stripped of leaves to be equally closed at Top & Bottom, in order that they may not be longer at one end than the other." (Greene, Jerome A, "The Guns of Independence – The Siege of Yorktown, 1781," p. 157.)

Basically, the gabions were large open bottomed baskets, made from intertwined branches, which were then filled with the dirt and stones the soldiers dug as they made the trench. With sharpened pickets placed in the ground they formed a kind of pre-fabricated wall or breastwork. The fascines were placed on top of this wall, parallel to the ground. They too were covered with earth, thereby increasing its height, shoring up the wall and providing further protection for infantry manning the parapets.

2) Cornwallis had employed hundreds of blacks to build the fortifications at Yorktown, when he initially established a base there. Some had been seized from plantations of patriots. Others had voluntarily joined the British forces in return for the promise of obtaining their freedom. With the arrival of the French and American armies and low on food, "hundreds of blacks were turned out of the British garrison, many of them stricken with [small pox.]" (Greene, p. 136.)

"Other pitiable refugees from Yorktown lay in woods near the allied camp, bands of sick and starving Negroes no longer able to work, most of them dying of smallpox." (Davis, Burke, "The Campaign That Won America – The Story of Yorktown," p. 202.)

Washington was greatly concerned that an outbreak of small pox would decimate his army. He ordered that British deserters be checked carefully for the disease and the Army's doctors "to be particularly attentive to removing without an Instants delay any soldier in whom the symptoms of small pox may appear." (Greene, p. 129.)

3) The average distance of the Allied trench, the first parallel, to the British inner defenses was about 800 to 1,000 yards. The British had two fortified redoubts on the far right of the American line, which ended at the swampy ground of the York River. The American line in front of the redoubts bowed out or away from them, making the distance to the inner defenses more than 1,000 yards. During

the night of October 5th and 6th, the British cannonade increased in intensity because of the digging and siege preparations. The American and French engineers used the British bombardment to pinpoint the location of British batteries and then to mark the positions where the Allies' cannons should be placed to best engage and destroy them. (Greene, pp. 151-153.)

4) Women at the time of the Revolution were well aware of the dangers of childbirth and the possibility of the infant being born dead or dying shortly thereafter. Abigail Adams wrote her husband John about her apprehensions that the baby within her had died. She later confirmed that while her spirits were better, the baby, "a much-hoped-for daughter," was delivered still-born." Another expectant mother wrote:

"O my dear Mother this is a trying situation to be in. Such an hour approaching, and little or not expectation of having the company, and the immediate sympathy of [my husband who was a prisoner of war, and mother.]" (North, Wedge, and Freeman, pp. 172-173.)

5) The distance from Trebell's landing on the James River, where the Americans' cannons and supplies were offloaded, to the artillery park at Yorktown was six miles. Bridges crossing an area filled with streams and marshes had to be strengthened to bear the weight of the heavy cannons. New bridges were constructed and older ones were reinforced. (Greene, pp. 112-113.) Unwilling to wait for the cannons to arrive, Washington ordered the construction of the siege line and batteries, in anticipation of placing the artillery in position.

6) Major Jean Bernard-Bourg Gauthier de Murnan, who was in the American corps of engineers, was in fact court martialed for various violent offenses and sentenced to be dismissed from the service. Washington initially "confirmed the opinion of the court, but . . . [b]ecause some of the testimony didn't appear to support the worst accusations, Washington reinstated Murnan." (Shepherd, Journal of the American Revolution 2017, p. 273.)

I have placed the reinstated Murnan at Yorktown supervising the construction of the siege lines, as would a Major in the corps of engineers. His presence and actions on the line are purely fictitious.

7) Malaria, called ague at the time, was a common affliction among the troops of both sides during the Yorktown campaign. The incubation period is from seven to thirty days and attacks last six to ten hours and recur every two days. It is assumed that because Cornwallis' troops had been in the Carolinas and in the Yorktown area longer than American and French troops, more of them were infected. Yorktown, located in the Tidewater was prime malarial country that Cornwallis described as a "sickly defensive post in this Bay." When Cornwallis surrendered he claimed that half his men were too sick to stand duty, although that was probably attributable to other diseases as well.

The usual treatment at the time was venesection or bleeding. Over a period of time, doctors drained a total of twenty ounces of blood, about ten percent of an adult male's total blood. This was sometimes supplemented with doses of mercury or opium. (McNeill, J.R., "Malarial mosquitos helped defeat British in battle that ended the Revolutionary War," The New York Times, October 18, 2010.)

An individual soldier's ability to survive malaria depended upon his immune system, that is whether he had been exposed to it before and built up immunities, his genetic makeup and probably pure luck.

8) At the start of the campaign, before the first siege line was even begun, General Knox sent Captain Thomas Shilds to get the wood for the gun platforms from Somerset on the Eastern Shore of Maryland. His orders specified he was to load ships

"with all the oak plank from 2 to 3 inches [thick] & from end 12 to 18 feet in length which you can find and also as much pine plank from 1 to 3 inches as well [will?] complete the loading of said vessels.

The plank being absolutely essential in the operations against the enemy, every method must be made use of to obtain it, and in case a sufficient quantity of it can not otherways be had you are hereby authorized to impress as much as shall be wanting . . ." (Greene, pp. 127-128.)

9) Knox planned to bring approximately forty-five artillery pieces from New York to Yorktown. That would have required about eight hundred men to provide gun crews for all the cannons, assuming the crews had duty on alternating days. On October 1, 1781, Knox's Corps of Artillery totaled 382 officers and men fit for duty. His Corps included the entire 2nd Continental Artillery Regiment of 242 and detachments from the 1st, 3rd and 4th Continental Artillery Regiments making up the balance.

On October 6, 1781, 420 auxiliaries from a Virginia State Regiment, Virginia militiamen and a Delaware Regiment were assigned to Knox's artillery park, bringing his total strength to about 800. These auxiliaries were used to guard the artillery park, maintain the fortifications, haul ammunition and supplies from the park to the batteries and work in the batteries under the direction of skilled gun crews. (Journal of the American Revolution, Reynolds, William W., "The American Gunners at Yorktown," All Things Liberty, May 9, 2017.)

Chapter 10 – The Fate of Officers

1) This scene is taken from a description of the Battle of the Hook on October 3, 1781 that took place on Gloucester Point, across the river from Yorktown. It was mainly a cavalry battle between the hussars of the Duke de Lauzun's Legion of about three hundred and twenty mounted troops, and Banastre Tarleton's infamous troopers and the 17th Light Dragoons. Each side was supported by infantry. In the initial clash of cavalry, Tarleton was thrown from his horse when the horse of one of his troopers was wounded and stumbled into Tarleton's mount. Other British dragoons protected Tarleton from

Lauzun's attempts to capture him. Lauzun and his hussars pursued Tarleton until driven back by British infantry. Tarleton then turned the tables and pursued Lauzun who retreated behind the protection of a line of American infantry that stood their ground and fired at least one volley at the British cavalry. Tarleton then withdrew to the defensive fortifications on Gloucester Point. The battle was basically over. British casualties were estimated to be around fifty. Lauzun's hussars lost three killed and sixteen wounded and the supporting infantry lost two killed and eleven wounded. (Greene, pp. 143-147.)

Washington treated the battle as a major success. It bottled up the British in Gloucester Point, (the Americans and French moved to within one or two miles of the British defenses), severed Cornwallis' lines of communication with the open Virginian countryside to the north and basically closed off any escape route by Cornwallis.

Washington's General Orders the next day stated:

"The General Congratulates the Army upon the brilliant success of the Allied Troops near Gloucester. He requests the Duke de Lauzern to accept his particular thanks for the Judicious disposition and the decisive Vigour with which he charged the Enemy, and to communicate his Warmest Acknowledgements to the Gallant Officers and men by whom he was so admirably seconded." (Greene, p.148.)

2) It was standard siege practice in placing cannons in the batteries not to unmask the guns' positions prematurely by cutting embrasures through the defensive wall. According to a French treatise on artillery:

"A Battery must not be opened the instant its cannon are mounted, because this would draw upon it the whole undivided fire of the place, . . .it must remain silent, on the contrary, until the whole of the batteries are finished, they should then be unmasked at the same instant, and the enemy[,] attacked from every point. . .can no longer act with the same precision, and is obliged to scatter his fire. . ." (Greene, p. 189, quoting from Lallemand's Treatise on Artillery.)

3) General Knox modified the standard mounting of mortars. Instead of being on heavy wheel-less wooden beds transported by wagons, Knox had them mounted on carriages, strengthened to bear the shock of recoil. Besides being more mobile, these mortars were able to fire with the muzzle at lower elevations. They were used to pound the British earthen fortifications and destroy them. (Greene, pp. 187, 379-380.)

4) The actual order of the American Army had Major General Lafayette in charge of the First Division with two Brigades, one commanded by Brigadier General Peter Muhlenberg and the other by Brigadier General Moses Hazen, the latter including Lieutenant Colonel Alexander Hamilton's Battalion.

The 2nd Division was led by Major General Baron von Steuben.

The 3rd Division under the command of Major General Benjamin Lincoln and its Second Brigade, commanded by Colonel Elias Dayton, included the 1st and 2nd New Jersey Regiments and the Rhode Island Regiment. I have moved these Regiments to Lafayette's Light Division because it was that Division that had the honor of opening the American trenches at the start of the siege on October 7, 1781. (Greene, pp. 82-83.)

5) A gill is five fluid ounces. While rum was severely rationed, there were other ways for the soldiers to obtain it. Colonel Lamb of the 2nd Artillery Regiment, complained "that altho' he has repeatedly Issued Orders, to the prevent the Soldiers' Wives selling Rum, the practice is still continued." There was a danger that the "unbridled profiteering" in the sale of rum "might jeopardize the performance of his troops." (Greene, p.231.)

6) As bizarre and insane as it sounds, once the Americans were in

the trenches, Lieutenant Colonel Alexander Hamilton, "ordered his troops to mount the epaulement and, fully exposed to whatever guns the enemy might open on them, execute the manual of arms from Baron von Steuben's Regulations. Incredulous at what their eyes beheld, many of the British held their fire." (Greene, p. 168.) Fleming attributes Hamilton's foolhardy action to his assessment that this was the kind of brash gesture the British admired and was consistent with their own traditions. (Fleming, p. 239.)

An American Captain who witnessed the incident wrote:

"Although the enemy had been firing a little before, they did not now fire us a single shot. I suppose their astonishment at our conduct must have prevented them . . . Colonel Hamilton gave these orders, and although I esteem him one of the first officers of the American army, must beg leave in this instance to think he wantonly exposed the lives of his men." (Fleming, p. 239.)

7) Chronologically, the troops occupied the trenches while construction was still ongoing for the batteries. The work was begun on October 8th. Once the gun platforms were assembled and in place, the embrasures were cut and the guns mounted after dark on October 9th. I have consolidated the time frame somewhat to move the plot along more quickly.

Chapter 11 – On the Siege Line

1) The American gun commanders "personally aimed the artillery" and when a shot had been "well directed," marked with chalk the positions of the wheels on the platform so that the carriage would be in the exact same spot for the following round. (Greene, pp. 192-193.) According to then current artillery theory for siege warfare, the first goal was to dismount the enemy's cannons and the second was to destroy the embrasures and earthworks.
The main American battery, in the early days of the siege, had three twenty-four pounders, three eighteen-pounders, two eight-inch

howitzers and two ten and a half inch mortars. (Greene, p. 187.) The guns were fired at ten-minute intervals and no more than fifty shots were fired by the same gun within a twenty-four hour period. (Greene, p. 194.) Most of the fire by the main American battery was directed at the two British redoubts that were about five hundred yards away.

2) George Washington himself fired the first shot from the American battery at about five p.m. on October 9. The ball from the eighteen-pounder, aimed by the gun commander, struck several houses in Yorktown and "finally crashed into the wooden structure where a coterie of officers had gathered for dinner." (Greene, p. 191.) According to Fleming, citing reports of Colonel Richard Butler and Dr. James Thacher, Washington fired the first gun but it was a twenty-four pounder. Colonel Philip van Cortlandt recalled one "could distinctly hear the ball strike from house to house." (Fleming, pp. 243-244.)

3) Mortar bombs were hollow, cast iron spheres, filled with powder. A twelve-inch bomb, designed as an anti-personnel weapon, would contain between from four to six pounds of powder. The fuse, a wooden tube containing powder and saltpeter, was driven in after the charge had been placed and was "intentionally slow burning to allow the projectile to reach its target before bursting." Once the bomb was in the mortar, and wooden wedges inserted to center it, "the fire of the discharged mortar triggered ignition of the bomb fuse." (Greene, pp. 380-381; Fleming, p. 240.)

Washington had issued an order requiring soldiers to yell "A shell!" whenever one landed in the works. Knox and Hamilton while in the trenches debated the merits, Hamilton believing it was unsoldierly and Knox stating that it helped to save men's lives. Two shells landed in the redoubt in which they were standing and several soldiers called out "A shell! A shell." Both Knox and Hamilton scrambled behind the blinds, sand-filled barrels in the trenches. Hamilton positioned himself behind Knox who was between Hamilton and the shell.

"Knox [being a very large man and Hamilton a small man] did not take kindly to acting as a human obstruction and a struggle ensued. The two men rolled over and Knox, being much stronger, threw Hamilton toward the hissing shell. Aghast, Hamilton scrambled back once more behind the blinds." After the shells had exploded, fortunately wounding no one, and it was safe to stand up, Knox said, "Now what do you think, Mr. Hamilton, about crying 'shell?' But let me tell you not [to] make a breastwork of me again." (Greene, p. 273; Fleming, p. 292; Chernow, Ron, Alexander Hamilton, p. 164.) Fleming attributes this story to an eyewitness account by Dr. Eneas Munson of Connecticut. (Fleming, p. 356.)

4) The inside of the cannons were treated with a mixture of water and vinegar to clean them out. (Greene, p. 194.)

5) On October 3rd, British deserters reported that two hundred artillery horses had been killed for lack of forage. "Dumped into the York, the carcasses bobbed out with the tide only to return with it a few days later to clutter the beach with decaying matter. By their return, remarked one officer, "it seemed as if they wanted to cry out against their murder after their death." (Greene, p. 140.)

6) The Allied firepower deployed against the British at Yorktown was formidable and unrelenting. The main American battery alone, from October 11 to October 12 "fired 336 24-pounder shot, 263 18-pounder shot, 199 10-inch mortar shells, 159 8-inch and 94 five-and-one half-inch howitzer shells." Other American batteries during the same period fired "166 10-inch shells. . . while gunners on the extreme left of the American sector of the first siege line, discharged 450 18-pounder balls." (Greene, p. 224.)

7) The capture of Redoubts 9 and 10 at the far right of the Allied lines was necessary to complete the second parallel from the French emplacements all the way to the York River. The Allies would then have Yorktown encircled in a tight noose and with possession of the two redoubts, be able to bring their guns to bear on the trapped

British at close range. (Greene, p. 224; Fleming, p. 273.)

General Knox assigned Captain William Stevens of the 2nd Artillery Regiment to command six three-pounders in support of the infantry nighttime attack on Redoubts 9 and 10. (Reynolds, Journal of the American Revolution, All Things Liberty, May 9, 2017.)

Chapter 12 - The Assault on the Rock Redoubt

1) The American attack force tasked with taking Redoubt No. 10, the so-called Rock Redoubt, consisted of four hundred men plus sappers and miners who would be in the forefront to clear away the defensive obstacles. General Lafayette had overall command and one battalion included soldiers from Captain Olney's 1st Rhode Islanders "and included a large number - perhaps a majority – of black troops." The commander of the leading column was Colonel Alexander Hamilton. (Greene, pp. 237-238.)

The "forlorn hope," were soldiers detached from each company who were to be the first over the wall. "The best and bravest men were usually selected." (Fleming, p. 282.)

2) Private Martin describes how, when they rushed forward in the darkness, many of the attacking soldiers fell into large craters made by bursting American shells, "holes sufficient to bury an ox in. . . I thought the British were killing us off at a great rate. At length, one of the holes happening to pick me up, I found out the mystery of the huge slaughter." (Martin, pp. 235-236.)

Captain Olney's attacking force did not wait for the sappers and miners to clear the obstacles. Instead, they rushed through the abatis and into the trench before the palisade, tearing at it and mounted the parapet. (Greene, p. 242; Fleming, pp. 283-284.)

3) Captain Olney, if not first, was among the first to gain the parapet and shouted for his company to form around him. On calling to his

men, "I had not less than six or eight [British] bayonets pushed at me." He parried them as best he could with his espontoon, but the blade snapped and "several enemy bayonets 'slid along the handle of my espontoon and scaled my fingers; one bayonet pierced my thigh, another stabbed me in the abdomen just above the hipbone.'" (Greene, p. 244; Fleming, p. 284.)

There were claims that Hamilton's troops attacking Redoubt No. 10 were instructed to take no prisoners, and many of the defeated defenders pleaded for their lives. Greene states, "Whether this is true has not been conclusively determined. (Greene, pp. 245-246.) Hamilton did restrain a New Hampshire Captain from killing the British Commander who had surrendered.

In another version of the same event, Fleming reports "one New Hampshire captain slightly mad, . . .lunged at the British commander, his bayonet raised, swearing he was going to avenge the slaughter committed by Benedict Arnold's raiders in New London. But Hamilton sprang in front of his captive, and sternly told the New Englander that not a single surrendered soldier was to be touched." (Fleming, p. 287.)

The entire night time assault on the Redoubt took about ten minutes. The Americans lost nine men killed, and twenty-five wounded. The British lost eight killed and seventy-three captured. The remainder of the garrison escaped, including thirty men who had ignominiously fled with their commander, British Major McPherson "the moment the firing began." (Fleming, p. 289; Greene, p. 245.)

The reference to New London, Connecticut is to Benedict Arnold's raid on the privateering capital of the east coast on September 4, 1781. According to the American version, Continental troops who surrendered Fort Griswold after putting up a stout resistance, were bayoneted by the victorious British. One historian claims that British cannon fire cut the lanyard on the flag pole and when the American flag came down, the British, thinking the Americans had struck their colors rushed forward only to be greeted by musket fire. Outraged by what they thought was American duplicity, the British troops, when they did breach the defenses, bayoneted those who attempted to surrender. Eighty-eight Americans were killed and thirty-five badly wounded out of a garrison of one hundred and forty men, including fifteen-year old boys and old men. (Randall, pp. 586-588.)

4) The French captured Redoubt No.9 in about thirty minutes. It was larger and defended by some one hundred and twenty British and Hessians. French casualties were much higher than among the Americans at Redoubt No. 10, probably due to confusion among the French troops who may have killed many of their own, thinking they were shooting and bayoneting Hessians who wore uniforms similar in color to those of the French. (Greene, pp. 251-252.)

Greene recounts an incident illustrating General Washington's calmness under fire. He, with Generals Knox and Lincoln and their aides, were observing the progress of the attack "from an exposed position in the Grand French Battery. Fearing for the safety of his chief on the open ground, Colonel David Cobb urged Washington to step back. 'Colonel Cobb," answered Washington, . . .'if you are afraid, you have liberty to step back.'"

Washington later wrote in his diary his admiration for the Allied troops: "The bravery exhibited by the attacking Troops was emulous and praise worthy. Few cases have exhibited stronger proofs of Intripidty[sic] coolness and firmness than were shown on this occasion." (Greene, p. 253.)

5) At four a.m. after the two redoubts were captured, the British attempted an assault at the juncture where the French and American lines met, designed to seize and silence some of the Allied cannons and perhaps extend the siege. The gambit was to gain time for a British fleet with additional troops to arrive at Yorktown and relieve the beleaguered garrison. The sortie achieved little other than

inflicting some casualties and spiking a few cannons with bayonets that were easily repaired when the positions were retaken. (Greene, pp. 262-265.)

6) Cornwallis's other desperate gambit to escape the deadly siege was to ferry his troops across the York River under cover of darkness and break out north into the Virginia countryside from the Gloucester shore. The effort began the evening of October 16th around ten p.m. as soldiers boarded sixteen large boats. Unfortunately for Cornwallis, his plan was thwarted by the weather – a storm arose with rain and strong winds and by midnight, Cornwallis called the effort off. The storm abated around two a.m. and by the time the boats attempted to return to the Yorktown side, it was in broad daylight. They were subject to intense Allied artillery fire. Miraculously, most of the soldiers who had embarked, arrived back in Yorktown by noon on October 17th, the anniversary of the surrender of General Burgoyne's army at Saratoga. (Greene, pp. 275-277.)

7) A 'chamade' is "when a besieged town wants to capitulate, or to make some proposals to the besiegers. In that case, one or more drums mount the rampart, and beat what the military calls a 'Chamade.'" (Greene, p. 457, note 14.)

Chapter 13 – Confrontation on Surrender Field

1) Except for the opening salutation and the deletion of the reference to William his brother, which I thought would be confusing, this letter is word for word, with the same emphasis, as Henry Knox' letter to Lucy. She was at Mt. Vernon, sharing her anxiety about the fate of the war with Martha Washington, and enduring the last month and a half of her pregnancy. (Drake, p. 70.) The full letter appears in "The Revolutionary Lives and Letters of Lucy and Henry Knox," by Phillip Hamilton, (pp. 160-161)

Knox refers to the harsh terms the British imposed on the Americans, when after a six week siege, General Benjamin Lincoln surrendered the American garrison at Charles Town (Charleston, South Carolina) in 1780. British General Clinton refused to permit the Americans the customary "honors of war." Under the rules of siege warfare, if a commander surrendered before the defenses were taken by storm and had put up a vigorous defense, the defeated forces were allowed to march out fully armed, with regimental and national flags flying. Further, and rather quirkily, the bands of the defeated army were entitled to play one of the victorious army's national tunes. Lt. Colonel John Laurens, one of the American Commissioners who had been the recipient of the harsh terms at Charles Town insisted that those same terms now apply to the British Army at Yorktown. (Fleming, pp. 321-322; Greene, pp. 287-288.)

2) Cornwallis himself of course did not lead his troops out and surrender. He pleaded he was indisposed but seems to have recovered nicely enough to accept invitations to dine with the French and American commanders afterwards. Instead, Brigadier General Charles O'Hara had the somber duty of leading the British troops to Surrender Field. At first he tried to surrender to the French Commander, Lt. General Rochambeau who directed O'Hara to General Washington. Washington, knowing that O'Hara was Cornwallis's deputy, in turn directed him to General Benjamin Lincoln, Washington's subordinate. (Greene, p. 297; Fleming, p. 329.)

Generations of American school children have been taught the British bands played "The World Turned Upside Down." The British were specifically prohibited from playing an American or French tune. "The World Turned Upside Down" was a popular tune of the period and one version was "When the King Enjoys His Own Again." Most accounts agree that the enemy bands played "an unpleasant march," "a British march," "the Sound of Musick, not Military Marches, but of Certain Airs, wch had in them so peculiar a strain of melancholy." Greene concludes that "what was played that day so long ago will probably never be known with certainty."

(Greene, pp. 295-296.)

The legend that the British played "The World Turned Upside Down," fit the American version of their tremendous victory – a rag tag army of shopkeepers, merchants, and farmers, whipped into a disciplined army defeated the career soldiers and trained professionals of the British and Hessian forces. The lyrics supported the fantastic nature of the victory. One version, although it is not certain when these lyrics were written, goes as follows:

"If the buttercups buzz'd after the bee,
If boats were on land and churches at sea,
If ponies rode men and grass ate the cows,. . .
Then all the world would be upside down."

3) The astute reader will question how the British cavalry at Gloucester Point crossed the York River and participated in the surrender ceremony. They didn't. The British cavalry were not part of the surrender of the Yorktown garrison. They remained at Gloucester Point and surrendered to the French and American troops there. The ceremony took place around 3 p.m. on the same day, the cavalry rode out with their swords unsheathed but their colors furled, the infantrymen grounded their arms and then the Americans and French occupied the redoubts of the British lines at Gloucester Point. (Greene, pp. 302-303.)

For purposes of the plot, I have had the 17th Light Dragoons ride down the road to Surrender Field.

4) Both Greene and Fleming accept eye-witness accounts that many of the British soldiers were "thoroughly drunk" and "marched irregularly," and acted "sullenly" and "swore terrible oaths," while the Hessians "performed . . .with stolid dignity. . .and precision and polish." (Fleming, pp. 330-331; Greene, pp. 297-299.)

5) The last American casualty of the siege was probably an American soldier guarding the public stores in Yorktown. He was bayoneted

by a drunken Redcoat who, in turn, was immediately struck down and probably became the last British casualty, The night of the surrender was "one long orgy of brawling and shouting and cursing and singing," by the drunken British soldiers. (Fleming, pp. 333-334.) Greene writes that an American sentinel was bayoneted by a drunken Redcoat. (Greene, p. 303.)

6) Those Negro laborers who had not been turned out of Yorktown, lay in the ruins dead or dying of small pox or other diseases. (Greene, p. 303.) Of the 4,000 to 5,000 black recruits at Yorktown and Portsmouth, about sixty percent died of small pox. Others died of wounds and typhus. Maybe 2,000 survived and "[i]t is impossible to establish what happened to them." (Black Loyalist, "Cornwallis and the Siege of Yorktown.")

7) A typical Affidavit of Parole, signed by British Officers after the surrender of Yorktown was:

"I (name and rank and regiment) Do Acknowledge myself a Prisoner of War to the United States of America, & having permission from His Excellency General Washington, agreeable to Capitulation to proceed to New York & Charleston, or either, & to Europe. Do pledge my Faith and Word of Honor, that I will not do or say any thing Injurious to the said United States or Armies thereof, or their Allies, until duly Exchanged. I do further promise that Whenever required by the Commander in Chief of the Army, or the Commissary of Prisoners by the same, I will repair to such Place or Places as they or either of them may require.
 Given unto my Hand at York Town __ of Octr 1781.

/s/_____" (Greene, p. 314-315.)

Note that no signature by either an American or British Officer as witness was required.

Treason and Triumph

Chapter 14 – The Aftermath of Triumph

1) Washington's General Orders of October 20th stated:

"Divine Service is to be performed tomorrow in the several Brigades and Divisions. The Commander in chief earnestly recommends that the troops not on duty should universally attend with their seriousness of Deportment and gratitude of Heart which the recognition of such reiterated and astonishing interpositions of Providence demands of us." (Fitzpatrick, John C., "George Washington Himself – A Common Sense Biography Written from His Manuscripts," p. 406.)

The text of the sermon closely follows the one delivered by Israel Evans, a Presbyterian Minister and Brigade Chaplain at Yorktown shortly after the surrender. (Headley, J.T., The Chaplains and Clergy of the Revolution, pp. 302-304.)

2) On October 21st, Washington pardoned all soldiers under arrest or confinement. It is not clear he was so merciful in dealing with deserters. At least a dozen deserters from Maryland Regiments were identified among the British soldiers by the American Commissary of Prisoners. They were court-martialed. The few who could prove they had never joined the American Army were treated as prisoners of war. "The others were convicted of desertion and hanged." (Fleming, pp. 335-336.) Another historian claims "... out of the many deserters discovered in the British ranks after the surrender, and sentenced to death by court martial, [Washington had] hanged but one... After holding the rest in nerve-racking suspense for many days, he pardoned them." (Fitzpatrick, p. 405.) Perhaps Fitzpatrick has confused the pardoning of the soldiers of the Continental Army incarcerated for various offenses with the deserters caught amongst the British army.

3) Private Martin refers to hunting pigs with dogs in the woods beyond Yorktown when during the siege, after twenty-four hours in the trenches, they had forty-eight hours off in camp only having "to

attend morning and evening roll calls and recreate ourselves as we pleased the rest of the time." (Martin, p. 238.)

After the surrender, the owners of slaves who joined or were seized by the British as they marched through Virginia, appeared in the American camp and "engaged some of [the soldiers] to take them up [catch the Negroes], generally offering a guinea a head for them." (Martin, p. 241.) The Black Loyalist estimates that maybe one thousand were "forced back into slavery."

George Washington himself retrieved two of his house slaves, "twenty-year-old Lucy and eighteen-year-old Esther – who had been among the seventeen who had escaped aboard the British sloop Savage six months earlier, thinking their freedom assured." (Chernow, p. 419.)

4) The surrender of the entire British Army under Cornwallis, together with the vast amounts of equipment and supplies led many of the Americans to believe the war was over or would be soon. The total of British soldiers and sailors, and Hessians captured was almost 8,100. Also taken were more than 240 cannons, mortars and howitzers, 80,000 musket cartridges, 2,800 muskets, 2,600 cartridge boxes, several hundred horses, wagons and British commissary stores of pork, flour, bread, beef, coffee, sugar and "more than 1,200 gallons of alcohol." (Greene, pp. 308-309.)

As for the human cost, it was relatively light on the American and French side in terms of battle deaths and wounds. The Allies sustained about 390 casualties with the Americans suffering one officer and twenty-seven men killed and ten officers and ninety-seven men wounded. However, it was disease that felled the vast majority of the soldiers. "[S]ome 1,700 Americans contracted illness or injury of one sort of another, and 1,000 of these were absent from duty and probably receiving treatment in Williamsburg." (Greene, p. 307.)

The British suffered 156 officers and men killed and 326 wounded, although another report set the total at 309 killed and 595 wounded. In addition more than 1,500 soldiers were sick or incapacitated on the day of surrender. (Greene, pp. 307-308.)

5) Private Martin writes of being stricken with a fever in March of 1782 and being bed-ridden and unable to eat his normal ration of beef and bread. A kindly widow woman, "[a] pitying angel, used almost every evening to send us a little brass kettle containing about a pailful of posset, consisting of wine, water, sugar and crackers. O, it was delicious, even to or sick palates." (Martin, p. 256.)

6) Sometime in September, Lucy Knox and her baby son Henry arrived at Mt. Vernon and she wrote her husband, then at Yorktown, "I met a very kind reception from that good lady of this place." (Stuart, p. 128.) After the surrender, Knox joined his wife at Mt. Vernon and then traveled to Philadelphia with General Washington and Martha who were grieving over the death, on November 5th of Washington's stepson, Jacky Custis from bilious or putrid fever. (Fleming, pp. 332-333; Stuart, p. 130.) He had contracted it at Yorktown where he had been serving as a member of Washington's staff, and racked by fever, had observed the surrender from a carriage and then been moved to a relative's home in nearby Eltham, Virginia where he died.

Henry Knox remained in Philadelphia with Lucy "until the moment of her difficulty shall be over." She gave birth to a son, Marcus Camillus on December 10, 1781. General Washington was the infant's god-father. (Callahan, North, Henry Knox, General Washington's General, p. 190.)

Washington praised Knox in his report to Congress stating "the resources of his genius supplied the deficit of means" and on November 15th recommended he be promoted to Major General. (Callahan, p. 190.)

7) Washington was not alone among the American Generals in owning slaves but, because he owned a plantation in Virginia, he probably was the only one at Yorktown to reclaim slaves "captured" or "liberated" by the British.

"All six of the major generals from states south of the Mason-Dixon line owned slaves while five out of the seventeen Northern major generals owned slaves. Rather than regionalism, slave ownership most closely correlated with income; the wealthiest major generals owned slaves." (Journal of the American Revolution, Procknow, Gene, "Slavery Through the Eyes of Revolutionary Generals," All Things Liberty, November 7, 2017.)

Chapter 15 – Reunion in Philadelphia

1) Philadelphia, with its Quaker heritage, was the center of anti-slavery sentiments in Pennsylvania. A racially mixed Quaker school was founded in Philadelphia in 1770. By 1773, Dr. Benjamin Rush was able to write "three-fourths of the province, as well as the city, cry out against [negro slavery.]" (Quarles, Benjamin, The Negro in the American Revolution, pp. 35-36.)

The Declaration of Independence, drafted in Philadelphia, originally contained a provision condemning the slave trade. It was stricken from the final draft due to the objection of many of the southern delegates (and some from the north as well.) (Quarles, p. 42.)

Author's Notes and Acknowledgements

"Treason and Triumph" encompasses the low and high points of the revolutionary struggle in 1780 and 1781 – the betrayal by General Benedict Arnold, a prominent patriotic hero, who almost succeeded in turning over the vital fort at West Point to the British in the fall of 1780, and the October 1781 victory at Yorktown with the surrender of an entire British Army under the command of General Cornwallis. Following Arnold's treason, the Americans feared an imminent British attack from New York City, the fall of West Point and the splitting of the New England colonies from the rest of country. Following the American and French triumph at Yorktown and the capture of more than 8,000 British and Hessian soldiers and vast amounts of equipment, most Americans assumed the war was won and independence assured.

This novel covers these two pivotal events through the eyes of Continental soldiers, some of whom are free blacks, a few officers – some fictional, some real – and women. The events described are true and are based on letters, diaries and analyses by well-known historians. At times, I thought I was writing a soap opera set in the Revolutionary War because some of the scenes are so over the top. This is especially true of Peggy Shippen Arnold's behavior, playing the faithful, innocent wife, presumed by General Washington and others to be driven temporarily insane by the exposure of her husband's treason and his abandonment of her and their infant son at West Point. It was an Academy Award winning performance, accepted by Washington, other Generals and senior staff. Not a single officer ever suggested that Mrs. Arnold be questioned about her role in her husband's treason.

Absurd as that may seem, Generals Washington, Knox and the other senior officers were governed by the views and understanding of women at the time. As an author, it is my obligation to convey as best as I can, the mores and culture of the 1780s and not mislead the reader by imposing 20th or 21st century sensibilities on my characters. Men in the 1780s believed women were the fragile, weaker sex, prone to excessive mood swings and displays of emotion. They were considered to have lesser intellectual abilities and thus, deemed incapable of engaging in complex schemes and plots.

This attitude is all the more incomprehensible because both Washington and Knox were married to women who, within their marriages, exerted a strong influence upon their husbands and displayed a deep intellectual capacity. For them not to recognize that Peggy Shippen was as intellectually capable as their wives is either a tribute to Peggy Shippen's acting abilities or a colossal failure to apply their own personal experience. When General Knox referred to Lucy as his "dearest friend," he meant it as the English philosopher Francis Bacon had written in his Essays of which Knox and other educated men of the time were aware:

"A man cannot speak to his son but as a father, to his wife but as a husband . . .whereas a friend may speak as the case requires."

Peggy Arnold got away with her act precisely because she knew how men thought and played into their misconceptions of the fairer sex. She was beautiful and coquettish – a flirt not restricted by conventions of modesty when it suited her purposes. One description of her during her "mad" scenes at her home at West Point was of a woman barely covered in her night dress, screaming there were hot irons being driven into her head and imploring the doctor and officers who had come to comfort her not to "murder" her little baby. She played her part to the hilt and was rewarded for her performance, not with an Oscar, but a safe conduct pass, from General Washington, to return to her family in Philadelphia. From there, she subsequently joined her husband in British occupied New York City and, for much of the war, lived the high life of society balls, elegant dinners and theater performances.

The same holds true with how whites thought of black men. The only person present on the fateful night of September 21-22, 1780, when Major John Andre met with General Arnold in a secluded wood on the west bank of the Hudson River, was a black man who held their horses. This was the moment Andre and Arnold concluded the details of their treasonous plot. Whether the Negro overheard their conversations will never be known because no one thought to question him. A black stable hand was deemed as dumb as a fence post or perhaps, just slightly more intelligent.

This perception of black men was challenged by the presence of free blacks in the Continental Army. Many of them were in major battles such as Yorktown and that presented a stark contrast between those blacks fighting for freedom and those enslaved, for whom there would be no freedom if the Americans triumphed. The British promised freedom to all slaves who joined their army. Many did, working in labor battalions or fighting in all black units. Black women performed washing and other camp chores. The surrender at Yorktown included not only British and Hessian soldiers but also the blacks who were within the British lines. Patriot plantation owners, who had lost their slaves when the British plundered their way through Virginia before being bottled up at Yorktown, quickly descended on to the battlefield to reclaim their "property." Many Negroes were taken by their masters back into slavery. George Washington himself recognized and reclaimed two slaves who had run away from Mt. Vernon and were within the British lines. I have tried, through the characters of Sergeant Adam Cooper and Private

Gideon Hazzard, to explore the conflicting feelings of free blacks fighting for the cause of freedom while observing the enslavement of other blacks for whom there could be no freedom.

Once again I am indebted to many friends who read the manuscript and offered helpful suggestions as to plot and character development. They have given me much encouragement both by their praise and honest criticism. My debt to them is all the more when I know of the demands on their time and the many books they have postponed reading to offer me their assistance. Dan Edelman, with his particularly acute eye and phenomenal ability of retention, spotted many an error and inconsistency I had passed over despite my numerous readings of the text.

My editor Ben West questioned lack of transition, omission of time and place, switches in point of view and pointed out confusion in the plot and dialogue that seemed too modern. I am once again indebted to him for protecting me from embarrassment and making this a better novel.

All remaining errors, including those of fact, grammar or spelling are of course my sole responsibility.

I have been heartened by my friends' comments on how much they have learned from the End Notes and how I have succeeded in making the history of our Revolution come alive. This was my main goal when I began the series. That I have achieved it in their eyes gives me both pride and pleasure. However, the concept of adding historical notes to a novel did not originate with me. I first realized I enjoyed George MacDonald Fraser's "Flashman" series so much because his end notes taught me the history behind his novels.

This is the fifth and penultimate novel in the series. I have written one per year. The two constants for the past five years have been the unselfish support of my son and wife. My son has done not only the formatting, a dreary and time consuming task, but provided his artistic talent in designing the covers. Each has been better than the last and this one for "Treason and Triumph" is no exception.

The other constant has been my wife's superb rewriting skills, her critical eye, and an amazing talent to identify convoluted or excessively detailed paragraphs that I regard as absolutely perfectly worded but clearly are momentum stoppers. In the words that Henry Knox sometimes used to begin his letters to Lucy, my own wife is truly "My Dearly Beloved Friend," to which I will add as well, my indispensable partner in life.

Martin R. Ganzglass
Washington D.C.
June 2018

Bibliography

The following are the books, blogs and websites I have relied up for historical accuracy. The Journal of the American Revolution and its blog, All Things Liberty, as well as Boston 1775 were especially helpful.

I continue to be amazed by the incisive observations and sharp writing style of Private Joseph Plumb Martin, a Continental soldier who served throughout the war. He participated in most of the important battles, including Yorktown where he was a member of the Sappers and Miners Regiment. I recommend his memoir, "Private Yankee Doodle – Being a Narrative of Some of the Adventures, Dangers and Sufferings of a Revolutionary Soldier." I have used the version edited by George E. Scheer. It is readily available as a used book and in my opinion, is the one essential read for those interested in learning about our war for independence, shorn of myths and heroics, from the viewpoint of an ordinary soldier. It is shocking to read of the extent of the suffering - starvation, disease, lack of clothing, blankets and shoes – and astounding that so many of the ordinary soldiers persevered and remained in service.

The two books cited below by Thomas Fleming, one of the battles around Connecticut Farms and Springfield, New Jersey in 1780, and the other about Yorktown, are full of details and personal observations of soldiers and officers and both make for terrific reads. Mr. Fleming died in July 2017 at the age of 90. As The New York Times obituary described him, he was "a prolific historian with a zealous interest in America's founding fathers, . . . [who] viewed America's struggle for independence as essential to understanding the history of what happened later." In an interview with the *Journal of the American Revolution*, Fleming said "[It] goes back to the sense that we were launching a revolution that would change the world. And it has!"

Since it is easy enough to search a book or article on line by author and title, I have omitted the customary reference to publisher and date of publication.

Angell, Israel,
Diary of Colonel Israel Angell

Brumwell, Stephen,
"Alexander Hamilton, Benedict Arnold, and a 'Forgotten' Publius," *Journal of the American Revolution*, 2017

Davis, Burke,
The Campaign That Won America – The Story of Yorktown

Callahan, North,
Henry Knox, General Washington's General

Chernow, Ron,
Washington – A Life,
Alexander Hamilton

Clarke, Jeffrey J.,
"March to Victory, Washington, Rochambeau and the Yorktown Campaign of 1781"

Drake, Francis S.,
Life and Correspondence of Henry Knox

Dunbar, Erica Armstrong,
Never Caught – The Washington's Relentless Pursuit of Their Runaway Slave Ona Judge

Fitzpatrick, John C.,
George Washington Himself – A Common Sense Biography Written from His Manuscripts

Fleming, Thomas,
The Forgotten Victory – The Battle for New Jersey – 1780, Beat the Last Drum – The Siege of Yorktown, 1781

Greene, Jerome A,
The Guns of Independence – The Siege of Yorktown, 1781

Hamilton, Phillip,
The Revolutionary Lives and Letters of Lucy and Henry Knox

Harrington, Hugh, T.,
"The Great West Point Chain," Journal of the American Revolution, All Things Liberty, September 25, 2014

Headley, J.T.,
The Chaplains and Clergy of the Revolution

Jacob, Mark and Case, Stephen H.,
Treacherous Beauty – Peggy Shippen, The Woman Behind Benedict Arnold's Plot to Betray America

Kelly, Jack,
"Revolutionary Tourist: Chastellux in America," Journal of the American Revolution, "All Things Liberty, March 4, 2016

Lengel, Edward G.,
The Glorious Struggle – George Washington's Revolutionary War Letters

Loane, Nancy K.,
Following the Drum – Women at the Valley Forge Encampment

Martin, Joseph Plumb,
Private Yankee Doodle – Being a Narrative of Some of the Adventures Dangers and Sufferings of a Revolutionary Soldier, George Sheer, Editor

McBurney, Christian,
Abductions in the American Revolution – Attempts to Kidnap George Washington, Benedict Arnold and Other Military and Civilian Leaders

McCready, Blake,
"Abigail Hartman Rice, Revolutionary War Nurse," *Journal of the American Revolution, All Things Liberty,* November 28, 2016.

McNeill, J.R.,
"Malarial mosquitos helped defeat British in battle that ended the Revolutionary War," *The New York Times,* October 18, 2010

Popek, Daniel M.,
"They . . . fought bravely but were unfortunate" The True Story of Rhode Island's 'Black Regiment' and the Failure of Segregation in Rhode Island's Continental Line, 1777-1783

Procknow, Gene,
"Slavery Through the Eyes of Revolutionary Generals," *Journal of the American Revolution, All Things Liberty,* November 7, 2017

Quarles, Benjamin,
The Negro in the American Revolution

Randall, Willard S.,
Benedict Arnold – Patriot and Traitor

Reynolds, William W.,
"The American Gunners at Yorktown," *Journal of the American Revolution, All Things Liberty,* May 9, 2017

Shachtman, Tom,
"The French Bread Connection," *Journal of the American Revolution, All Things Liberty,* September 12, 2017

Schellhammer, Michael,
"Mutiny of the Pennsylvania Line," *Journal of the American Revolution, All Things Liberty,* January 14, 2014; "Mutiny of the New Jersey Line," *Journal of the American Revolution, All Things Liberty,* March 19, 2014

Shepherd, Joshua,
"Temper, Temper: Officers and Gentlemen Go Beserk," *Journal of the American Revolution,* 2017

Smith, Jr., John L.,
"How Yorktown Almost Couldn't Afford to Happen," *Journal of the American Revolution,* 2017

Stoltz, III, Joseph F.,
"Le Plus Detaillee: The July 1781 Reconnaissance of New York," *Journal of the American Revolution, All Things Liberty,* June 12, 2017

Stuart, Nancy Rubin,
Defiant Brides – The Untold Story of Two Revolutionary-Era Women and the Radical Men They Married

Wakin, Daniel, J.
"Sermons of 1776, With a Spirit of 2003; Newly Found Papers Reflect New York's Mood in Time of War," *The New York Times,* March 16, 2003

Walker, Paul K.,
Engineers of Independence – A Documentary History of the Army of Engineers in the American Revolution, 1775-1783

The thrilling saga of our War for Independence concludes with . . .

Book of Negroes

Sarah sat in a quiet corner of the Knox's warm kitchen, humming softly to herself. Reaching down she gently rocked the wooden cradle containing her son, born the second week of November. She loosened the blanket swaddling his small body. With his eyes closed, one could not see they were grey green like hers, though he had Adam's high forehead and broad nose. Maybe, she thought, that was due to nursing and his nose would be less flat, more like hers, over time. It did not matter. To her, he was a beautiful baby.

She had never seen Adam so happy, so filled with love for her and adoration of their little boy. When Adam had chosen the name Emmanuel. Sarah had not objected. Her own father was unknown. Most likely he was Willis Parks, the master of the Tidewater Virginia plantation where her mother was enslaved. How else had Sarah acquired the color of her eyes and her lighter skin? She knew of at least four pregnancies her mother had endured to breed more slaves for Parks. And that was before Sarah had been sold to Reverend Penrose of Hackensack, New Jersey, seven years ago. She had not seen her mother since.

To banish these gloomy thoughts, she recalled Adam dancing around the room, embracing Emmanuel, so tiny in his father's muscular arms, telling him he would teach him to catch the biggest fish, weave the tightest nets, forge the strongest hooks, carve the best oars, tar the finest hull, row the fastest dory, until laughing at her husband's exuberance, she had to tell him to stop before their son became frightened by the torrent of words.

With the arrival of their son, she and Adam were enjoying the most joyful and blissful time of their lives. General Knox, Lucy and their two children were temporarily residing in a spacious solid brick home, for the duration of Mrs. Knox's pregnancy. She was due around the beginning of December. Adam, as a member of General Knox's staff had been assigned a small attic room for himself, Sarah and their child. She surmised Mrs. Knox had her hand in this. Sarah was, as well as Mrs. Knox's favorite baker, now the nanny for Henry, their sixteen-month old boy. On occasion Sarah would also take care of little Lucy Knox, bringing the five-year old girl down to the kitchen and letting her help make the dough or place the cut and cored fruit in the pies.

Sarah enjoyed baking and the friendship with the cooks and other servants in the house, although most were white, as well as the wages she received in hard coin. Admittedly, she missed being an independent businesswoman, providing baked goods for the social events of other prominent Philadelphia families. On the other side of the scale, she owed the Knoxes. It was the General who had proposed to Adam the dangerous bargain that had made her a free woman. In return for engaging in a year long spying mission, Knox had agreed to arrange for the purchase Sarah's freedom. When Adam had thwarted the plot to kidnap General Washington from the Ford Mansion in Morristown, General Knox had swiftly made good on his promise. The precious papers certifying her freedom signed by Reverend Penrose, along with a letter verifying her status signed by General Knox himself, were hidden beneath her clothes in their locked trunk, in their small room in the attic.

Not that she had felt unwanted in Mr. and Mrs. Jeremy Absalom's home where she had lived since coming to Philadelphia until Adam arrived from Yorktown. But there was no comparison between the home of a respectable, elderly free black couple, living at the edges of the established boundaries of the city and the Knox's elegant residence located in the center of the bustle of Philadelphia and the social swirl that occurred within the house. Besides, the Knoxes had been most generous, giving Sarah and Adam a crib, some baby clothes and most importantly, prevailing upon Dr. Rush, when he came to examine Mrs. Knox, to look at Emmanuel as well.

She was surprised to see Jeremy Absalom enter through the rear door of the kitchen, rather than coming down the three steps from the dining room. But then she realized, as a black man, even a free one, he would have known not to come to the front door of the Knox's residence to ask for admittance to see her. Jeremy was a tall man, now stooped with age and required the use of a plain black cane. She wondered what had made him come this distance over the rain-slicked cobblestones to visit her. With preparations underway for the dinner meal, the kitchen was now full of commotion. She waved at him and quickly skirted the large oak table in the center, heaped high with uncut vegetables. Sarah helped him off with his coat and hat, hung them on a hook near the fireplace to dry and offered him a chair near the cradle.

"Ah, this is your son," he said sighing, as he settling himself against the hard wooden seat and bent stiffly down to peer in. "His name is Emmanuel," he said more as a statement than a question. "There are not too many black men named Emmanuel," he said softly. "Most are given the names of ancient Romans by their masters to show how clever and educated they are in the classics." His voice, although low enough so only Sarah could hear, had a bitter edge to it.

"I heard a sermon once, a long time ago," Mr. Absalom continued, looking up at the beamed ceiling as if the words would descend from heaven through the roof. "This preacher taught that Emmanuel means 'God is with us.' At the time I was not yet free. My every day existence under the threat of the whip and the constant hard labor with little sustenance, convinced me of the very opposite." Again the strain of bitterness.

"But now, I see free blacks in an army fighting for independence from a brutal tyranny, your own husband, himself freeborn, who risked all to purchase your freedom and," he nodded toward the cradle, "your own infant babe." His tight lips formed a grim smile, although his eyes betrayed a greater joy. "A second generation born free. I think perhaps I was wrong all these years." He exhaled deeply, placed both hands on the knob at the top of his cane and rested his chin upon them. "I hope your son's name is a prophecy for a better life for him." He sat there lost in thought, his clouded eyes staring at the brick wall behind the cradle.

Abruptly, remembering the purpose of his visit, he straightened in the chair and glanced around the room, taking note of the white cooks and servants close to them. "I have received a letter that I believe pertains to you. I would have preferred to meet with you in private, but this will do." Absalom bent forward and brought his head closer to Sarah's.

"An acquaintance of mine, Peter Williams, a Sexton at the John Street Methodist Church in New York City, has written to me." He paused and waved one hand dismissively. "Not only to me but others as far south as Baltimore and north to Boston, where there are significant populations of free blacks. Peter is a religious man with many friends within our communities," he added by way of explanation. What had this black Sexton written that affected her, Sarah thought apprehensively. Mr. Absalom was telling the story at his own pace however and would not be rushed. She rocked the cradle and hoped Emmanuel would not interrupt him by waking.

After another lengthy pause, Jeremy picked up the thread, this time speaking even more softly. Sarah leaned forward straining to hear him above the voices of cooks and servants, the banging of pots, the thwock of a cleaver cutting a haunch of meat, the constant coming and going and banging of pantry doors and pots and pans.

"Sexton Williams has in his employ at the Church, two blacks who fled Virginia, and reached the British lines on the coast. Fortunately, they were able to stow away on a British ship that made its way to New York City. One is a woman, perhaps close to fifty years of age, the other is a young boy, maybe fourteen or so." He rocked from side to side as if seeing the two Negroes in his mind. "The boy has a brand burned on to his forehead for attempting to run away before." He sniffed deeply, taking in the cooking aromas filling the kitchen and nodded appreciatively. "He must have spirit since it did not deter him from trying again and, this time succeeding."

Abasalom pulled his chair closer so that the two were now almost head to head and placed his hand on Sarah's bare forearm. "According to Sexton Williams, the woman is looking for the whereabouts of a daughter named Sarah, the only one of her girls sold to someone in the north."

Sarah could contain herself no longer. "Please tell me the woman's name."

"Lettia. The boy, who is her son, is called Jupiter," he said with disgust. "They do not use their master's name but it was Parks."

Sarah cupped both of her hands over her mouth and nose. Her eyes filled with tears. "It is my mother. My poor, poor mother."

"Sarah," someone called. "Mind the breads and cakes in the oven."

She rose, wiping her hands wet with tears on her apron. "It is my mother," she said, repeating the phrase over and over as she made her way to the side of the hearth to remove the loaves from the Dutch oven.

When she returned, Absalom was rocking the cradle and peering down at Emmanuel who had awakened and was staring up at him with a furrowed brow. The infant made tiny sucking noises, unsure whether to cry or smile. Sarah picked her son up and held him tightly.

"Adam and I will find the money and bring them here. I will take care of her. And my brother can be put to work. Will you write your friend? Tell him to inform my mother I am in Philadelphia, married and a free woman. Will you help us? To be reunited with my mother after all these years," she said through tears of joy. "It is another blessing for us." In her mind, Sarah already saw her mother settled in somewhere in town, a room of her own, or in the Knox's kitchen, helping out, staying warm in the winter, minding her grandson.

Absalom sighed and shook his head slowly. "Sarah, my child. Even in Philadelphia where the devout Friends and influential patriots have strong anti-slavery sentiments, slave catchers and bounty hunters prowl the wharves and streets. These are evil men. Your mother and brother are not safe here. I am sorry to say they are only free in British occupied New York."

"Then, I will go to her," Sarah said defiantly. One or two of the servants looked at her curiously, having heard her loud declaration. Emmanuel whimpered and nuzzled her bosom. If she were still nursing when she left for New York, she would have to take the little one with her. Adam would help her plan the journey and what to do next. He would know how to reunite her with her mother and brother and get them to safety.